1995

Designing Training Programs

The Critical Events Model

Second Edition

Gulf Publishing Company
Houston, London, Paris, Zurich, Tokyo

Designing Training Programs

The Critical Events Model

Second Edition

Leonard Nadler
Zeace Nadler

Designing Training Programs
The Critical Events Model, *Second Edition*

Second edition copyright © 1994 by Gulf Publishing Company.

First edition copyright © 1982 by Addison-Wesley Publishing Company, Inc.

Gulf Publishing Company
Book Division
P.O. Box 2608 □ Houston, Texas 77252-2608

10   9   8   7   6   5   4   3   2   1

Library of Congress Cataloging-in-Publication Data

Nadler, Leonard.
    Designing training programs: the critical events model.—2nd ed. / Leonard Nadler, Zeace Nadler.
        p.   cm.
    Includes bibliographical references and index.
    ISBN 0-88415-100-X
        1. Employees—Training of. I. Nadler, Zeace. II. Title.
    HF5549.5.T7N285 1994
    6583.3'12404—dc20   94-637
                                                                  CIP

Printed in the United States of America.

iv

Contents

CHAPTER 1

❖
Designing and Using Models

This book is concerned with learning, or more specifically, with designing learning experiences provided by employers. Various names are given to this activity, but we prefer human resource development (HRD), which is defined as organized learning experiences provided by employers within a specified period of time to improve performance and/or promote personal growth. Each element of this definition is discussed in *Developing Human Resources* [80].

Within HRD, there are three learning activity areas: training, education, and development. Training involves learning that relates to the *current* job of the learner, education relates to a *future* job of the learner, and development refers to learning that is *not* job-related.

The first eleven chapters of this book discuss the Critical Events Model (CEM) and ways to design training with it, while Chapters 12 and 13 explain how the model can be modified for education purposes. This book will not discuss a model for development.

Within the HRD field, some people make decisions about learning programs, while others actually design them. We call those people "Designers." Although the major focus of this book is on using the Critical Events Model (CEM) in the actual design process, it will also help people who are even peripherally involved. The book should enable managers and supervisors to understand what the HRD Designer does. Therefore, HRD designers can use this book to communicate with their supervisors about designing learning experiences, particularly when they use the CEM.

THE DESIGNER OF LEARNING PROGRAMS

Human resource development personnel can fill many roles in an organization. We have identified the roles and sub-roles in *Developing Human Resources* [80, p. 127]. They include:

1

Learning Specialist
  Facilitator of learning
  Designer of learning programs
  Developer of instructional strategies
Manager of HRD
  Supervisor of HRD programs
  Developer of HRD personnel
  Arranger of facilities and finance
  Maintainer of relations
Consultant
  Expert
  Advocate
  Stimulator
  Change agent

This book focuses on one of those sub-roles, the "designer of learning programs," who will be referred to in this book as the "Designer."

Of course, the Designer should be familiar with the other roles and sub-roles, particularly those in the learning specialist area. As appropriate, we will discuss how the Designer works with the "facilitator of learning" (facilitator) and the "developer of instructional strategies" (developer). Indeed, in some organizations, one person fills all three roles, though people are increasingly specializing as Designers.

One reason for this is that organizations have learned that it is possible to contract for the facilitator and developer. Although it is also possible to contract for the Designer, many organizations favor keeping a Designer on staff who knows the organization and the personnel involved.

LEARNING

As learning is the core of this book, let us take some time to discuss what is and what is not learning, as the term is used in this book. A more detailed discussion of learning theories will be found in Chapters 7 and 13. For now, let us examine the general area of learning.

Learning is the acquisition of new skills, attitudes, and knowledge. (The learning psychologist refers to these as "domains.") This definition does not tell us anything about how learning is acquired or whether the learner can actually use the new learning outside of the learning situation. These are both major areas of consideration we will explore in depth as we move through the CEM.

Although some people include behavior in this category, we contend that a person does not learn behavior. Rather, behavior is a possible result, an application, of learning. That a person fails to use (that is, behave) what he has been taught does not mean that he has not learned. Since there can be many reasons to explain his unexpected behavior, his failure to act reveals something about the constraints on behavior. It also suggests that we should avoid teaching people things they cannot possibly use, unless the goal is to learn with no intent to apply. Although this would be a valid goal in development, it is inappropriate for training and education.

Incidental Learning

We learn through different modes. One is *incidental,* and we encounter it all the time. As we engage in various social activities and entertainments, such as watching television, reading, talking with neighbors, logging into electronic bulletin boards (BBS), we learn. This kind of learning is not planned, nor is it the primary reason for doing these things.

Although this area of learning is important, it is not our concern in this book. On the other hand, we cannot totally ignore incidental learning since it can be transmitted through the company culture and in other informal ways. We must be sensitive to incidental learning so that it reinforces rather than conflicts with intentional learning experiences.

Intentional Learning

In this book the focus is on *intentional* learning, that is, a learning experience in which the individual expects to be a learner. This learning experience consists of identified learning objectives, a specific time (allotted by both the individual and the organization) dedicated to learning, and some form of evaluation, planned either during the program or after it has been completed. From the organizational viewpoint, intentional learning requires an appropriate allocation of resources if learning is to take place.

Generally, large organizations allocate the physical and financial resources needed to provide intentional learning—the training and education activities of HRD—while small organizations, which contend that they cannot afford these expenditures, do not. Although learning continues to occur in those organizations, it becomes incidental.

Organizations of any size that provide intentional learning (HRD) reap many benefits, as will be demonstrated later in this book. The organization that does not provide HRD forces its people to rely on incidental learning, and often pays the price when employees learn the wrong things.

Shea demonstrates this problem in his discussion of new employees [99]. If an organization does not have a well-planned orientation program, one that goes beyond merely filling out the appropriate forms, the new employee is forced to learn by the incidental mode. The employer, who has no idea what the new employee is learning, may be surprised by the unusual behavior that results. It may prove more costly to correct the effects of incidental learning than to provide a good intentional orientation program.

Incidental and intentional learning can compete with each other within an organization. The grapevine (incidental learning) that exists in every organization may send out signals about how a particular job is to be done. If, in the absence of intentional learning, the performance of that job is below standard or even at variance with what the organization needs, the organization may have to counter the negative results through an expensive learning program. It is much more difficult to unlearn than it is to learn.

In the CEM, as described in Chapters 2 and 13, there is an event called Evaluation and Feedback, which enables the Designer to identify some of the behaviors that are acquired through incidental learning. Rather than looking at incidental learning as negative or undesirable, the Designer must be alert to the serendipitous possibility of integrating incidental learning into intentional learning.

As this book will essentially focus on intentional learning, the qualifier "intentional" will be dropped. The reader should recognize the two modes and remember that in this book, "learning" refers to intentional learning.

Teaching and Learning

Two words are often used interchangeably, in spite of their different meanings:

Teaching—what we do to others.
Learning—what we do for ourselves.

Teachers have many roles, but let us focus on that of being a facilitator.

Facilitation is the general process of enabling individuals to acquire learning. It uses people and machines to cover a wide range of behaviors. There are many variations. Facilitation can range from the "stand-up classroom presenter" to fully machine-mediated instruction. For example, teaching can involve a facilitator who does little more than help the learner find the appropriate resources for learning.

A common example of machine-mediated instruction is the use of computers and videos. Even though the facilitator and learner may never see each other, they may communicate through the machine, using a computer modem to contact each other. What the facilitator does, in that situation, changes dramatically—instead of being a presenter, the facilitator becomes a coach and a resource.

Both the facilitator and the learner are essential to the learning process. In some carefully designed learning situations, it is even possible to have them reverse their roles for the benefit of either or both.

The cliché "you can't learn nobody nuthin" may be ungrammatical, but it expresses the truth that even the best facilitator is useless if the learner will not or cannot learn. The too often used saying "If the learner hasn't learned, the teacher hasn't taught" makes the situation one-sided. Learning is a transaction that requires both parties, actively engaged, even though they may not be interfacing.

We will continue to discuss the learner throughout this book. Too often the learner is ignored or overlooked, while teaching is emphasized, as if the same teaching is appropriate for all learners.

If good teaching is to take place, the instructor must prepare and apply a carefully designed learning program. Keep in mind, however, that even a well prepared session can seem spontaneous and be enjoyable.

In any effective design process, the learner should be involved. It may not be possible to involve each learner in each event, but provision should be made to include all the learners. As we develop the CEM, we will make suggestions and give examples of ways to involve the learner. Indeed, being part of the design process can be a very effective part of the learning process.

Learning and Performance

Employers, who pay the HRD bills, are not as interested in the learning they have provided or the learning their employees may have acquired as they are in results of that learning; that is, improved job performance.

Learning does not necessarily improve performance and this is the challenge addressed throughout this book—how to improve performance through more effective learning programs.

The emphasis in this book is on learning for performance (training and education). We believe that other purposes of learning (development) are important, but they are beyond the scope of the model discussed here.

MODELS AND DESIGNING PROGRAMS

Individual creativity is wonderful—it should be encouraged and rewarded. Despite this, Designers should first explore existing models before they design a new one. Too many Designers start their work without realizing that many models already exist and that such models can be extremely helpful. Perhaps there is an ego factor involved, and a Designer would rather create something new, but using an existing model shows that a Designer is aware of resources and knows how to use them.

The Designer should not, however, take a model and apply it without some prior exploration. Before discussing some of the variables to consider when selecting a model, let us first discuss the concept of models.

Uses of Models

Models are meant to represent the reality of their developers. Developing a model is not a unique experience reserved for the privileged few. All of us "design models" as we try to make sense out of the everyday world. Without those models, it is doubtful if we could solve our daily problems.

Take a simple but common experience. You have decided to drive from New York City to Chicago. Before you start your trip, you do some planning (designing your trip), and a significant part of that process involves consulting a road map. The map identifies the roads you can take, as well as the major cities or other discernible points you will pass. The map can help you make estimates about the time it will take for such a trip, and even some of the costs.

You know that using a map will simplify your trip. In your planning process for that trip you are actually using a model. The road map is the basic part of your model. You know that it shows the roads, but they are not actual roads. You know that you could not put your car on any part of the map and achieve your goal. The map is merely a representation of what you can expect to find when you get on the road.

By consulting a map (model), you have a much greater chance of having a successful trip than if you started without it. Of course, it is also important to have the correct map—the appropriate model. Not every map will help you plan a trip from New York City to Chicago. Although airline maps, railroad maps, or a map that showed the routes from New York City to New Orleans have their uses, none of them are appropriate for your trip.

Viewing a road map as a model should illustrate some of the questions you should ask when you choose a model for learning, such as:

• What is the purpose of the model?
• For what kinds of learning is it most appropriate?
• Does it tell the Designer what to look for in the process, or only the road to take?
• Does it help the Designer anticipate possible challenges and opportunities?
• Does it provide alternatives?

As we will see, the CEM provides positive responses to each of these questions.

An effective model is one that helps a Designer understand an essentially complicated process. Good models have foundations in theory. The Designer should ascertain the concepts that are embodied in any model. Von Bertalanffy notes that conceptual models represent reality in a simplified and therefore comprehensible form [115]. Not all models must be simple, but because a model appears to be simple is no reason to reject it. Rather, the potential user should ascertain if the theoretical base from which the model has sprung provides the tools needed.

Models do many things for the Designer:

- Explain various aspects of human behavior
- Bring together what is known through research and observation
- Simplify complex human processes
- Provide help in observing a situation.

A model is a starting point, not the final guide. No one model will suffice for every design situation, nor can most models be used without some customizing by the Designer.

A model should not be confused with reality—it is only a representation. The Designer must seek that model closest to the situation in which it will be used. As with any attempt to reduce a complex process to a one-dimensional representation (diagram or flow chart), some things will be lost. The utility of the model depends on the Designer's understanding of the real situation and the flexibility of the model to be customized for that situation. Within those limitations, models can be important for the Designer. There are those who feel that using a model makes them appear dependent. They think that their organization or client might doubt their professional competence if they rely on a model. As in the travel example discussed earlier, does relying on a map disparage one's driving ability? Quite the contrary. Anyone who has been a passenger in a vehicle and felt insecure because the driver hesitated when faced with unforeseen alternatives, knows that using a map (model) could have made that trip much less harrowing and more successful. The same can be said for using a carefully selected model when designing HRD learning experiences.

Open and Closed Models

There are different types of models, but most of them can be classified as either open or closed. Each type is based on a different theory or philosophy that needs to be considered when a Designer selects a model for a particular task.

An *open model* assumes that external factors can affect the design process. In creating an open model, the model builder is accepting the fact that some external forces may be beyond the scope of the model, but that such factors must be considered in the design process.

An open model is a working hypothesis. It provides the Designer with possible courses of action and enables the Designer to anticipate outcomes. The open model is descriptive; it endeavors to describe what will happen if the model is used. It makes no guarantees as to outcome at the initial stages of the design process. Rather, it alerts the Designer to possibilities and to the major decisions the Designer must make.

An open model tends to be a verbal model, whereas a closed model tends to be mathematical. This diminishes the open model's importance for some Designers. However, even as knowledgeable a model builder as von Bertalanffy begrudgingly acknowledges that verbal models have contributed to our understanding of human behavior and should not be shunned in favor of only mathematical models [115].

One of the weaknesses of some open models is that feedback during design is not automatic. The assumption is made that the user will recognize the need for feedback, but it is generally not built into the model. However, there is nothing to restrict an open model from having a feedback component. In looking at the CEM, the "Evaluation and Feedback" event is prominent and it must occur at the completion of each event.

A *closed model* assumes that every input in the design process can be identified. Some theorists even go further and claim that all the input can be controlled. Closed models endeavor to build all possible variables into the model. The underlying concept of a closed model is that anything that can possibly have an effect on the design process has been identified and integrated into the model.

The closed model is predictive, for it is intended to be used exactly as designed—conclusions and outcomes are predetermined. That is, if the Designer uses the closed model as indicated by the model builder, the learning program will go forward exactly as promised by the model. The Designer has few options. If the Designer strays from the closed model; the model is not being used for the purpose for which it was developed.

This was the case with the original Instructional Systems Design (ISD model). This model has gone through many iterations, and it is no longer possible to know what a person means when referring to the "ISD." However, the first model was developed to provide education programs for military personnel who were involved with the Minute Man missile. Everyone who went through the program was required to learn to perform in a specifically prescribed manner, so that each member of the team knew exactly what to expect from every other member. The model was well-suited for its original purpose and for similar programs that require that exactitude today. Unfortunately, it is used by some, with necessary modifications, to provide training and education where the final behaviors are not expected to be absolute. As noted earlier, closed models tend to be mathematical, at least in concept. They use algorithms, or "yes-no" choices. The movement through the model tends to be linear, either going in one direction or in specific feedback loops. The early engineering/mathematical influence is quite apparent in closed models.

The contrast between open and closed models can be seen in Figure 1-1. Clearly, we favor an open model (such as the CEM), but we recognize that there are times and situations when closed models have their advantages.

Open	Closed
Outside factors exist which cannot be identified at the outset	All factors can be identified or accounted for in the model
A working hypothesis	Outcomes predetermined
Descriptive	Predictive
Verbal	Mathematical

Figure 1-1. Contrasting open and closed models.

VARIABLES FOR SELECTING A MODEL

In selecting a model, a Designer should consider some of the variables discussed in this section. The list of variables is not complete—it probably never can be comprehensive enough to serve the needs of every Designer. However, it indicates the factors to be considered when choosing the model to be used.

Training, Education, and Development

We defined these terms earlier in this chapter. Let us now look at them in terms of models for designing learning programs. When *training* is the purpose of the design, the model should relate to individuals and their present jobs. It is essential that trainees (individuals or group) are actually doing those jobs when the design process is started.

The CEM can also be used for *education,* but some of the activities will be changed because the focus is not on the present job, but a future one. Therefore, the data base gathered by the Designer will have to change. The reasons for this are explored in Chapters 12 and 13.

It is possible to modify the CEM significantly for *development,* but the process is not explored in this book.

Skills, Knowledge, and Attitudes

It is generally agreed that there are three areas of learning: skills, knowledge, and attitude. When choosing an appropriate model, the Designer must ascertain how these areas figure into the project. When selecting a model, the Designer must consider which model is most appropriate for the particular learning experience, or the mix of the three needs.

When emphasis is on *skills* and there is only one way for performance to take place, a closed model might be more appropriate. When a task requires a lot of skill, but individual differences must be considered, an open model might just as readily be used.

For *knowledge,* similar considerations apply. If what is to be learned is exact, specific, and not based on previous experiences (work and/or learning), a closed model might be more appropriate. Some closed models were used in the early years of computer-assisted instruction because the emphasis was on absolute and predictable behavior. As we learn to use the computer as an instructional strategy, rather than an end in itself, open models are proving just as appropriate.

Some specialists contend that little can be done about *attitudes.* They argue that learning should only address overt behavior. Such people generally favor closed models. Those who prefer open models tend to be more humanistic, and they consider attitudes as one area of learning. Indeed, in using an open model, including the learner early in the process is a key element.

It is the Designer's responsibility to select the model that reflects not only the objectives of the design, but also individual and organizational understandings and practices regarding skills, knowledge, and attitude.

The Learner

A Designer should not begin the design process without considering the learner. Learners are not empty vessels into which learning can be poured. They are human beings with much to offer and learn.

When a Designer believes that the learner should be involved in the design process, a model should be selected that requires such involvement. Of course, if the learner need not be part of the design process, the model should reflect that point of view.

Chapter 7 (Build Curriculum) discusses the adult as a learner, particularly in the workplace in greater depth, but a few items should be mentioned here about selecting a model.

The learner's previous learning experience is important. Many people have had extensive learning experiences both in school and out of school. Perhaps they have even been in previous HRD programs offered by the organization. Other people may not have even completed high school or had any other learning experiences since attending school. Each group will view learning and the design process differently. Those with extensive learning experiences would probably want to be included in the design process. Those whose previous learning experiences were less than satisfactory may also need to be included. These varieties of experience must be considered by the Designer when selecting a model.

The Designer must also consider how physical distance or geography will affect the use of the model. If it would be too expensive or logistically impossible to communicate directly with the learner, another model might be selected that would not require close interaction between the Designer and the learners.

This distance barrier can be overcome if the Designer has access to technical resources. Technical devices, such as modems, conference calls, FAX machines, or two-way television, can assist the Designer to communicate with others. Technology already exists that allows the Designer to observe the performance of potential learners even though they are miles apart.

Of course, the use of that technology requires resources and support. If those resources are not available to the Designer, then the model being considered should take into account the geographical limitation.

The Facilitator

The training model chosen should clearly reflect the relationship of the facilitator to the design and to the instructional process. As noted earlier, the facilitator's duties may range from stand-up presentations on a face-to-face basis to providing facilitation from a distance or through electronic devices. It is also possible for the facilitator to be away until called upon by the learner.

There are times when the Designer and the facilitator are the same person, such as in a university. Even in that situation, however, increased use of electronic technologies is changing the roles of university professors. Increasingly, the people doing the designing are not the same ones as those doing the facilitating. Once the learning program starts, the Designer is generally out of the picture unless a pilot program is being designed, as described in Chapter 10. If the facilitator is allowed to make changes in the learning program without consulting the Designer, the model should reflect that possibility. In large organizations, the physical distance of the Designer and the facilitator may inhibit communication between them, unless they use available electronic and other aids to communication.

The level of the learner in the organization is another factor the facilitator must consider. That is, different levels of employees tend to be assigned different facilitators (from internal and external sources). The higher the level of the facilitator, the more likely that modifications of previously designed programs will be permitted.

The instructional experiences of the facilitator should be considered when a model is chosen. For example, if the facilitator is relatively inexperienced, as in peer-mediated learning, it is important that the Designer produce a program that can be conducted by a person with little experience. Other considerations as well as the range of instructional strategies are discussed in Chapter 8.

Experienced facilitators tend to want to leave their professional fingerprints on any design. The Designer must consider that in choosing and using a model.

Culture of the Organization

The Designer must also consider the culture of the particular organization when selecting a model. The concept of organizational culture emerged in the 1980s, although there was some discussion of it before that time [75]. When someone says "Everybody knows," the statement generally refers to cultural behavior. However, it is usually only the people of the particular organization or group who can follow the point being discussed without further explanation.

Culture can be viewed as habits and customs people develop to cope with change.

Because they are habits and customs, cultures are observable. Habits and customs are developed by people, and are not genetically transferred. If nothing in a culture changes, behavior becomes institutionalized. That is, a behavior occurs so often, over such a long period of time, that it becomes automatic and less susceptible to change. The important factor is change. And, one of the goals of HRD is to bring about change. Therefore, the Designer must consider how the model relates to the particular organization. Although the outcome of the program will be change, it is also possible that just using the model can require some changes in the organization, particularly the cultural behavior.

For example, if the culture of the organization calls for a high degree of interaction among all levels of employees, then a design model should provide for that. If the culture of the organization is such that people are expected to have specific jobs, receive assignments, and get the job done, the Designer should consider these factors when selecting a model. If the culture of the organization is one of participative management, the Designer might want to select a model that encompasses that kind of cultural behavior.

Identifying organizational culture is not an easy task. Much work has to be done in this area. A Designer must learn something about the concepts of organizational culture, and how design models relate to that element. It is not possible, however, for the Designer to wait for the definitive work before designing.

The Designer must also consider the culture in terms of reactions to names and/or labels. In the early 1970s the U.S. Marine Corps was faced with some problems and decided to implement sensitivity training. It soon became obvious that the term "sensitivity training" evoked negative responses in the Marine Corps. The name of the activity was changed to something like "social responsibility," and the training gained acceptance and resulted in some excellent programs.

On the international scene, at one time many learning programs were designed to encourage people to limit the size of their families. However, the phrase "limiting size" was not considered appropriate in some religious countries. The focus of the program was changed to "responsible parenthood" and proved successful in those countries.

The issue here is not just a matter of wordsmithing, or trying to fool the public. Rather, it is important to recognize that the same word, in different cultures, can communicate many different things. It is important for a Designer to determine, for a particular cultural group, which words are acceptable and which will evoke a negative reaction.

There are times when this means changing some of the terminology within a model. For example, in some organizations the word "feedback" is viewed as jargon and therefore perceived negatively. When that is the case, the Designer can still use the model, but change the word to one more culturally acceptable in that organization.

Some of the more frequent statements a Designer may encounter in an organization are:

- Learning is a waste of time.
- If you want them to learn, just tell them.
- The only true learning takes place when the learner is involved.
- Anybody can learn anything.
- Give an intelligent person a job, and it will get done. Learning is not necessary.
- No learning can take place without some risk.

You can obviously add many more such statements to the list. They are all reflections of the various kinds of organizational culture that will influence the kind of model the Designer chooses.

Likes and Dislikes of the Designer

You, the Designer, are a person who has your own likes and dislikes in many matters, and you should certainly like the model you select for designing a learning program. If you are not comfortable with the model, you are less likely to use it effectively.

There are many questions you need to ask yourself. Do you prefer to work alone, with a small group, or with the total organization? The models you consider should clearly indicate the kinds of behavior expected from you in those areas.

How do you want to be seen by your organization? Do you want to have greater visibility in your organization? Some models are constructed so that you can design with a minimum of visibility by the organization. On the other hand, if you believe that visibility is important, then choose a model that either allows or provides for that.

If you move around your organization asking questions as part of your design process, will you be viewed as a help or a hindrance? Given your response to that question, you might want to choose a model that does not require you to involve others in the design process. If, however, you believe that asking questions of others while you design is preferable, choose a model that encourages or requires that behavior on your part.

How do you want to spend your time? As any Designer knows, the design process takes time. Within the process, there are many tasks, and how many depends on the model you select. You need to be able to see from the model how you will be spending your time. Will it be on writing lesson plans, meeting with others, or preparing budgets? Many designs include all of those elements, and more, and you should look at the model in terms of what you will be expected to do, and whether that is what you want to do.

These questions, and many more like them, must be considered as you choose a model for designing learning programs. If you are not comfortable with a model, you will probably be less successful in using it. You may need to "try on" several models before you find those that are best for you. You might find a model that can handle most of your design needs, with some modifications.

THE CRITICAL EVENTS MODEL

In this book, we present the Critical Events Model, which we first developed in 1965 and called the Process of Training. Since that time, CEM has been used extensively by us and others in work situations with clients as well as by in-house Designers, and with students (mainly graduates who were also HRD practitioners). It has been modified somewhat throughout the years, and

THE CRITICAL EVENTS MODEL

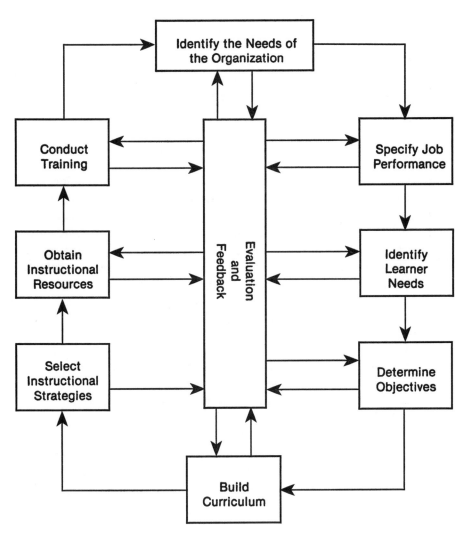

Figure 1-2. The Critical Events Model.

we have gained a great deal of experience in a wide variety of situations. Our experience has been very useful, and we offer it for your consideration.

Figure 1-2 presents a diagram of the CEM. This book discusses each event in the diagram as it relates to training and education design situations.

Before going into the CEM in depth, some general observations can be helpful.

AN OPEN MODEL

The CEM is an open model. It recognizes that organizations and individuals are complex, and identifying and determining all the variables when a program is being designed is not always possible.

It is not unusual to find that the actual work of designing brings to light organizational policies and practices that must be re-examined. The policies may have been forgotten, overlooked, never known, or non-existent. However, they may be crucial to performance, and identifying them sometimes makes it unnecessary to design a learning program. This is discussed in Chapter 3.

The CEM depicts what may happen, but it cannot be used to make predictions. Factors may intervene between the time the design process starts and the time the final design is actually delivered for implementation.

After using the CEM several times, a Designer should have some idea of the responses to the various questions found within the chapters, particularly at the end of each chapter. The Designer will understand how various parts of the organization will respond to being asked to be part of the design process.

Designing a learning program takes time. There is no exact formula that can tell us how much time will be needed.

Evaluation and Feedback

The CEM open model approach recognizes that the problem or opportunity that existed when the design process began may cease to exist or cease to be relevant by the end of the process. Therefore, the CEM provides specific opportunities and requirements that will keep the Designer in constant touch with the organization.

It presents a specific activity called "Evaluation and Feedback" at the end of each event. This activity enables the Designer to evaluate whether the problem or opportunity has changed while the design process has been going on. This activity is so important that Chapter 2 deals specifically with that event.

CHAPTER 2

Evaluation and Feedback

Although the Evaluation and Feedback (E&FB) event will not be implemented until after the Identify the Needs of the Organization event, it is necessary to discuss it first (see Figure 2-1). In this chapter the initial discussion will be general, but at the end of each subsequent chapter Evaluation and Feedback will be specifically related to the event discussed in that chapter.

As noted in Chapter 1, the emphasis on E&FB is one of the important elements of the CEM. It provides a constant tracking of the progress of the design process, and demonstrates the way each event relates to the current activities of the organization. It combines the design process with organizational activities so that the design process does not become irrelevant.

E&FB functions much like the "hold pattern" built into space flights. It does not signify that anything is wrong, but it alerts everyone to the necessity for some decision making before proceeding further. The Designer should not proceed to the next event until agreement is reached on what has been accomplished during the particular event and that it is appropriate to proceed to the next event.

As there can be confusion about the terms "evaluation" and "feedback," let us look at them before discussing how they will be used.

WHAT IS EVALUATION?

Evaluation is the process of relating outcomes to objectives or purposes. In the CEM, it must take place at the end of each event as a way of determining what has happened during that event, and how the outcomes relate to other events in the model.

Many people are familiar with evaluation when it is used in learning situations, job performance, or performance appraisal. In the CEM, evaluation is used to examine the processes and results that have taken place during one or more of the events.

THE CRITICAL EVENTS MODEL

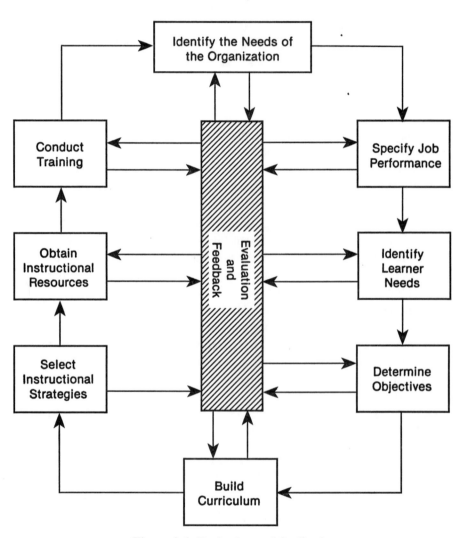

Figure 2-1. Evaluation and feedback.

During the design process, the Designer works for and with others in the organization—and perhaps even with some people outside the organization. During the CEM, the use of E&FB is not to evaluate the performance of the Designer, but rather to assess what has taken place during the design process. It is an evaluation of the outcomes of the design process, for which the Designer has responsibility.

A distinction should be made between evaluation and research. The essential difference is that evaluation should be designed to determine *what* happened, while research should be designed to determine *why* something happened [74]. Making this distinction enables us to decide which is more relevant. During the design process, evaluation is not only relevant, but essential. Every Designer must be competent in evaluation, though not necessarily in research.

There are different kinds of evaluation, and suggestions will be made as to those most appropriate at different stages of the CEM.

WHAT IS FEEDBACK?

Kurt Lewin was the first to apply the term "feedback," an engineering term, to his work in behavioral science. Many behavioral scientists continue to use it, although there are those who dislike the term. In the absence of a better, generally agreed upon term, we will continue to use it.

Feedback requires that those involved in the design process share what they have learned during evaluation. The specific people with whom the Designer must share will vary with each event, though there may be some overlap. It should become obvious that selecting those who will be directly involved in the feedback process requires care. The selection will reflect the Designer's knowledge of the organization, as well as its politics and culture.

This event underscores an important part of the CEM, which is that the Designer should not work alone. People from inside as well as outside the organization must be involved and the roster of those people will change from one event to another. Some people will be involved in almost every event, while others only in one or more.

The feedback may take place in a meeting or a series of meetings, and this may require that the Designer have small group skills to facilitate those meetings.

The feedback also may be in the form of written reports, particularly for individuals who should be informed although they are not directly involved in the process. This requires the Designer to have skills in written communication also.

EVALUATION AS A PROCESS

Evaluation is not a single activity, but a process with many models to choose from. Figure 2.2 shows a process of evaluation that can be helpful for the E&FB event of the CEM and for other design activities as well.

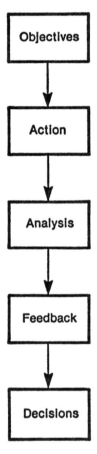

Figure 2-2. Evaluation process.

When using this model in the E&FB event, remember that it is the progress of the design process, not learning, that is being evaluated.

The process of evaluation is shown in Figure 2.2, but the process should be used in the reverse order: identify who will be getting the feedback, then identify what form that feedback should take.

Decisions

The Designer should begin by identifying who must make the decisions about the particular event. Those people will fall into several categories. Some of them will have the authority to make such decisions. For example, the individual who controls the budget must be involved in making money decisions.

Sometimes it is also necessary to involve those people who might be affected by the decisions. Although they cannot make the decisions, it can be helpful for the decision makers to know what those people think. This is particularly important when a customer service element of the design is being worked on.

Generally, for training, the immediate supervisor will be involved in making decisions during the development of the training model. For education, others, such as possible future supervisors, will be involved.

Feedback

Here the Designer must identify how the material will be disseminated to the various decision makers. If they are internal to the organization, the Designer must determine what channels of communication are available.

The Designer must determine whether the recipient prefers direct or indirect communication, a one-on-one meeting, or a written memo. The recipient may want to receive communications on his computer or voice mail or even on his personal fax machine. As time goes on, other methods of communication will provide exciting possibilities for the Designer to communicate to a variety of individuals.

The form of the feedback must be relevant to the recipient's usual work procedures and should include the ideas presented below.

Analysis

It is possible to analyze the results of any evaluation in a variety of ways. The Designer must consider who will receive this analysis and who will be involved in making decisions regarding this analysis.

Too often, a Designer will produce material that is "professionally" commendable, but of no use to the intended audience. A prime example is in the use of statistics. There are times when hard data (statistics) is preferable, and in those situations the Designer must ascertain the recipient's understanding and receptivity to statistics. Using statistical measures that the recipient will not understand, can hinder rather than enhance E&FB.

There may be more than one analysis of the results of the particular event in the CEM. This does not mean that the Designer will alter the information and data collected. Rather, it means different treatments (analyses) are required by recipients who plan to use the results in various ways. Some recipients just need to share information, while others need the analysis to make a decision. Certain recipients may merely request a one-page executive summary, while others may require a full report.

Action

This term denotes what is done within a particular event of the CEM, which will obviously be different for each event.

Objectives

These will be the specifics for each event of the CEM as discussed in the relevant chapters.

Note that although the flow of activity starts with "Objectives," the flow of planning for E&FB starts with "Decisions". The Designer must have as clear a picture as possible of what might be required for analysis, feedback, and decisions, because the Designer's perception will influence the actions that need to be taken.

The E&FB activities are repeated at the end of each event of the CEM in order to test the appropriateness of the design process. Sometimes this can prove frustrating, particularly when it takes time, a lot of time, to prepare for and involve the necessary people. Because E&FB is a way of assuring continuing relevancy of the design process, it must be done before proceeding to the next event. If the Designer meets resistance, it is possible that the original reason for the particular program being designed no longer exists.

ORGANIZATIONAL CULTURE AND HISTORY

If it is to be successful, the design process cannot exist in a vacuum. The Designer must be able to identify the culture and history of the organization and may also have to consider micro-culture, or the differences in culture in a specific unit of that organization [75].

When the Designer is external to the organization, he or she must identify and understand the cultural factors before choosing a model. An internal Designer, who is part of the culture and perhaps even of the history of the organization, may not be as sensitive to this need.

When designing E&FB, the Designer must be familiar with the cultural patterns that exist in the organization regarding individual involvement and the sharing of information. There may be a cultural pattern that determines how material is shared, whether by writing, orally, by computer, voice mail, or other channels. The culture may call for personal interaction, rather than written correspondence. The Designer must choose not only which option is "best," but which is culturally relevant.

The organization may have a history, as well as culture, of how decisions are made. The history of an organization is sometimes more readily accessible than the culture. Individuals may say, "Well, in the past we . . . ," or "Remember when . . .?" Such comments should signal the Designer that history in the organization is an important factor to be considered when planning for E&FB.

The Designer and E&FB

Through careful planning and attention to culture and history, the Designer can avoid becoming isolated from the rest of the organization during the design process. Where there is no prior history of E&FB, the Designer must plan these activities very carefully so that E&FB is seen as an identifiable activity that cannot be separated from the process.

Because other people will be involved in E&FB, the Designer must be able to coordinate its activities and outcomes. Although the Designer does not have to be in control, he or she is expected to assert the initiatives necessary to make this a positive experience for everyone.

The E&FB is a cumulative activity. It is impossible to overlook E&FB for the first part of the CEM and then introduce it at a later event. E&FB must be prominent and observable at each event of the CEM. That is the only way to ensure that a training program will be relevant to the changing needs of the organization.

As the design process progresses through the CEM events, the Designer can expect E&FB to take more time than during the earlier events. There will be more information to be processed, and more options are likely to open up. The Designer must allot additional time proportionately. There is no formula for a balance between time devoted to the E&FB and the time for the other events. There are too many factors, beyond the control of the Designer, which must be considered.

Effectively using E&FB depends on the history and culture of the organization. Knowing if the E&FB or something similar has been used in previous design experiences, or if project work or participative behavior is encouraged will influence how to plan and use E&FB.

Let us look at two major patterns of organizational behavior.

No Previous Participate Behavior

In organizations where there is little experience in participative behavior, there is no crossing of unit lines, no matrix organization, no project work groups, no task forces, or any other forms of participative management. As the E&FB is based on bringing individuals together from different parts of the organization, the Designer must be aware of the need to change some norms. Using the CEM, particularly E&FB, encourages participative behavior.

Many organizations attempt to introduce or reinforce participative behavior, and the Designer should be aware of that goal. This is only one example of how the CEM does more than just produce a learning program, and why it is necessary to tailor the program to the particular organization.

Organizations that do not have a history or culture of participate behavior can be identified in many ways, in spite of managers and executives who protest that they seek participation. When the Designer hears, "Don't bother me with the details. I am only interested in results," he or she should realize that it will be difficult to involve those people in the design process. However, if they are not involved—if they do not participate—they will probably not know what to look for in results.

In order to encourage reluctant individuals to participate, the designer must explain how each of those who should be involved in E&FB could benefit from the experience and the outcome. When people in the organization can readily see how a well-designed learning program could benefit them, they are more likely to participate. They must be encouraged to see the design process as their process, not something being foisted on them by the Designer. They must be shown how their participation in E&FB will benefit them, and their organization.

There are situations in which participative behavior exists in some parts of the organization, but not in all. The Designer should seek the areas where participation is being practiced, and build on that experience.

For example, if production people are involved in sales meetings, the Designer can build on this by showing that participating in the design process, through the E&FB, is much the same. One unit works with another for the benefit of all. You can make it a win-win situation by showing them that their participation is to their benefit, just as it is in a sales-production meeting.

Participating in E&FB takes time. At the outset, the Designer cannot tell how much time it will take, although time will be required away from daily tasks. For most people in an organization, time is a scarce commodity. Those who have little experience in participative behavior may need help in understanding how devoting some time to E&FB can save time later.

When you work with people who have not been involved in participative experiences, a sharp distinction must be made between influence and control. The E&FB allows for both, but the Designer should help the participants understand when each is appropriate. The Designer must retain ultimate control because the design is the Designer's responsibility. The Designer, through E&FB, seeks to give others the opportunity to influence the design and the design process.

There are those who will seek to control when they take part in a participative endeavor. Indeed, if they do not see the possibility of being in control, they may choose not to participate. If possible, such people should not be part of E&FB. If it is expedient to include them, the Designer may require some private meetings prior to an E&FB meeting to clarify the different responsibilities and expectations of each member of the E&FB group.

Previous Participative Behavior

Working with an organization where participative behavior is the norm is much easier. The challenge to the Designer is to identify the most acceptable and successful participative practices and build on them for using E&FB.

It may be necessary to adjust terminology to the customs of the particular organization. For example, instead of calling this event "Evaluation and Feedback," the Designer may choose to call it "Task Force on the Design," or another name that communicates the intent more effectively and according to the customs in the particular organization.

Even when participative behavior may be the organizational norm, there may be individuals who are not comfortable with participation. Therefore, the Designer should consider the needs of each person as an individual.

PREPARING FOR E&FB

Whether the organization is participative or not, the Designer must still prepare for E&FB, especially just after the first event, "Identify the Needs of the Organization" (Chapter 3). Here, we can explore some generalities that will apply to all the events of the CEM with respect to E&FB.

Composition of E&FB Group

It is unlikely that exactly the same people will be involved in E&FB for every event. As early as possible, the Designer should begin to identify the types and specific people to be involved in each event. Some people will be fairly obvious, such as supervisors for training, and potential supervisors for education. Customers might be involved in events related to customer service.

The Designer might also consider some other people as part of an E&FB group. At some events it might be helpful to include the "realists," who want to deal with hard data and the bottom line. For other events, "conceptual thinkers" might be helpful.

Internal and External People

Even though the Designer might be external, those taking part in an E&FB group will generally be from within the organization. They can be from a range of areas, depending on the problem or challenge identified in "Identify the Needs of the Organization" (Chapter 3). The group could include supervisors, managers, potential learners, shop stewards, others who have dealt with a similar or related problem, others who might be affected by the learning experience, and those who can be resources as internal subject matter specialists.

There are situations where external people might be helpful. "External" means those people who are not directly employed by the organization.

They could be customers, franchisees, union members, subject matter experts, and even government employees. The Designer's choice depends on the purpose of the design, who the learners will be, and the available internal resources.

An E&FB Workshop

It may be possible for the Designer to identify a core group that will be involved in the E&FB for most of the events of the CEM. Because that group will be working together, the Designer can bring them together early to become familiar with each other and to learn what will be expected of them during the E&FB meetings. At this time, the Designer can give the group a learning experience in group process. While some members of this permanent group may already have skills in group process, others may be very new to them. Because these skills are used in an organization, this training can have benefits for the groups beyond the E&FB.

E&FB MEETINGS

It is the Designer's responsibility to make specific preparations and arrangements for E&FB meetings, but it is not necessary, at the outset, to plan all the meetings. A pattern can be identified to help the Designer and those expected to participate.

One major point is to be sure that every member of an E&FB group knows the CEM in general. They do not need to know the specifics for each event, but they should have an overview so they will know how their E&FB group relates to the total design process.

For example, the pre-meeting reading material provided to members of an E&FB group might be a list of job performance requirements, with several levels of details. It is unlikely that the entire E&FB group for that event would be interested in how the list was derived. Some of them may even have been involved in that process, and therefore are already familiar with it. The Designer should have additional materials prepared for clarification. Those materials should not be distributed, as discussed below, but members of the group should know that they exist and are available.

For a specific E&FB meeting related to a specific event, each member of the E&FB group should have additional information on that particular event. Exactly what that should be is a decision to be made by the Designer. It will vary with each design, each organization, and the specific individuals taking part in that E&FB meeting.

Preparing for an E&FB Meeting

There are some general rules to follow when preparing for any meeting, and they can be helpful to the Designer. Some of them, however, have special application to an E&FB meeting.

There are times when a *design committee* is established by the Designer or some higher level manager in the organization. This is often necessary when there are some political concerns within the organization or when the Designer wants to broaden the base of those involved in the design process. For such a committee, the Designer should be a member, but definitely not the chairperson. The selection of the chairperson can be a political decision. The discussion that follows covers both situations: the use of a design committee and the Designer being in charge of the design process.

An E&FB meeting will review what has taken place during the particular event of the CEM. In most cases, it will be important to share at least the outcomes of that event, and perhaps even the process—how it was done, and who was involved.

This information can be shared in *writing* before the E&FB meeting. Generally, it will be in the form of a status report from the Designer. When a design committee is being used, the chairperson should send out that information, even though it would probably be drafted by the Designer. It is important that the tone of the report be one of sharing, rather than pushing towards any particular decision.

As the design emerges through the CEM, the amount of information available to the E&FB group will increase. This will require careful screening by the Designer to ensure that all members feel fully informed, yet not overwhelmed by paper pollution.

In some situations this material could be sent in writing via in-house computer linkages. If that is the case, the Designer must consider whether there is a need for privacy. When using the computer, for example, it is possible to send a private message to selected recipients. When using other forms of communication, such as a fax, it may not be as easy to restrict the output.

There may be situations when the preparation for a meeting requires *face-to-face* meetings between the Designer and individual members of the E&FB group. These should not be attempts on the part of the Designer to manipulate people or to plan the outcomes of the meeting. Some participants might want more information about particular points than others. Such pre-meeting conferences should be carefully planned by the Designer so that there is no implication that the Designer is doing something behind the backs of other E&FB group members.

For the E&FB meeting, as for any other well-planned meeting, a *notice* should be sent to all concerned. The notice should contain the basic information as to time, place, and anything else that would help them prepare. The Designer should recognize that, no matter how important the design process is, it is generally not of prime interest to those who will attend. They usually have other priorities. The time of the meeting should be carefully selected to meet the needs of as many of the E&FB participants as possible. Whenever possible, the expected duration of the meeting should be specified.

There should be a meeting *agenda,* which will be fairly obvious, as it is based on a particular CEM. Because the design process may not be foremost in the minds of most members of the E&FB group, it will help them to know what is planned and how they need to prepare. The *site* where the meeting will take place is also important. Here we get into the concept of the "territorial imperative," which states that where the meeting takes place has a significant impact on the behaviors during the meeting and the outcomes. Because the site of the meeting will send a message to those who are invited and others who know about the meeting, the Designer must seek a site that the organizational culture perceives as being of some status. It might be the office or conference room of the chairperson of the Design Committee, particularly if that individual holds a significant position in the organization. In some situations, it might be advisable to have the meeting close to the job site, where the results of the designed program are expected to have an effect. Unless there are some good reasons otherwise, the Designer should consider not having the meetings on the "Designer's turf" because that could convey more control than the Designer intends.

The site of the E&FB meeting can change depending upon the particular event, and members of the various E&FB groups should know that.

Despite the best efforts of the Designer, reality dictates that not everyone who is invited will attend every E&FB meeting. This will be explored further under the section on "Follow-up."

The Meetings

There may be more than one E&FB meeting at the end of each event. The Designer should plan for each meeting to build on what was done previously. If possible, and as needed, a commitment should be obtained from those attending to be present at the next meeting.

It is also possible that, as the result of a meeting, particular topics or tasks will be assigned to smaller groups within the E&FB participants. It may also become obvious that others need to be involved who are not currently members of the particular E&FB group.

The Designer must be sensitive to the possibility that calls for a sub-group or other people may indicate that those present do not want to stay involved. At this point, the Designer should re-examine the composition of the E&FB group. Are they the right people? Why do they want to involve others? There might be problems with the membership of the particular E&FB group or their tasks. It may well be, however, that the members of the E&FB see a need for other resources to enable them to process the information and arrive at a decision.

The various roles of the individuals participating in the meetings should be made clear. For example, it is generally best for the Designer to be the convener and not the chairperson. The E&FB group will probably want the Designer to serve as a secretary so that the work of the group will not get lost. The Designer should consider using technology to help. Recording the meeting could be as simple as using "newsprint," large blank pages on an easel or posted on the walls. Or, the entire meeting could be video taped. (More information on these technologies can be found in Chapter 8.)

Although the Designer may serve as secretary, that role should not inhibit full participation. It is probable that the Designer has more information and experience about the particular design event than anybody else in the room. Therefore, the Designer needs to be available as a resource, and not just a record keeper.

The norms for conducting the meeting should reflect those already established in the organization. This will probably not be the first meeting within the organization that the members of the E&FB group have participated in. The organization probably has a record of the history of such meetings and perhaps even indications of the cultural behavior in those meetings. The Designer must be aware of that history and the way such meetings were conducted.

The Designer should seek answers to questions, such as What is the range of behaviors expected during small meetings in the organization? Can everyone ask questions? Who chairs the meeting? What are the procedures? (Be sure you are not trapped into using Robert's Rules of Order, which can be deadly for such a meeting.) Are decisions reached by consensus or voting?

Physical factors must also be considered. Is it customary to have coffee or other beverages available during a meeting? Are finger foods (cookies, fruit, pastries) generally provided? Is everybody expected to sit during the entire meeting, or is it permissible for people to take a stretch when they wish?

Effective meetings are crucial to the implementation of E&FB. The Designer, as well as the participants, may need some work on group skills in small meetings.

Follow-up

At the end of an E&FB meeting, specific decisions must be made. One of the most significant could be the decision not to proceed! This may be considered heresy by some, but one of the important benefits of using an open model like the CEM is that the Designer and organization are not trapped into designing a program that may no longer be relevant or necessary.

Deciding to proceed, which is more likely, should be a positive decision arrived at by the process (consensus, majority vote) the E&FB group has previously agreed upon. Whatever the decision, it should be communicated to all concerned, so there is no ambiguity as to what will happen next. Until that is done, the Designer should not proceed to the next event of the CEM.

One technique is to use a "memo to files" or "memo to myself" [77,78]. This is a written document that sets forth at least the decisions reached by the group. It should also contain relevant information as to the data gathered during the event, particularly that which will be helpful for the next event. Not every member of the E&FB might want such a document, but it should be available to all.

The written document, as part of the follow-up at each event, needs to be different from the minutes of a meeting. Some Designers choose to send a draft of the document to the E&FB group before making it "official." Once again, such a practice should be relevant to the communication cultural practices in the organization.

There are times when particular members of an E&FB group might not be able to attend a meeting or the final meeting. This may make it even more important for the Designer to make sure that everyone has the relevant information. Although some members may not have been at the particular meeting, they might need to be involved in some of the later events of the CEM. They should not be dropped out of the loop. They should not be made to feel inadequate or asked to make special efforts to catch up with the process.

CONCLUSION

As noted earlier, E&FB does not end with the close of this chapter. In every chapter after this, E&FB will be one of the final activities discussed. It must be, for without E&FB built in as part of each event, the value of the event is lost.

It is possible that the E&FB group might meet even before the end of an event of the CEM. In the course of working on an event, the Designer may discover contradictions or ambiguities that were not previously apparent. By using the CEM, the Designer can readily move to another event as appropriate. The Designer may then exercise various options, such as returning to the current event, going back to a previous event, briefly exploring a future event, or suggesting that further work on the design process would not be helpful.

We will now return to the regular flow of the CEM and start with the event, Identify the Needs of the Organization.

CHAPTER 3

Identify the Needs of the Organization

Every organization has needs. These are defined as requirements the organization must meet in order to attain its goals, while recognizing that constraints exist on the kinds and number of resources available. Essentially, an organization's resources are the physical, financial, and human resources that it has or can obtain.

The focus of this chapter is on human resources, but by no means can we exclude the other resource areas. We will constantly refer to all the resources as we progress through the Critical Events Model.

An organization consists of people, and although this chapter discusses the needs of the organization, the emphasis will be on people who are part of the organization or in some way related to it.

The objectives of this event of the CEM are

- To determine the needs of the organization as they relate to HRD
- To identify which problems are related to training
- To explore options, other than training, that meet the needs of organizations.

THE NEEDS OF THE ORGANIZATION

We are now at the first event of the CEM (See Figure 3-1). All models are built on assumptions, and the first one in the CEM is that organizations will not provide training unless there is a specific need. Until that need is sufficiently defined, it is not possible to move on to the next event. This can be frustrating for Designers who want to get on with the work and begin the learning process, but this first event of the CEM is part of designing learning. Rushing ahead to the next event, before concluding this one invites disaster.

THE CRITICAL EVENTS MODEL

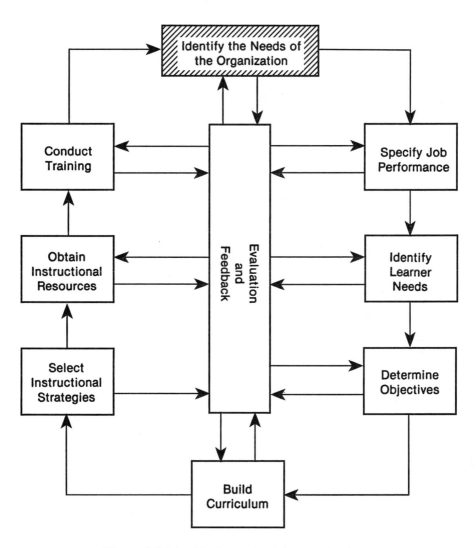

Figure 3-1. Identify the needs of the organization.

If training is a solution, it is important to first know the nature of the problem. Without that clarification, training can accomplish absolutely nothing except wasting resources.

This first event of the CEM contains what has been called "front-end analysis." Don't begin the design process unless there is some assurance that there is an agreed-upon problem, that training is an appropriate response to that problem, and that the response will not prove more costly than leaving the problem unsolved.

Problems arise within groups (the total organization or parts of it) and with individuals (employees and external customers). The needs of individuals and the organization do not have to be in conflict, though such a conflict sometimes exists. Generally, the needs of both the individual and the organization have to be identified. However, because HRD is provided by the organization, it is necessary to first look at organizational needs. This can be done without demeaning or ignoring individuals.

Individual Problems and Group Problems

A dichotomy sometimes exists. How would you respond to the question, "Which is more important, individual development or organizational development?" This question was actually asked in a survey in the 1960s, and it is still being asked by some people today. It assumes that these two factors are at opposite ends of a continuum, and that the answer is either/or. It ignores the possibility that both might be appropriate, depending on the needs of the individual and of the organization.

There are times when the purpose of training is to bring about modification of individual behavior, for example, a training program to teach a learner a specific skill to be used with a piece of equipment. There are other times when the training program is concerned with learning behavior that affects others. This is an organizational concern.

To be more specific about designing learning programs, it is necessary to look more closely at what is an organizational need (related to training) and how it arises.

WHERE DO NEEDS COME FROM?

From Others

Picture a time when you are sitting at your desk, and you receive a phone call. You are told that production in a particular department has fallen below quota, and you are asked to design a training program to increase production. There is no doubt that there is some kind of production problem; therefore, there is an organizational need. Before rushing into design, however, it is important to stop and determine whether or not training is an appropriate solution to that need.

From the tone of your caller, it may be possible to determine that the need is an urgent one. As production performance can be quantified in terms of output, any variation below a determined figure becomes a problem (need) for somebody in the organization.

If the call had been from the service area, identifying the problem could have been more difficult. The problem may not be one of output, which can be quantified, but that does not mean that a problem does not exist. If a manager (your caller) thinks that there is a problem, you must at least make some kind of positive response. To do less would reduce the possibility of future phone calls when help is needed from the HRD unit.

Although quantification is lacking in the service area, it is still possible to have very specific needs. A common one is an increase in customer complaints. In a supermarket, long lines at the checkout counters could encourage consumers to take their business to a competitor. The problem is certainly visible, even though it may not be readily quantifiable in terms of sales.

At first, managerial requests for a program may be very gratifying. Although it is necessary to respond hopefully to your caller, do not rush out. First, you need to know much more about that problem. Let us look at some of the possibilities that need to be explored when trying to identify the need of the organization, as related to a possible training program.

From Your Past Performance

People in your organization may be coming to you because you have an admirable track record. In the past, you helped them solve problems through the training programs you designed. The new request may be completely different from anything you have done in the past, but you are still looked to for the solution rather than part of their problem solving process.

It takes a strong will and a good self-image to respond by slowing down the enthusiasm and focusing on the design process. By introducing the CEM design, particularly this event, you are indicating your willingness to respond, but indicating that some up-front issues must be explored first.

If you have been doing a good job of helping managers solve their problems through training, of course you will get repeat calls. That provides one measure of feedback on your performance. Once you have been accepted as part of the problem-solving resources of your organization, you will find that it is relatively easy to advocate a design process over a quick response based on inadequate data.

When the Designer is new to the organization, particularly when the HRD activity is just starting, it may be necessary to respond fairly rapidly with a training program just to gain validity and acceptance. You should, however, recognize that you are doing it for those reasons, and you may not be coming close enough to the real need of the organization. You should be able to differentiate between those programs you are designing to gain acceptance and those that are directed towards meeting the identified needs of your organization.

Production or Service

Before 1960, most needs arose from some area of production, where most of the U.S. workforce was engaged. With the explosion of technology, the workplace changed, and by 1990, it was estimated that an overwhelming part of the workforce was engaged in service areas. This includes the exchange of information, as well as direct customer service.

The comments below can only address generalizations; each organization is different. Some organizations focus on production, some deal only in service, and others have both elements within the same organization. The factors discussed, however, can give you some indication of what you can look for in your organization.

Equipment

Given the constantly changing technology, it is not surprising that one of the major forces that creates training needs is the introduction of new equipment or the need to update existing equipment. This is certainly not new. When electric typewriters were introduced in the early 1950s, people assumed that the change would not pose any problems or needs. With this new technological wonder, typists would just be able to type faster, with no need for training. The keyboard was the same as the old manual ones, so it would be easy for a typist to sit at the same desk, replace the manual typewriter with the electric machine, and just start typing.

In practice typing output decreased measurably. The morale of typists took an appreciable slide down, and grumbling was audible. Researchers were called in. After exhaustive studies, they determined that one of the problems was the lack of training to facilitate the changeover. In addition, they also found that it was much more difficult to teach a manual typist to work the new electric machines than to teach a person who had never worked on a manual. In both situations, a learning program was essential, but in the case of the manual typist it required a design to provide for unlearning.

More recently, the introduction and availability of personal computers has presented problems for organizations. As computers became more common, it was assumed that every executive and manager would have one. Frequently, little was done to provide the learning that would enable those people to effectively use the new technology of the computer.

Any new technology introduces the need for some behavioral change and some training. Too often, however, the new technology is introduced before the training, and usually even before the organization has fully considered its implications.

Introducing the computer into management changed the way people had traditionally communicated since the introduction of the telephone. With computer technology, it is possible for managers to "talk" to each other without leaving their offices. One person can now leave a message on another person's computer at any time of the day or night. It is no longer possible for a person to say, "I never got your message." If the message did not go through, the sender would know that. If it did go through, it was just waiting for the receiver. This communication mode required significant changes in behavior within and among organizations. The need arose for learning to use this mode of communication, as well as the other virtually instantaneous forms of communication such as the fax machine. We are nowhere near the end of the introduction of such technology or the needs they constantly generate.

Regulations

Regulations come from many sources, internal and external. Internal regulations may be called many things. They often reflect the written and unwritten policies and practices of the organization. When regulations are written, as in a personnel manual, it is much easier to recognize them. Written regulations can also exist for standards of production, customer service, or virtually any aspect of organizational life. The unwritten regulations that "everybody knows" are much more difficult to deal with.

Whatever the regulations are, they are sure to change, and such changes frequently create needs. Designers must be alert to the possibilities that might involve training. They should try to anticipate the changes in regulations and work with those who promulgate changes so that the organizational need which might require training can be identified early enough.

External regulations principally come from the government. Complaints about government regulations can be found in almost every daily issue of a newspaper. Columnists and reporters thrive on this subject. Politicians, running for office find the topic of regulations very convenient as a rallying cry against the incumbents.

Designers should not become embroiled in the debate over government regulations. But there is no question that a constant flow of governmental regulations exists and some of these will create needs in the organization that Designers should consider.

Professional Society Regulations

Given the impact of expanding technology, it is no surprise that an increasing part of the workforce involves various professional societies, organizations, and groups. (For reasons of simplicity, we will refer to all of them as societies.) As can be expected, the societies establish various criteria for performance.

This has long been the case in areas such as health and accounting. It has now spread to other areas, and the Designer must be familiar with those which might influence the work force of a particular organization.

When there are several societies in the same area, the Designer must be cautious and not identify with any of them. That is the choice of the employees whose work is controlled, or at least influenced, by those societies. In designing a program for employees in those areas, the Designer should reflect the regulations of the organization, with due deference to the regulations promulgated by the societies.

As the regulations from those societies change, some of them will require training programs. The Designer must be sure to work closely with the groups within the organization who are or will be affected by those changes, and design appropriate training.

Organizational Changes

The curve for activity in mergers, acquisitions, and diversification tends to have peaks and valleys. Generally, those activities are driven by financial considerations. Too often, the human element is not given adequate attention.

Consider an executive decision to diversify. The organization is in sound financial condition and has a good market position, so the executive level may decide to reach out into different areas to diversify. Such decisions are not uncommon, and they produce a new set of organizational needs that did not exist previously.

In a dizzying series of cycles, we have witnessed acquisitions and mergers. Each one of these causes organizational changes. Too often, the human resource part of the organizational change is overlooked.

Another form of organizational change takes place when a new company is spun off as a subsidiary of a parent company. This has become more common as organizations recognize the need that some people have to be entrepreneurial, a need which can infrequently be met in large organizations.

Consider the decision to add a new product line to an existing organization. This may be desirable for any number of reasons involving market share, new technologies, or changing consumer composition. It may not seem to be too great a decision, but it can introduce new supplies, customers, and processes. All of these can create organizational needs for which training might be an effective response.

Customers

For this discussion, the term customers will include external customers (sometimes called consumers) as well as those within the organization, where one unit "sells" its product or services to other parts of the organization.

At one time, it was thought that customers need not influence the organization to any great degree. Increasingly, however, the customer has begun to influence how an organization functions. As has been noted, "customer expectations have been raised to new levels and fresh requirements established" [42, p. 274–275]. The passive customer of the past has generally disappeared. As more organizations involve customers through activities such as feedback mechanisms and focus groups, it can be expected that customers will either identify or create organizational needs that previously had not been apparent. Many of those needs will require training.

One of the most obvious needs is in the area of quality. For a variety of reasons, more customers have been concerned about quality and look for it in the goods or services they purchase. Quality must be designed into the product/service, but that design may also create a training need.

External Pressures

Organizations exist in some "community" that surrounds them. This community consists of many elements, and any of these can bring about needs that did not exist previously.

One kind of pressure starts from the outside, but the Designer meets it as a *request from a company officer.*

Picture the situation of a Designer who is called into a manager's office and asked to design a training program about _____ (you can fill in the blank with almost anything) because one of the company officials heard that a competitor was using that training program.

This happens when a fad or gimmick catches the corporate fancy. It is not too difficult to look back over the past years and produce an impressive list that would include things like sensitivity training, transactional analysis, transcendental meditation, programmed instruction, video-tape recording, behavior modeling, quality circles, or total quality management. Actually, each of these does have something to offer. At this point, we use them to illustrate that sometimes a need seems to arise when a company officer wants the organization to be able to report that they are in the forefront of a trend in training, whatever it happens to be at the time.

External pressure can also come from *suppliers* or those who sell various kinds of training programs. As an organization recognizes the importance of training, so does the marketplace. The proliferation of suppliers in this field is one of the major growth areas in recent years, and it is destined to grow even more. At one time, those applying such external pressure were called vendors, but they prefer the term suppliers. Some people (and firms) dislike even being called suppliers, preferring the more glamorous title of "consultant." In terms of designing training programs, suppliers usually sell a product or design a training program.

As a group, suppliers include those who provide training designs (which can be used as purchased, or can be customized as needed), sell hardware (equipment), sell software (computer, psychological inventories), and supply facilities or sites. This is only a short list for illustrative purposes. Suppliers have more to offer, and what they offer changes with the marketplace. If you are interested in the length and variety of the list, just check out those publications in the HRD field that have monthly or periodic buyers' guides. Notice that they are consistently growing and that suppliers are showing wide varieties of offerings. In addition, the daily mail (and fax) brings attractive brochures, and the ringing of a Designer's telephone often heralds the approach of a supplier's salesperson.

There is certainly nothing wrong with this situation, since increased competition can be helpful, both in quality and cost. But, just as a Designer receives this input from suppliers, so do some other members of the organization. They then turn to the Designer and ask, "Why don't we have that kind of _____ ?" (The blank line represents whatever the supplier is offering.) "How come you are not smart enough to know that such a _____ exists, and that we 'need' it?" Too often, the tendency of the Designer is to acquiesce and purchase the program to show others that the Designer and the HRD unit know what is current.

The variety and volume of offerings by suppliers will depend upon the economic conditions and the introduction of new technology or concepts. A Designer must keep up-to-date and help the organization assess the validity of needs created by suppliers.

Competition

Most organizations have to consider the marketplace. Even nonprofit or government organizations, which may not have direct "competition," have to consider the alternatives in the marketplace. For example, the US Postal Service, must consider what the private carriers (Federal Express, UPS, and others) are now doing and planning for the future.

The competition for a particular organization is generally identified by executives and managers. Some of the responses they plan to make to the competition can be expected to generate organizational needs.

Government

This is not the place to argue about the role of government in the private sector, but rather, to recognize that in every country in the world, organizations are affected by the laws and regulations governments pass. The organization can also be affected by the absence of some laws and regulations, such as in the case of foreign competition.

There are times when the actions of a foreign government, will also produce some needs. Indeed, the world appears to be constantly shrinking in terms of how the government of one country affects companies in other countries. For example, at the end of the 1980s, the government of Thailand made a positive decision to move from an agricultural economy to an industrial economy. This movement caused companies in Singapore to change some of their practices in order to discourage foreign companies from moving from Singapore to Thailand.

In any event, the government must always be seen as a force that creates needs for an organization, although only a limited number may fall in the area of training.

Changing Workforce

There were times, when the workforce in any country and in any organization was fairly predictable. That is no longer the case in most countries because of several factors.

One is the increasing movement of people from one country to another, principally from lesser developed countries to developed countries. The former tend to be agricultural, with fairly low levels of school achievement. The latter are more likely to require higher levels of school achievement for the workforce.

In addition, in some developed countries, there have been increasing efforts to include more people in the workforce who in earlier years would have been on the fringes or not in the workforce at all. This includes those who lack the basic literacy competency required in the workforce, women, or some minorities.

These changing populations in the workforce create organizational needs that might not be apparent. The 90s has been emphasizing "basic skills." This includes, of course, the usual arithmetic and communication skills, but also workplace behaviors.

In summary, then, these external pressures are pervasive and emphatic. Some of the needs they create require training, but not all. It takes a great deal of strength to resist some of those pressures, where training may not be an appropriate response, particularly when the budget is in the hands of others. If the HRD unit (Designer) does not respond, it is not difficult for those others to use their budgets to purchase training programs externally and bypass you. In very few cases will "they" (whoever controls that budget) admit that perhaps the external training program they purchased did not really make any difference in their operations. At that point, the Designer should refrain from saying "I told you so," and be ready to assist when training is an appropriate response.

ORGANIZATIONAL DIAGNOSIS

Diagnosis is a continual process. Managers continually diagnose as they solve problems, even though they may not use that word to describe their activities and may not use standardized instruments or available organizational diagnostic models. They do, however, continually ask questions, and if you as the Designer can be part of that questioning process, you are closer to helping provide some of the appropriate solutions. This first event of the CEM is directly related to the diagnostic activities within an organization.

How Are We Doing?

This question is frequently asked in many parts of the organization, though in different ways. It may be expressed in terms of the "bottom line"— are we making a profit or taking a loss? Or, it may be related to the goals and mission of the organization. Sometimes it is asked as an organized data-gathering process, while at other times it may be one of the standard items on the agenda of staff meetings.

How Can We Do Better?

The pressures of the marketplace or the demands of the customers dictate that organizations that do not change are doomed to die or spend much of their resources attempting to survive. One need of the organization is to constantly seek ways of doing things better in order to retain or improve its position.

This search for improvement is generally stated in terms of financial resources. In some situations, it is possible to do better, but the cost of improving could price the organization out of the market. There are alternatives, and training could be one of them, but careful exploration is required before a Designer rushes to start the design process. The Designer must avoid the possibility that the cure (training) could turn out to be worse than the illness (the need).

A different but related approach to doing better has evolved with quality *circles.* (This should not be confused with quality *control,* which is a different activity.) This technique for exploring ways in which an organization could do better was started in the United States in the late 1950s and early 1960s, generally as part of activities in the area of participative management and suggestion systems. Its use in Japan attracted a great deal of attention during the 1970s, causing many people to consider it a Japanese management technique. Applications of quality circles are based on the premise that those who are doing the work are likely to know their own problems and possible solutions.

If your organization uses such an activity, no matter what it is called, there are needs that are relevant for the Designer. The first one may be to design training for participants who need to learn how to function more effectively in quality circles. The Designer might try to encourage quality circle participants to allow the Designer to sit in on some of their meetings. One purpose would be to listen carefully and to identify those needs of the organization for which training could be a response. If a Designer is accepted by such a group, he or she can also help them avoid the "training is the answer" response before exploring the need further.

Not all organizations function in the same kind of marketplace. Some government organizations do not face competition. Although lack of competition has been blamed for the government's lack of efficiency, we have only a limited understanding of the forces that influence the behavior of government employees. They are always under the microscope of the media, citizen groups, and special interest groups. Some governmental structures may even have special oversight groups that look closely at operations.

Nonprofit organizations may not have to face marketplace competition, but they must constantly seek ways to do things better. They have very limited financial resources and are under constant pressure to improve the job performance of all their employees and volunteers. This is a constant organizational need for them.

What Problems Do We Have?

Every organization has problems, and new ones always arise. Traditionally, it is the job of managers to solve problems. Designers can help them by working on solutions for which training could be an effective response.

Increasingly, people at all levels of the organization are being involved in solving problems, and this suggests that they should also be involved in designing the training programs that will be provided to address those problems. There are many dimensions to involving many different kinds of people in organizational problem solving, because the range of problems is great. Some of the problems involve only one kind of resource (for example, physical), but most problems involve all three resources (physical, financial, human). Some of the problems concern only a single individual or a small group of individuals, while other problems involve the entire organization.

Constantly solving problems is a basic need of any organization. One difficulty is determining whose problem it is and how important it is to that individual and to the organization. For one person, solving a particular problem could be the most important immediate task. For another person in the same organization, solving that particular problem could have a very low priority.

What Problems Can We Anticipate?

It is not enough to solve the problems that exist—consideration must also be given to anticipating problems that might arise. A common problem, exacerbated by the continuing use of new technologies, is the introduction of new equipment, such as word processors or lasers. It includes any equipment that requires a change in performance by those who, on their present job, will be required to operate the new equipment.

The organization needs to anticipate the future and to take appropriate action as soon as possible so that the organization's leaders are prepared for changing conditions. Despite the urgency of this need, some of the leaders ignore obvious sign-posts. Perhaps there is a tendency to think that one can solve some problems by ignoring them, or to react only to those problems that verge on becoming a crisis.

What is being done in your organization to prepare for the future? Take one area, the changing diversity of the work force. This has many dimensions, including age, ethnic origin, and level of schooling of employees. Some organizational leaders have recognized the problems and opportunities of a changing work force, while others have not.

Consider the following. A fast-food chain in the U.S. conducted a comprehensive market study on ways the changing population affects what they sell and the methods they used to market their products and services. The results were astounding, and the company entered into a massive effort to develop significant changes to accommodate the data provided by the study.

At the same time, we met with the HRD officials in that company on some current problems. When we learned of the marketing study, we wondered aloud whether any efforts were being made to relate that data to HRD. We asked what changes might be required due to a different workforce in those areas and the new products and services? Given those changes, what training programs would need to be designed? Up to that point, nothing had been done to relate the extensive, important data and the impending managerial decisions to the HRD effort of the organization. The practice in that organization had been to first make changes and then implement training. Fortunately, they realized how inconsistent this approach was, and HRD was included in the project early enough so that training could be assigned for the anticipated changes.

Timing

Organizations always have problems. What a Designer must determine is the reason a particular problem erupted *now,* and who or what caused the problem to surface at this time.

The answers to these questions are crucial, for if training is to be used as a solution to a problem, the Designer must know the time frame and who will seek the solution.

PERFORMANCE ANALYSIS

Training is essentially concerned with performance. Therefore, it is important to ask: What performance is required? How do the needs of the organization relate to a performance problem?

How Did The Need Arise?

Once again the Designer must determine how the need arose and who identified it. As discussed earlier, needs can arise from either internal or external sources. From whatever source, there will be some person within the organization who has responsibility related to that need.

For example, there may be complaints about the quality of merchandise, late shipments, damaged materials, or incorrect invoicing. Particularly where service is involved, customer complaints can arise quickly and require immediate actions.

The source of the need, and the individuals involved, must be carefully identified. During this event, agreement must be reached that, no matter what the source, it is a human performance problem for which training is a solution. Otherwise, the design process ends here.

Which Human Resource Area?

As we have noted in *Developing Human Resources* [80], the human resource area is broad and covers many different aspects. One topology is to see the HR area as shown in Figure 3-2, Human Resource Areas. This is a "snapshot" of the HR areas in the early 1990s. It has changed over decades, and can be expected to continue to change. However, it will serve to illustrate what a Designer must look for.

Note that HRD is only one of the four major areas. Each of the other areas also has implications for solving performance problems. Some of the specifics related to this are discussed below in Alternatives to Training. Before starting any design, the Designer must be sure that the major solution is in the HRD-training area, though some part of the solution may also rest in one of the other HR areas.

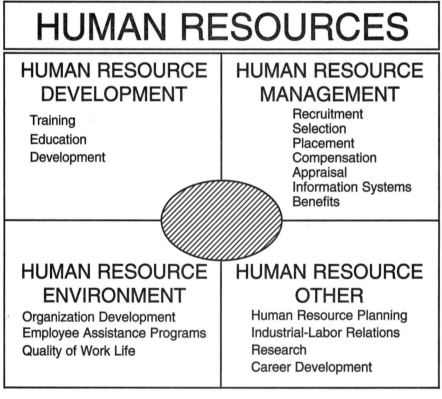

HUMAN RESOURCES	
HUMAN RESOURCE DEVELOPMENT Training Education Development	**HUMAN RESOURCE MANAGEMENT** Recruitment Selection Placement Compensation Appraisal Information Systems Benefits
HUMAN RESOURCE ENVIRONMENT Organization Development Employee Assistance Programs Quality of Work Life	**HUMAN RESOURCE OTHER** Human Resource Planning Industrial-Labor Relations Research Career Development

Figure 3-2. Human resource areas. Reprinted with permission [80].

Cost/Benefit

As with any other solution, consideration must be given to the cost/benefit relationship. That is, will it cost more to solve the problem than to leave the problem unsolved? This is an extremely difficult question to answer, but it is one that must be asked.

One difficulty is with actually determining the *cost*. In some areas, this can be done easily. In manufacturing, for example, it is easy to calculate loss due to waste, poor quality during manufacturing, reworking, and similar quantifiable costs. For service and knowledge, it is not that easy. Customer complaints can be quantified, but there may be customer dissatisfaction that does not result in complaints but in customers just going to other organizations to have their needs met.

Another element of cost is the amount of money it would take to "fix" the problem. If training is being considered, what would be the cost of that training? It may be difficult for the Designer to calculate that figure this early in the design process, but some kind of professional guess should be made.

Similarly, the *benefit* of the training may be difficult to quantify. For manufacturing, once again, it may be relatively easy to calculate what can be saved by doing it right the first time. For service and knowledge, the direct benefit may not be easily quantified and weighed against the cost.

Using cost/benefit as a major part of the front-end analysis may not be sufficient. Other factors must be considered besides the "bottom line." Consideration must be given to the people concerned so they are not treated as machines or fixed elements in the cost/benefit relationship. That does not mean that a cost/benefit relationship should not be developed, but it should not be the only factor considered.

ALTERNATIVES TO TRAINING

Up to this point, the focus has been on training to meet the needs of the organization. Consideration must also be given to alternatives for meeting those needs. Although the implementation of those alternatives is outside the scope of the Designer, it is important that the Designer be aware of them.

Training should not be considered the last resort, nor should it be considered the only response to an organizational need. Before making such a commitment of time and resources, before going on to the next event of the CEM, the Designer should at least help the organization explore other alternatives.

The Designer who does not help the organization explore possible alternatives is courting disaster. Though the range of alternatives keeps expanding, the need for training programs may still exist. A Designer should not feel threatened by being asked to explore alternatives. Rather, it helps the Designer and the organizational leadership focus on what training can and should do and how training can relate to some of those other alternatives.

Searching for alternatives will show the organizational leadership that the Designer is not so myopic professionally as to consider training the only response to every problem. It is even possible that some of those alternatives could be enhanced by a training component, though training is not the major thrust.

Hackman and Oldham [33] have suggested four widely used alternatives. They are

1. Change the people who are doing the work.
2. Change the people who are related to those doing the work.
3. Change the workplace.
4. Change the contingencies, benefits, and rewards.

Let us look at some of these and other alternatives that should be explored as part of this first event of the CEM. Although the Designer may decide that the design process should not be continued, the information gathered in exploring alternatives can be helpful to the Designer.

Fire and Hire

Firing some people and hiring others may seem cruel and inhumane, but sometimes it is the best way to solve a problem. This, of course, should not be done lightly, and not by the Designer. However, the Designer may have to consider that alternative.

For example, some years ago we were asked by a major bank in New York City to design a sales training program. This was at the time when banks were struggling to become competitive in New York, and selling was being introduced into banking as a new and necessary activity. The bank hired a vice-president for marketing (an almost unheard of position at the time) and set up a marketing unit (really a sales unit). They asked us to design a training program for personnel who would be selected from among their regular employees to work in that new unit. The trainees would be what are called "platform" people.

This type of employee goes back to the early days of banking in the U.S., and at that time, employees actually sat on a platform or behind swinging gates. One reason for this was to separate them from the public, until the platform person was ready to speak to the applicant. In more recent times, "platform" people are the people seated in bank lobbies at desks, away from the tellers' windows, and sometimes still behind a swinging gate that limits the access of the public.

In the banking world, a platform position was a step up from teller and similar entry level positions. It was a position to which many lower level bank employees aspired. It meant being in control, making bank assets available, and was generally considered prestigious. The essence of the platform position was that the employee sat at a desk, and the public came to the desk, sometimes at the discretion of that employee.

The change that the bank officials wanted to bring about, through training, was for the platform person to get out from behind the desk, visit customers at their work sites, and sell banking services. The goal was commendable, but the bank's new approach caused some difficulties. As part of this first event of the CEM, we interviewed some of the platform people to focus in on the new problem/opportunity. We found, in private interviews, that many of the platform people had no intention of getting out from behind their desks. They had worked for years to reach the point where the desk was a reward, a symbol of success on the job and in the organization.

We reported back to our client in the bank, as part of this first CEM event. After some discussion, we suggested that training was not the first step to bring about the change they wanted. First, it was important to assess each platform person and decide either to retain that person in the present position, reassign to another position in the bank, or terminate. It would also be important to recruit new employees who would not see sitting behind a desk as a reward for good performance. The organization was asking for too great a change in behavior through a training program. Some of the platform people were not prepared to do the job as redesigned, and training would not change that attitude.

Despite this, we were still offered a contract to design a training program. We turned down the offer for this design project, although we did continue to do other work with the bank. Our suggestions on this project were ignored, and a contract to design a training program was given to another external Designer. Subsequently, a training program was conducted.

Within six months the vice-president for marketing was fired, and a different person was hired for the job. Simultaneously, some new people were recruited and selected for the redesigned platform job and were assigned to go out of the bank and sell. Some of the former platform people were retained for those activities that still needed to be done behind the desks, and a few more were kept who agreed to sell outside the bank site.

There are times and situations when a training program cannot bring about the massive change in job performance that the organization expects. Designers need to have the courage to say this during this first event of the CEM and not wait until a final evaluation of the training program discloses that the anticipated performance change was not possible.

If the decision is to hire new employees, then consideration should be given to designing and providing education for those new employees.

Redesign the Job

An effective response to an organizational need might be design of the job instead of design of a training program. For example, several years ago, a nuclear accident occurred in the U.S. at the Three Mile Island nuclear plant. After much time and investigation, the final report by the concerned U.S. agency noted that this accident had multiple causes. One, as determined by the investigating group, was the lack of sufficient training and education, and another was a lack of adequate standards of performance. It was also found that no amount of training or education could have helped because the workplace had been designed in such a way that no single employee was capable of performing all the functions that were required. The immediate solution was to redesign the jobs, which highlighted the need to continually check job design.

Performance is a result of multiple factors. There are situations where redesigning the workplace and specific jobs may meet organizational needs and solve problems far beyond what might be accomplished by training.

That is not to say that a Designer must be able to design or redesign jobs or the workplace. There are others who are experts in those areas. The Designer might find it advisable, in some situations, to call upon those people for their advice before starting to design a training program.

Change Equipment or Regulations

Sometimes the need for training arises because of an inconsistency between the requirements of the job and the equipment provided to do the job or the regulations that affect the job.

This becomes obvious when there is a management/labor conflict and the employees say they will "work by the book" (stick strictly to the contract and regulations.) It then becomes evident that in order to get the job done, it may be necessary for employees to use equipment in ways not intended or to overlook some regulations.

The Designer should not wait for a conflict before becoming aware of possible discrepancies. They do not always exist, but the possibility is always present. There are many reasons why this situation can occur, but that is not within the scope of the CEM. Rather, if the Designer suspects that the equipment being used on the job is the cause of the problem, then others need be involved. These people may be engineers, purchasing agents, or maintenance personnel. Indeed, their involvement may highlight a hidden need for some training for them as well, but that should not be the reason for involving them. Rather, the Designer must be sure that the equipment is not the cause of the problem before beginning to design a training program.

Regulations can be even more complicated because this area can involve government officials at all levels. Private organizations hesitate to open their doors to those officials and generally try to abide by the pertinent governmental regulations. This leads some organizations to ignore or bury factors related to some government regulations, particularly in the area of health and safety.

Before Designing for a problem related to equipment and regulations, the Designer should work with others to determine whether any changes have to be made in those areas. If not, then training might be the appropriate approach.

Organizational Change

The concept of "organization development" has been in vogue since the middle 1960s. Over the decades it has changed, and rightly so. The broader concept of organizational change can include many elements, one of which could be organization development. A related approach is to look at the organizational changes that might require different ways of organizing, or what has been called organization architecture [72].

Various kinds of organizational changes are possible. To make a unit more effective, it might be desirable to change the reporting direction or the placement of the unit within the organization. There are many changes that can improve performance, and they should be tried before contemplating a training program.

Organizational relationships will be highlighted in the next event, Specify Job Performance. At this first event, however, consideration should be given to looking only at the overall organizational relationships and ways in which they may contribute to an organizational need. If it appears that changes are required, the consideration of those changes should precede attempts to design a training program. The very changes may contribute to a need to train.

Traditional organizational patterns are slowly giving way to more innovative relationships in order to improve organizational and individual effectiveness. For people who thrive on the ambiguity of some of those relationships, there may be few problems. For others, training may be helpful to minimize the ambiguity and lead towards more effective performance.

EVALUATION AND FEEDBACK

This first event of the CEM explored some of the reasons organizations have needs related to HRD. It also explored some non-HRD alternatives that a Designer must consider. Before going on to the next event of the CEM, some specific questions should be addressed and specific decisions should be made.

At this point, the Designer moves into the Evaluation and Feedback event.

Whom to Involve

During this first event, a wide variety of individuals may have been involved in the meetings and data gathering. It is unlikely that all of them need to be or should be involved in evaluation and feedback.

At the very least, however, those people who are the *decision makers* should be involved. They would be the people who can authorize the Designer to proceed to the next event.

These people should be in the position to authorize:

- the involvement of others, particularly those at the job site
- the identification of the specific learners
- time release, if needed, to attend the program
- budget for the program.

This last item would depend on where the budget will come from. This will be discussed further under the event Obtain Instructional Resources.

Consideration should also be given to involving one or more of the *supervisors* of those who are expected to be in the program. One or more of them will probably have been in the group that met during this first event.

Decisions

The following are the questions that must be asked and the decisions that must be made before going on to the next event:

1. Is there agreement on what the problem is?

   To avoid ambiguity, it is helpful to have the problem stated in writing so everyone can see it. This will also be helpful when setting up objectives and evaluating the results of the training.

   It is not necessary to have any "sign-offs" on the written statement, unless that is the practice in the organization. It is not meant to be a legal document, but rather an internal "memo of understanding."

2. Is it agreed that training is important to solving the problem?

   For some problems, there may be a variety of responses to this question. The general scope of training should be agreed upon, even though the details cannot be specified until more of the CEM has been accomplished.

   The Designer should avoid making promises for what training can do, because all that can be said at this point is that learning will take place. Actual job performance is not under the control of the Designer and the HRD unit. It is the responsibility of the supervisor and the learner.

3. Is there a specific decision to start the design of the training program?

   It is important that the decision be clear and specific. It must encompass more than a wave of a hand or the nod of a head.

One is reminded of the confusion that frequently occurs in negotiations between the U.S. and Japan. The U.S. negotiator asks if the Japanese negotiator understands, and receives "Hai" in return. Generally, the U.S. negotiator thinks this means "yes," for that is the dictionary definition. In usage, however, "Hai" also means "I hear you." It is much like a U.S. person just shaking the head to signify hearing, while somebody from another culture might consider it agreement. Within the organization, the Designer must be perfectly clear on what constitutes agreement to a decision.

MOVING FORWARD

When the decision is clear and specific, the Designer can proceed to the next event, Specify Job Performance. If time allows, the Designer should stop at this point and reflect on what happened during the present event. While the experience is fresh, the Designer should note ways in which to use this first event more effectively the next time the CEM is used.

Some of the discussion that has taken place may signify paths to explore or bypass as the Designer moves on to the next event.

CHAPTER 4

Specify Job Performance

With the completion of the previous event, it becomes important to look at the specific job for which the Designer is asked to design a training program. The job currently exists in the organization, but some individual (or group) has determined that its performance needs improvement. As noted at the end of the previous chapter, it was agreed that training could be a solution to that problem.

It is crucial that this event follows directly after Identify the Needs of the Organization (Chapter 3). This is one way that the CEM differs from other models, which often identify the needs of the learner first and assume that the problem rests with the learner rather than with the job itself.

It is essential that agreement exists within the organization about the job that is to be performed. Until agreement is reached on what the job contributes to the organization, and how, it is meaningless to attempt to improve performance on that job.

The Designer should not be chagrined if, at the end of this event, it is determined that there is no need for this job. Indeed, it is much better to discover that before going through the costly process of designing.

Some controversy exists regarding the use of the words "behavior" and "performance." Earlier versions of the CEM used the word "behavior" for the label of this event. Historically, that was correct. But, over the past years there has been a growing tendency to use "performance" to describe what is done on a job. By the end of this event, the Designer will be able to specify the performance expected of an employee who is doing that specific job.

WHAT IS JOB PERFORMANCE?

To effectively look at a job, the job must be separated from the person who does that job. The separation, of course, is only temporary and specific con-

THE CRITICAL EVENTS MODEL

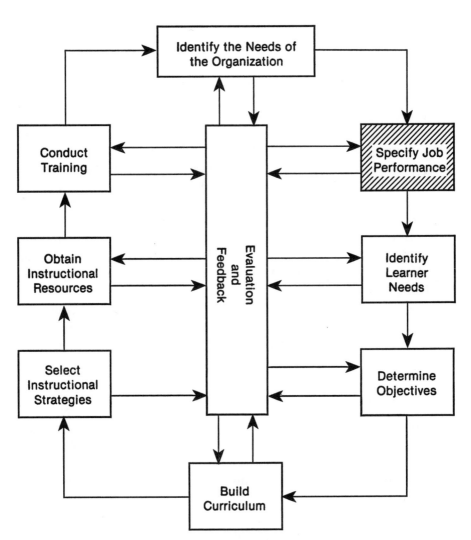

Figure 4-1. Specify job performance.

sideration will be given to the individual in the next step of Identify the Needs of the Learner.

An essential part of job performance is the concept of what people do; that is, what *job* they perform. The term "job" is used to represent the work that anybody does in an organization, from the lowest to the highest. Many people at the executive level do not see themselves as doing a job. If they wish to use a different label for this discussion, that is acceptable. The label can change, but what must be done to reach the objectives of this event will remain the same.

Perceptions of the Job

When designing a training program, the job for which it is intended already exists. The output of the job can frequently be measured or determined in many ways. However, what may be more difficult to determine is the perception of the job; that is, what various people think that job is and what it is intended to contribute to the organization's mission and goals. Therefore, a significant focus of this event is on gathering and clarifying perceptions of the job for which training is being considered.

The Designer should not be dismayed, once perceptions have been clarified, to discover that there is not a need for training. This recognition can arise during the event, but it will certainly be one of the factors to be checked out during evaluation and feedback.

The perceptions of a job are, in part, based on expectations. The question is: What does the organization expect to take place when the job is accomplished? This answer can vary among individuals and groups, so it is important to work towards that clarification before moving ahead in the design process.

The Supervisor

Every job in an organization has some kind of *supervisor* with the possible exception of the CEO. In this discussion, the term "supervisor" is used very broadly. The most obvious use, and the one that encompasses the largest number of individuals, is what is commonly called the first line supervisor; that is, the first level at which an employee gets the work done through the efforts of others.

Currently, discussions and explorations are in progress to redefine what a supervisor does. This is due, in part, to the fact that new technology is changing the nature of work. It also is due to the differing expectations of employees. The name, and even the duties, of a particular position may change, but there will still be some individual or group to whom employees are responsible at all levels of the organization.

Unless the workplace changes more drastically than any current predictions, the supervisor will remain, although there may not be a straight hierarchical line from the top to the bottom of the organization. For example, a CEO who has a private secretary, supervises that secretary. The form and process of that supervision may differ greatly from what a supervisor does on a production line, but the activity of supervision still exists.

Perceptions of Those in the Job

The Designer must at least be in contact with those currently doing the job. But, caution must be exercised so that the emphasis is on the job, not on the individuals.

The people doing the job have much to offer. This is not new, and that treasure house within organizations is slowly being explored through approaches such as participative management, suggestion systems, and quality circles.

Some Designers hesitate to go directly to the person on the job, expecting defensive behavior or a reluctance of the individual to share relevant data. If this is the case, there may be some problems for which training is not the correct response. If a low level of trust already exists, it may be the problem that is affecting job performance.

The Designer should not be surprised if an employee counters with a statement such as, "I would like to do the job better, but 'they' won't let me." Finding the elusive "they" can be the Designer's most important activity in this situation. If the previous event, Identify the Needs of the Organization, has been done well, this situation (if it exists) should already have been uncovered. If not, it may surface here, and the Designer should recognize that possibility and perhaps even anticipate it. As the Designer works further with the employee, it may appear that there is no "they," but rather some misperceptions.

In one situation, we were designing a program for the managers of a multi-site company. Thirty managers were brought together, and we explored some of the concepts and practices expected of managers in that company. At one point, to test their perceptions, we presented a case concerning an employee who handled a difficult problem and brought about unexpected financial benefits to the company. One group of managers suggested offering employees a bonus when they made unexpected contributions to the company. Some of the managers immediately protested that the case solution was not appropriate because the company did not permit bonuses, because of union problems in the past. The group of managers who presented the solution questioned the source of that information. It turned out that there was absolutely nothing that prevented a manager from authorizing a bonus, though the perception of this limitation existed.

Perceptions of Others

The Designer should not be surprised to find that there are those in the organization who only know how jobs are done through second hand information and the perceptions of others.

When a problem arises, possibly some employees will blame the job, even though they do not really know what the job is supposed to contribute to the organization. These employees have perceptions and expectations, and the Designer must verify these before starting to design.

Some of the perceptions may have evolved over a long period of time, while others may be more recent. There are the perceptions of those employees who have actually seen the job done or seen the results of the job. These are also perceptions of those employees who have only heard about the job being done and have not actually seen the results.

These differing perceptions frequently give rise to a good deal of erroneous information. They also contribute to the "grass is greener" feeling. It is not uncommon to hear, "If I had that job, I could do it much better." This sentiment is sometimes voiced by people who do not know the job, but have a perception of it. They might be able to do "it" better, but they are not always even sure what "it" is.

In a large or complex organization, perceptions may be contradictory or in conflict. When viewed from one perspective, the job appears one way; when viewed from another, it appears much different.

In every organization there are *peers,* except in those situations where there is only a single CEO. Peers are usually people at the same level in the organization, but not necessarily in the same work unit. The peers holding similar positions to the job for which design is being considered can be a good source of information about the job, but care must be taken to focus on the job and not on the individual doing that job. The Designer should not be surprised to find differing perceptions about the job among the peers.

Time and Perceptions

Over time, jobs change. Unfortunately, sometimes perceptions do not. This happens often when a person moves from a nonsupervisory position into a supervisory one. If the new supervisor remains in the same unit, that person usually expects the job to be done exactly as before. Over time, the job may change, but the supervisor's perception of the job may not.

It is important for the Designer to identify perceptions of the job for which training is being considered, because these perceptions will influence the kind of data collected and the way in which it should be analyzed and interpreted.

INTERDEPENDENCY OF JOBS

People working together in an organization depend upon each other, so job performance must be viewed as being interdependent. The very nature of an organization is that the tasks that must be accomplished to reach goals require more than one person.

This dependency is illustrated in Figure 4-2. Stated simply, one employee's output is another employee's input. When people work in groups, one group's output is another group's input. Although this may seem to be an oversimplification, it is a core concept related to work and one that too frequently is not recognized.

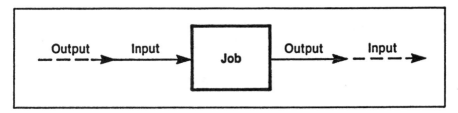

Figure 4-2. Interdependency of jobs.

As part of understanding job performance, the Designer must look at the input side of the job under examination. The Designer should consider where the input comes from and where the output goes. The two major sources, for both, are from within the organization and from outside the organization.

From Within the Organization

When the input is from within the organization, the Designer must trace the source. In the process, the Designer may discover that part of the problem is that there is a default on the input side and no amount of training for the job under observation will improve the situation.

An example of this situation occurred in the assembly operation in a manufacturing plant we were working with. The problem identified in the first event of the CEM was that the assemblers were not working up to the quantity standard that had been set. Repeated trial runs showed that it was possible for the tasks to be performed in the time specified, but actual production was still suffering. In this plant, work came to the assemblers by forklift trucks from other points in the plant and stocks were piling up on the floor creating a safety hazard.

After the first event of the CEM, the decision was made to train the assemblers to improve the way they received, handled, and processed the materials. Forklifts were always scurrying around, so the problem was not one of having to wait for parts.

On closer observation, the Designer (working with the assembly group supervisor) determined there was a fault in the input. Sometimes, for example, there was a surplus of part A but not enough of part B, and the assemblers were not able to complete a unit. The supervisor acknowledged that this happened, but thought that this possibility had been built into the assembly group production quota. Further examination showed that it had not.

The assembly group supervisor then worked with the Designer to identify the source of the problem. The forklift operators were part of another unit under a dock supervisor. As the parts were unloaded (from either a railroad siding or from trucks), they were stacked into a holding unit. The supervisor of that unit had to get the parts moved out as rapidly as possible so as to clear the way for new parts coming in. If he did not, it could mean extra cost to the company for demurrage (costs of holding the railroad cars and trucks).

However, the output of the forklift truck unit and that of the assembly unit did not match. The output of the forklift truck unit had not been coordinated with the input needs of the assembly group. No amount of training could handle that scheduling problem.

When the input comes from within the organization, adjustments are possible. They may involve scheduling, the state in which the input arrives, or the storing of the input until needed. If those situations are at the core of the problem, the Designer can uncover the problem and solutions can follow, even though training may not be one of them.

From Outside the Organization

Input may also come from outside the organization. The sources can be suppliers, subcontractors, or customers. In a retail establishment, customers are very important, for if there are no customers the organization will probably not survive. Providing additional training for salespeople will not increase sales, if the customers are not giving orders.

Input from external sources may be more difficult to identify, but the process must still take place. In the assembly group incident described earlier, another problem arose in a different part of the plant. The problem was quality control and rejection of some of the finished assembly. Once again, probably because of faith in the HRD department, the department manager requested a training program.

The Designer assigned to this project, using the interdependency approach, began looking at the input side of the situation. (On the output, it was clear that there was a problem, by the level of rejects.) Some of the parts were manufactured in-house while others came from external suppliers.

Presumably all were carefully examined before being sent on to the assembly department. It was determined that internal production was very carefully examined and tested, but, for what appeared to be a good reason, the external parts were receiving only a superficial examination. The receiving dock manager could only provide examination and/or testing of a few items out of each shipment.

The result was that faulty materials were being moved into the plant and not identified until they were assembled. The solution to this problem proved complicated. It required that additional space be provided for incoming shipments, additional personnel be assigned to inspection of incoming parts, and a training program be provided so that these inspectors could work efficiently to make the whole effort cost-effective. That was not the training program originally contemplated, but it was the training program that was needed when job performance and interdependency were considered.

Once the training program was designed and conducted, and records of rejects were maintained, the suppliers were forced to improve the quality of their shipments. This incident does not mean that input is always somebody else's problem. However, the Designer must be very sure that the fault does not lie in input before going further with the design process. If input is a problem, the Designer should determine whether someone on the input side needs training in order to provide the appropriate output.

Satisfactory input and unsatisfactory output may indicate that the problem is within the job. The employee may be working well, but the output being produced is not what is required for somebody else's input.

A Designer should not be misled into thinking that this is only a production situation. It happens just as frequently in office or managerial situations. A manager looks to subordinates to provide reports so the manager can make decisions. These reports are the manager's input. If the reports are not done correctly, perhaps there is the need for some training down the line so that this output will provide the necessary input.

Standards of the Job

The output of the job must be stated in some kind of standards. The two most common are quality and quantity. These appear to be easy areas to work with, but actually they are very difficult to determine. Until agreement is reached on these two components, it is not possible to specify the job performance that can produce the desired quality and quantity.

In each organization, these terms have different meanings. The Designer must determine specifically what is meant by those terms within this organization and by the people who are involved with the job. Quality can either be very observable or extremely elusive. When the output of a job is in a manufacturing situation, it can be compared to a specific standard, and quality can be determined. The most obvious case is either the output works, or it doesn't. When Chrysler went through its critical financial crisis in 1980, the company stated that from that time on, cars would be produced at such a quality level that they could be driven off the line. To the ultimate consumer this may not mean much, but the message to the workers was clear and strong and to the point. At the end of the assembly line, if a car met at least basic quality standards it could be driven off the production line. If it had to be pushed off the line, the work was not up to the quality that had been engineered into the car.

By contrast, and with a different product line, GM ran television commercials about the locomotives they manufactured. They emphasized that careful quality control and high standards of work performance meant that the completed locomotive could immediately be driven off. (Have you bought a locomotive lately?) Obviously the message to the average consumer was the idea of quality of work, not the product.

It is possible to hedge on quality by using alternative approaches. When we lived in Japan in the early 1960s, we bought a Japanese combination radio-record player. At that time, quality control in Japan focused on service to the consumer, rather than on quality in the manufacturing side. The set we received did not work after just a few days. The manufacturer sent a team to our home, and the repair men spent several hours making the necessary repairs to correct the errors of production. When they left, the set worked fine.

Within a week, the set once again was not working. We notified the manufacturer. Another group of men showed up and spent several hours making repairs. Ultimately, we returned the set and bought components. Later, when working with Japanese industry, we asked about this practice of making repairs at the consumer's site. We found that in Japan this was the general practice at the time and extended far beyond just consumer goods. It was partly a cultural factor. Providing service in the consumer's home or plant indicated the manufacturer's concern for their customers. Culturally it was appropriate, but economically it was a disaster!

As the Japanese expanded into the international market, they discovered that quality had to be built in during production and not handled as part of service. They trained their production workers and their inspectors so that quality became a reality.

Quantity is easier to deal with. For a job, either things are counted or they are not. If there is no quantification, the Designer should consider other alternatives. The increased emphasis on productivity (which implies measurement of quantity), provides further insights into ways of counting and measuring. As a Designer and an organization work to specify job performance, they may discover that methods should be introduced to quantify a job that previously did not have that dimension.

It is not possible to consider quantity alone. It must be related to the amount of time used to perform the tasks as well as to input/output consideration. The interdependency of jobs should never be overlooked, particularly when measurement is required. When a job is quantified, it can create problems elsewhere in the organization.

During the late 1960s, Americans became more concerned with hiring disadvantaged people. An interesting incident occurred in a Westinghouse plant. A "new hire" (one euphemism for the disadvantaged) entered the workforce at the rank of sweeper, which was the general entry level for all new employees in that plant [76]. He rapidly showed his ability and in a very short time was promoted to machine operator. His job (input) was to receive materials, process them on his machine, and put them (his output) into a basket to be taken by a sweeper to the next operation.

At first, the HRD people received accolades for doing such a good job with this new employee and he was soon given a merited promotion. Very soon thereafter, however, disaster struck. The floor supervisor visited the HRD unit and complained bitterly that what they had done in their training and education program was a waste! No sooner did the new employee get his promotion then he began "goofing off."

The employee's shift was to end at 2:30, yet after 12:00 he was nowhere to be found. "A lot of good your training did," said the supervisor. The HRD manager talked with the supervisor and then suggested they talk to the new employee. The following is what transpired.

New Employee: "What did ya hire me for? You keep telling me I got 'ta do the work and do it right. What's the beef? Did you have to throw out any of my work?"

Supervisor: "You left your machine!"

New Employee: "It was shut down."

Supervisor: "Of course, because you weren't working. You were supposed to be at your machine until 2:30."

New Employee: "I done the work."

Supervisor: "Not if you left early."

New Employee: "You told me to do all the pieces in the three bins the sweeper got me. I finished the three bins and took off."

Supervisor: "But you are supposed to stay until 2:30."

New Employee: "Do you pay me for the time or for how much work I do?"

And therein is the conflict! Managers may talk of production and productivity, but they tend to pay people for elapsed time. If an employee works more than a certain number of hours, he or she is often payed time-and-a-half, but usually an employee is not paid for production-and-a-half. The message being sent to the person doing the job is that time, not production, is important. Yet, should organizations allow a training program that encourages employees to work more slowly to fill up the amount of time the worker is expected to remain on the job? This is a conflict that can be identified by the Designer but must be reconciled by management.

There must be clear agreement about the standards for the job. Establishing this agreement is important in this event and it will become even more important when we encounter learning evaluation. If the Designer is to show benefits from the training, there must be baseline data on standards to compare with. This is the time when agreement must be reached on quality and quantity.

Group or Individual

For the most part, there is a tendency to look at a job as if only a single individual is doing it. More and more, however, jobs are being done by groups. This fact complicates the situation, particularly when employees are free to rotate jobs within limits. It does not mean that it is impossible to specify job performance, but such a specification must relate to the reality of how the work is actually done.

Until now, training programs have been designed for situations where one person was working alone or alongside others. Working with others has not been fully explored in terms of job performance. Of course, we do have those situations where people must work together, and this has produced training programs in team building and similar activities to improve group performance. Too often such programs deal with interpersonal relations, but not with job skills. There are few published examples of situations where people had to be trained to be substitutes for each other on a regular but unplanned basis. Yet, this is the direction the workplace is moving at this time.

Group performance patterns should be recognized and built into the specification of job performance. There should be two sets of specifics: one for what an individual does on that job, and the other for what the individual does when exchanging or substituting for another member of the same work group.

GATHERING DATA

To specify job performance, it is necessary to collect data. There are many ways to do this, and no one way is best. Each method has its exponents and its critics. The Designer must identify and select the method that seems most appropriate to the Designer, the job, and the organization.

Each Designer has certain competencies, and can be expected to use those methods which proved successful in the past. However, success can be a trap. A Designer may continue to use the same methods even after discovering they are not relevant for a particular task. Therefore, Designers must develop a wide range of competencies, in a variety of methods, for gathering data about job performance. There are several tested and commonly used approaches for doing that. The Designer should be familiar with these and know when to use them.

In a sense, these approaches are "safe" because they have the validity of having been published. Somehow publication lends credence even to a seldom used methodology. The professional journals have a constant flow of "How I Did It" type of articles. Some of these can be very helpful to the Designer in opening up new vistas for gathering the required data.

A shortcoming in many of these articles, however, is that they usually do not tell the whole story because of the limitation of space and the need to appeal to a wide readership. If a Designer is interested in a data-gathering experience shared by an author in a magazine article, he should write to the author for any additional information that may be helpful. A Designer with experience will realize that methodologies can change, and that those changes can be the result of many factors.

Constant changes are occurring in the culture of the workplace, and in some organizations, a greater openness now exists for providing data. A trend toward a higher level of education has produced people who are more articulate and who can provide more data. The use of data-gathering instruments instead of interviews requires a higher rate of literacy. But, on the other hand, employees can be "instrumented" to exhaustion and completely overwhelmed by the constant flow of forms that must be completed to gather data.

The Designer must continually ask: Why am I using this particular method for gathering the needed data? Is there another way? Is there a better way? When I used this method previously, what did I learn about ways to do it better?

Some Designers find it helpful to maintain a file on the methods used and suggestions for improving those methods. The Designer then, of course, must be sure to read that file before the next activity in data gathering.

A particular job can influence the source and methods for gathering data on job performance. Some jobs are readily observable, and gathering the data does not pose any particular problems. Those are the easy ones. They are jobs in which the output is immediately and easily discernible, such as a production job or a service job. In production, the output is always observable and almost always measurable. The way the job is being done tends to be standardized. The job is generally composed of small units or tasks that must be done exactly the same way by anybody who is doing that job. Of course, individual variations do exist, and some of these can be important in understanding how job performance can be improved.

Jobs in the service area are also easy to observe. The clerk servicing a customer, the waiter in the restaurant, or an employee working at a similar service job can be observed. It is also possible to establish quality measures in such jobs.

However, when the Designer looks at supervisory and management jobs, his work becomes more complicated. The output of these jobs is the result of many more factors than just the performance of these jobs. The quality of the job is only generally measurable. At higher management levels, there tends to be less agreement on how the job should be done. At those levels in the organization, employees are not eager to have data gathered about their performance or to have any significant inquiry made into how they do the job. The emphasis is on the results of the performance, not the performance itself. This makes data gathering about the job extremely difficult, and in some organizations, almost impossible.

The Designer should consider the complexity of the job when selecting a method for gathering data. The more complex the job, the more difficulty can be anticipated in collecting the data. In some complex jobs, collecting the data must be done in a way that will avoid interfering with the job. Continuous or complicated operations require the complete attention of the employee, and the data-gathering process should not be allowed to interfere with the performance of the job.

When the Designer is not adequately familiar with the job or the operation, other resources should be used for data collection. The Designer should discuss this possibility with both the supervisor and the subordinate to be sure that the alternative resource is acceptable. That resource could be someone else within the organization who knows the operation and who can observe without interruptions, questions, or explanations or it can come from an external resource. If an external resource is used, it should be carefully checked out. Some individuals within the organization may not be in favor of bringing in an outside resource. However, there may be positive results if the external resource brings to this activity some information on similar jobs in other organizations.

As with any job under scrutiny, the Designer must be aware of the Hawthorne Effect. A famous study conducted at the Hawthorne Plant of Western Electric in the 1920s found that workers being studied tended to behave differently than those who were not being studied [92A]. As soon as the Designer starts looking at a job, the job can change.

For example, in the 1960s, as one consequence of the British Industrial Training Act, a need arose for more people with competencies in designing training programs. In 1966 we were invited to England to conduct a workshop and used the CEM (then called the Process of Training) as the core of the workshop. The participants were asked to actually design a program as part of the workshop, and we sought a common job that everyone could see and would find familiar. At the first tea break, we found that job. All of us could have firsthand observation of the woman serving the tea and therefore could use her job as the basis for designing a training program.

Picture what happened during the tea break following the session on Specify Job Performance? As each participant passed the table where the young woman was pouring, he (an all male group) took quick mental notes on how the job was being performed. By the time the young woman experienced the piercing scrutiny of the first five participants, her performance deteriorated. After serving the next five participants she fled crying to the rest room! The remaining participants never did get to see the job performance.

Of course, a Designer usually would not ask that many people to observe a single employee in such a short period of time, but even over a longer period, the depth and intensity of observation could be just as disruptive to performance. A Designer must recognize that a worker under scrutiny may no longer perform the job in the usual manner. This is applicable to all levels of the organization.

Another important consideration to make when gathering data is the difference between a job being done by an individual and one performed by a group. Different methods are required, as some are more useful for individuals than for groups. Also, some group methods are irrelevant when individual job performance is the factor. A third variable must also be considered: the organization.

The Designer is always trapped, at the beginning, by organizational history. It is possible to get out of the trap, but the Designer must start by determining if the trap does exist. Often a Designer is told, "But Designers never asked for this information before. They sat in their offices and did the design without bothering us." When comments like these are made, the Designer may get a signal to gather the data without observing the actual job site. If so, a Designer should not go against history just to be different. If, however, onsite presence is necessary for understanding the job and the environment, a Designer should not hesitate to develop the strategies that will induce the people on that site to extend an invitation. If they view the Designer as being helpful, it should not be difficult for the Designer to receive such an invitation.

Every organization has a climate, even if we cannot always be sure of what it is [106]. As climates change, a Designer may be required to change previously selected methods. What worked last time might not work this time. It is not possible to provide a list that says, "If this is the climate, then . . ." The variations in organizational climate have not been categorized to that extent.

It becomes incumbent on the Designer to continually sense the subtle changes in climate that occur in every organization. The wind is constantly shifting. There are times to go against the wind and times for the "bamboo approach" of bending with the wind. The Designer must relate closely enough to the entire organization to be able to sense the changes and to know the appropriate design behavior that will be congruent with the current climate of the organization.

In general, when gathering data for this event, the Designer should consider sources and methods. In some models, these two elements are considered as one activity. That approach deprives the Designer of some of the alternatives that are possible within this activity. Therefore each of these will be discussed separately.

SOURCES

The Designer must identify the sources of the information necessary to specify job performance. Before actually gathering the data, the Designer must do some intensive planning. In some situations, it will not be possible to go back to a source a second time.

Sources can be inside the organization, or outside, and cost may well be a factor in determining which source to explore. Sources, may be people or records and reports. These are not mutually exclusive.

Gathering data from people may not produce all the information needed. In that case, the Designer must go to the records and reports as well. Let us start by looking at people as a prime source of information.

People

When dealing with people, their perceptions and biases must always be recognized. This should not, however, dissuade the Designer from using people as a source.

A major factor to be wary of is employee confusion between "what is" and "what should be." People may confuse one with the other while presumably telling the Designer what is actually being done on the job. Both of these factors are helpful in understanding job performance, but must be separated within the data. A prime source for information is the *person actually doing the job*. Here too, however, the Designer should be cautious that a job description a worker gives him is actually the way the job is done and not just a description of how the person would like to do the job. The employee may consider this a good opportunity to influence changes in the job. The Designer should take note of this data, because the person on the job is a very good source of ideas on job improvement, but those ideas should be kept separate from the reality of the job performance.

Because jobs are interdependent, before any changes are made based on a single source, employees on both the input and output sides should be consulted. At this juncture, it is important to separate the job from the individual. The focus here is on the job, no matter who is doing it. Interdependency requires that a job be done within the organization. How the individual is doing the job will be explored in the next event of the CEM.

Groups within an organization that usually work at the same level can be called peers. Peers will often provide different data regarding the job being looked at, especially if they anticipate that their data could bring about changes in their jobs.

By stretching the peer concept, the Designer can also identify people outside the organization who perform the same kind of work. For example, salespeople from outside the organization selling the same general product line could provide significant data. Of course, the performance of competitors in such a situation is extremely important, but very difficult to determine.

The *supervisor* is another good source. Indeed, the supervisor was probably the person who called the Designer in to start the design process. If that is so, the supervisor must certainly be included as a source. However, if the supervisor's supervisor (i.e., a manager) requested that the program be designed for subordinates of the supervisor, then a different situation exists. The supervisor is still a good source, but may be overly cautious or even hostile. The Designer needs to gain the confidence and trust of the supervisor, if that supervisor is to be a valuable and reliable source.

Consumers can be external or internal, but the term usually applies to those outside the organization and more generally describes the ultimate purchaser. The consumer is the individual or unit that receives the output of the job under consideration. The consumer can also be someone or some unit in the organization that is influenced or affected by the output, but does not directly receive it.

The data from the consumers are usually gathered by others, in which case, the Designer would rely on the records and reports gathered by these people. When the consumer is internal (for example, in another part of the organization), the actual consumer is more readily available.

Another source of outside data comes from *conferences and meetings.* There are various trade associations, professional groups, and other temporary meetings (also called institutes, workshops, and so on) where job performance is discussed. The content of these conferences and meetings can be related to a specific job or to what is happening in the general field and can be expected to influence the job under design.

The Designer may also be invited to *internal meetings* called by others in the organization. Such meetings may be very general, not job specific, but can be of help to the Designer in understanding the broader context and trends.

Professionals outside the organization also constitute a valuable source of data. These include university faculty who are teaching and researching the same kind of job for which the CEM is being used, engineering and management faculties, suppliers of services, and product suppliers who have broad knowledge of the field.

Records and Reports

Written documents seem to have a life of their own. Though there is some indication that this is changing, we are still people who put a great deal of value in the printed word.

In recent years, technological advances have increased the storage and dissemination of written material and can be expected to have an even greater impact for the future. One innovation has been the *computer.* With the proliferation of microcomputers, a great many employees have desk terminals and personal computers. The computer makes a vast amount of information available, and therefore, becomes an important source for designing training programs. It is important that Designers either develop computer capabilities or find someone with that competency who can join the Designer's staff. Word processing, through computers, allows for the production of much more written material than in the past. Whether for better or worse, computers put more written information into various channels and into filing cabinets. (Of course, a great deal can be stored in the megabytes available on even a personal word processor, but there is still a great deal of printing and filing.)

Despite technological innovations, some sources of data can still be found in standard filing cabinets, on bookshelves, piled on desks and tables, and stored in other exotic fashions. A major source of data are *production records.* Included within this category are those records that can tell the Designer about sales, customer complaints, back orders, and all the other data related to production. For a non-manufacturing organization, the term production may have to be modified, but those records contain information that indicates how the organization is meeting its goals or accomplishing its mission.

If the Designer finds *performance appraisals* among the various records, attention should only be paid to the criteria for performance appraisal, not the appraisals themselves. That data, if available, will be helpful in the next event, but could be confusing here.

One frequently used source is the *job description.* Indeed, some Designers go to the job description as the primary source, but then get trapped in the past. For the most part, a job description does not tell what is expected in the way of job performance at present, but rather what was expected when the job description was written. An analogy can be found in the dictionary. People go to the dictionary to find the meaning of words. Yet, dictionaries do not tell us what words mean but what they meant at the time the dictionary was published. To test this, if necessary, write down meanings for words such as mediocre and sanction. Then, look at the dictionary and see how these meanings have changed over the years.

The job description is important and should not be overlooked, for it is the agreed upon document which is relied on to indicate something about job performance. It should not be ignored, but it should not be accepted at face value. The Designer should not put the personnel office in the position of defending the document, for that is not the purpose of obtaining it for the CEM. As a result of looking at the job description and at actual job performance, the description might be changed. In some organizations, the job descriptions are written in very broad and general terms because the personnel office recognizes that actual job performance cannot be fully stated in such a document.

It is a rare organization that does not have meetings and produce *minutes of internal meetings*. Some of those minutes have very limited distribution, and it may be inappropriate for the Designer to be on the route slip. However, if the designer can be included on the route slip as a routine step, he will have another source of data concerning job performance. Reviewing the minutes will probably require a great deal of reading about extraneous factors. So, if possible, the Designer should evolve a screening mechanism to avoid having to read the unrelated material. A common practice is to have a staff member (if the HRD unit is more than a one-person operation) read all the minutes and highlight those parts that relate to job performance. With either the computer or word processing, some of this information can readily be "filed" for instant recall as needed.

Despite the movement towards the paperless office, it will probably be years before this is a general practice. Therefore it can be expected that the flow of *memos and reports* will continue. Because memos and reports can also be a source of data about job performance, the Designer must take steps to be on distribution lists for these as well, and set up a similar screening and filing process so the relevant data on job performance can be retrieved.

A common practice in many organizations is the *reading file*. This may contain minutes of meetings, memos, reports, correspondence, and so on. In fact, it becomes a significant vehicle for keeping everybody informed about each others activities, and if such a reading file exists, the Designer should certainly be on the route slip. If it does not exist, the Designer will have to devise alternative methods for gaining access to the various printed pieces of data that circulate within an organization. As the use of computers expands, much of this written material will be put into the computer, and the Designer may find more ready access. It can be anticipated that not all of the various kinds of written reports, memos, and so on will appear in the computer for general consumption, as a limited distribution may be essential for some. Whatever the mode, the Designer must stay alert to the various ways in which these source materials are circulated and stored.

As stated earlier, conferences and meetings can be a valuable source of data. Very often this source is reduced to a report referred to as *conference proceedings.* In the technical fields, those conference proceedings can be extremely valuable and often represent the state of the art. Many items will be reported on during the conference and will appear in the conference proceedings. The material can contribute to the general understanding of expectations of job performance. This source can also be helpful in indicating trends and future directions. It can enable the Designer to raise questions about how the job is changing or can be expected to change. This can help the Designer avoid the trap of designing for a job that is becoming obsolete or is on the verge of being changed by new technology or processes.

The Designer is not expected to be an expert in the various technical fields, and therefore, the kinds of proceedings that he can read, understand, and use may be limited. This limitation must be explored by each Designer. A Designer should not try to become an expert in a field that takes years of study. The role of the Designer is not as an expert in the subject matter, and the Designer must avoid the temptation to become an instant expert.

Literature is another source of written data available to the Designer and includes the two major categories of magazines and books. Many occupational fields have specialized magazines that can be a source of data about job performance. These range from a simple one-page flyer or newsletter to a several-hundred-page quarterly. Once again, the Designer should not try to become a subject matter specialist, but should be familiar enough with the terminology and trends to be able to understand what constitutes job performance possibilities in a particular field. If it is a completely strange field, the Designer must find other people as the appropriate resource, as discussed earlier in this chapter. Books in the field are a similar source. The same advantages and limitations exist as for magazines. Given the wide coverage of a topic presented in a book, the Designer might seek help from others in the organization as to which parts of the book are relevant to understand performance on the job under scrutiny.

There is a tendency to scoff at *government documents,* but they can be a very valuable source. Frequently large sums of taxpayers' money have gone into the research and related work to produce some of the government documents pertinent to occupational fields. In the U.S., the Government Printing Office is probably the largest publishing organization in the country, and their output is available to everybody at relatively low prices. To ignore this source is to refuse to accept the results of some of your organization's tax dollars.

METHODS

There are different ways to use the sources that have been discussed. Some of those are fairly easy to use, while others require significant levels of skill in order to be effective.

It would be relatively simple to make a laundry list out of this section of the chapter. Instead, it might be more useful to discuss the various methods by grouping them. For example, the heading "Questionnaire" includes checklists, various types of data gathering instruments, closed questionnaires, and so on. Each of these is different but will be discussed under the same heading.

Questionnaire

The methods under this heading concern some type of written data-gathering device. The Designer could develop the questionnaire or use some of the available standardized instruments. The data can be hand-processed or machine-processed, depending upon quantity and complexity.

Of prime importance is the effect of the questionnaire on the respondent. If that person has a low level of literacy, the questionnaire can be a frustrating experience. (One alternative in that case is the scheduled interview, which will be discussed later.) At the other end of the scale, a highly literate respondent may react negatively to a forced choice questionnaire and prefer an open-end type of questionnaire.

Before using a questionnaire, the Designer should be sure that the data are obtainable and that it is possible for the respondent to supply the required answers. The results might be less than satisfactory if, for example, the respondent was a machine operator and was asked to "Indicate the ways in which technological advances of your machine could contribute to increased productivity of your unit." The operator may have some ideas, but the question is possibly asking for something that is beyond the understanding of the operator. The question also assumes that productivity (as differentiated from production) is a concept that the operator can deal with even though many managers have not been able to cope with the concept of productivity.

If the data are obtainable, will the responses be helpful? What could the Designer do about them? Some responses are predictable. "Get me a different supervisor and I would work better." Or, "If they let me design this car, we could save a lot of money. It has too many unnecessary gadgets on it." If the questionnaire is well designed, it should produce data that the Designer can then use to specify job performance. The questions should all be tested in terms of the possible responses and their use by the Designer.

When developing a questionnaire, the Designer should avoid the common trap of a "fishing expedition." Do not throw a broad net hoping that at least some of the questions and responses will prove useful.

To be effective, the questionnaire should be long enough to gather the necessary data, but short enough to be completed in a reasonable period of time. The length of reasonable time will vary from one situation to another, but for each situation there is a limited period of time that the respondent can be expected to devote to the questionnaire.

It is important to pilot test the questionnaire; that is, to administer it to a selected small group (even two people) and ask their feedback about the clarity and form of the questions. For job performance, testing the questionnaire on the supervisor is essential. If the supervisor will not participate in this phase, the problem may not be with the job performance of the subordinate.

In some situations, sharing the data with the respondents is helpful. This builds a level of trust for similar activities in the future, as well as providing for another check on the quality of the data gathered.

Questionnaires can take many forms. A common one is the *checklist*. The respondent is presented with a series of statements and essentially is asked to check off those items that are a part of the job. A variation of this form would be to list the various tasks of the job and ask the respondent to prioritize them in order of importance. Depending on the problem that triggered the request for the training program, the respondent might be asked instead to number the tasks in the order in which they are performed.

A variation of the checklist is the *Likert Scale,* named for the eminent behavioral scientist, Rensis Likert, who introduced it. Statements are presented to the respondent who is asked to rank them on a linear scale. The respondent is provided with a definition of the scale (for example, 1 is low and 6 is high, or some similar distinction). The statements should all be linear; that is, the respondent should be able to select some appropriate point on the scale without having to qualify the response. Note the use of a scale, 1 to 6, which does not have a midpoint. If the scale were 1 to 5, there could be a tendency to select 3, which is a noncommittal way of responding. The scale could be 1 to 4 or 1 to 10 depending upon the nature of the statements, the respondents, and the way in which the data will be used.

Another type of scale is the *semantic differential.* It is much like the previous scale, but the difference is that the respondent is usually presented with words that are diametrically opposed, with a line between them. The line will have gradations, which can be numbered or unnumbered. The respondent is asked to circle the point on the line that represents the desired response. It is important that the words selected be direct opposites.

There are many other ways of constructing questions, such as forced choice, multiple choice, and even the old standby, true and false. In each case, the Designer should keep in mind the factors discussed earlier concerning the respondent, the nature of the data, and the use to be made of the data.

Another type of questionnaire is the *open-ended*. Many people know it as the essay examination question given in school. Although this type of questionnaire appears simple, the questions for this instrument are difficult to construct. The questions must seek the data, without indicating any bias on the part of the questioner. The questions must be clear enough so that the respondent does not have to seek assistance just to understand the question. Provision must be made for the response. For example, space should be made available on the same page as the question or the respondent should be given additional paper on which to answer the questions.

Another type of open-ended questionnaire is the *completion* format. The respondent is presented with the statement, "If I could change any part of this job, I would . . ." The same considerations about length of response that applied to the open-ended question should be applied here. Although similar to the essay, the completion format tends to stimulate the respondent's thinking more than the essay-type question and some designers report better results.

It is possible to have a questionnaire that *combines the checklist and the open ended*. The respondent is asked to complete the checklist and is given space to write something under each item. This space is usually labeled "comments," but better data can be obtained if the checklist item is followed by either a completion option or a question that focuses the attention of the respondent.

The type of questionnaire will be influenced by the number of respondents. If there are many respondents, it might be easier to use a checklist or closed type questionnaire. These types make for uncomplicated processing and comparison of the data obtained. Where large numbers of respondents are involved, the data usually have to be presented in some quantified form, and the checklist questionnaire is well suited for that.

It is difficult, if not impossible, to quantify the responses to open-ended questionnaires. Each must be read, and the data assigned to preconstructed categories. This is acceptable and even desirable for research, but can be time-consuming and counter productive for specifying job performance. If the number of respondents is small enough or if the job is sufficiently controversial (as in management), the open-ended questionnaire will gather more substantial data and will be worth the additional effort and resources required to process the data.

If a Designer anticipates using questionnaires frequently, developing a file of questions related to particular jobs can be helpful. Then, at successive times, in this event of the CEM for the same job, a questionnaire can be readily constructed. Before using the questionnaire, the Designer must review the usefulness of the questions in prior situations, as well as any changes that have occurred in the organization or unit since that time. The Designer should also consider any additional competencies he/she has acquired since the last time.

For some jobs, it is also possible to use external sources. There are companies that produce standardized questionnaires for some common jobs, such as those in supervision and management. Other suppliers produce questionnaires that relate to specifics, such as morale, interpersonal relationships, and communications. These materials vary from year to year, so it is not practical to attempt a list of what is available. However, the companies that provide such products are usually listed in buyers' guides published by the American Society for Training and Development and by other organizations in the HRD field.

Interview

The interview is a face-to-face situation between an interviewer and one or more people. The interviewer is either the Designer or someone who represents the Designer. The interviewee (or respondent) is the person from whom data, information, or opinions are being sought. Interviews can be done either as with a *group* or *individual.* It is a very active process in that the respondent will do most of the talking, with the interviewer listening and possibly using some data retrieval device such as note-taking or a tape recorder. Interviewer competencies will be discussed later in this chapter, but at this point note that one factor that determines whether group or individual interviews are appropriate is the skill of the interviewer. Where job performance is the result of group behavior, a group interview might be more appropriate. Conducting individual interviews, in such a situation, could communicate that someone is trying to split up the group. The interviewer may gather the data, but at the cost of reducing the morale and perhaps the effectiveness of the group.

A serious limitation of the group interview, obviously, is that if everybody takes part, the work stops. If the interviews are to take place "on the clock," particularly, if the output of this group affects the work of others, provisions must be made to take care of this situation. To do the interviews "off the clock" raises other issues. It could communicate that management does not consider the process sufficiently important to use company time, and such a perception can seriously limit the validity of the data gathered. Another factor to consider if the interview is held after work hours is whether the respondents will be paid for their time or given compensatory time. These issues should be clarified before an interview is planned.

The individual interview must be handled very openly but cautiously. When an employee is taken away from work for an interview, rumors can be anticipated. When the employee returns to the worksite, he may be greeted with questions such as, "They had you on the hot seat, didn't they?" or, "Do you still have your job?" Unless the situation is clear to all, negative implications can be expected. To prevent these, everybody who is concerned should recognize that those being interviewed are valued resources and that the work of the Designer could not be accomplished without significant help through the interview process.

To get the most from an interview, careful attention must be paid to *climate setting*. The interviewee and those associated with the interview must receive prior notice. This should include the time, place, purpose of the interview, and a clear indication that the interview process has the support of the interviewee's supervisor. The place of the interview is extremely important as it relates to the concept of the territorial imperative. The site communicates, nonverbally, the importance placed on the interview by all concerned. The two places that should be avoided are the work site itself (unless it is necessary to provide some specifics about job performance) and the office or desk of the supervisor. It is best to find some neutral space. This is not always easy to find and some compromises will have to be anticipated. If there are no other alternatives, the office of the supervisor could be used with the explicit agreement that the supervisor will not be present—and that the supervisor will not stroll in and out of the office with muttered excuses. If the interview process calls for the supervisor to be present, and that is an acceptable approach, it is not desirable to use the supervisor's office unless there is absolutely no alternative site.

The interviewee should be put at ease. For example, in the United States, offering coffee is an accepted practice. When both parties sip coffee, a friendly and sharing atmosphere often results. However, the Designer should consider how coffee drinking is viewed in this particular organization. In some organizations, drinking coffee at or near the work site is absolutely forbidden. In others, no restrictions exists, while in others, the employer actually provides a coffee pot and a continuous flow. ("Coffee" includes other drinks, such as tea and soda, depending upon the norm in the organization.) Do not make too big a production of serving something to drink, such as providing a big tray of donuts, pastries, or other confections, unless that is the culture in the organization. Overabundance of these amenities can impede the interview process and even produce a negative effect.

In setting the climate, the interviewer should have some opening questions that will establish the norm. The first questions should be those that can readily be answered, so the interviewee experiences success in the initial stages of the process. As the interview proceeds, it can be anticipated that more specifics will be required, with the possibility of arousing some internal conflicts in the interviewee.

There are different *types of interviews*. One is closely allied to the questionnaire and actually uses questionnaires, which have been discussed earlier. The difference, of course, is that during the interview the respondent is not expected to write the answers. As the questions are asked and the interviewee responds, the interviewer records the responses on the questionnaire form. This method can be used with almost all of the questionnaires that have been discussed. The interviewee can be given the questionnaire so as to follow the questions as they are being asked. If the interviewer does not want the interviewee to see the questions until they are asked, the questions can be put on individual cards and handed to the interviewee as the questions are asked.

When specific questions are being asked and the order is predetermined and not to be changed, the questions are referred to as an *interview schedule*. A schedule is particularly important where similar data are being sought from different people and when more than one interviewer is involved.

It is also possible to have some key questions, the open-ended type, which serve to stimulate the interviewee to talk about specific aspects of the job. Such an interview can probe in-depth issues, but can also provide a good deal of extraneous data. In one interview situation, for example, the following took place. The interviewer was an upper-middle-class woman and the respondents were generally blue-collar workers on the lower fringe of the employment ladder. They were employed at the Sparrows Point Plant (Maryland) of Bethlehem Steel and had been in a company-union-government program on literacy. The purpose of the individual interviews was to gather data on the workers' perceptions of how the program had influenced their job performance.

At first, we were hesitant about the comparative socio-economic gap between the interviewer and the interviewees, but we agreed to permit the interviewer to at least try. After the first few interviews, the interviewer met with us and we discussed the process and the data. We were prepared to offer the interviewer the opportunity to disengage from the project.

Quite the contrary. The interviewer had done a good job on climate setting and her only problem was that the interviews were taking much longer than anticipated. Her reading of the situation was that these respondents did not lack oral or verbal skills, but rather they had few opportunities on the job for conversation and they had acquired the reputation of being verbally inadequate, as well as illiterate. This was not the actual situation. The interviewees wanted to tell her how the learning program had improved their family life as well as their job performance. For many, it was one of the first times that anybody with the aura of management had ever asked their opinion.

A general limitation of the interview process is the difficulty in organizing and analyzing the data. A closed-end questionnaire should not present any problem. More commonly, however, an interview is used to allow the interviewee flexibility of response. This provides data with a wide scatter. This data definitely would not be quantifiable, though some interviewers then take the raw data, put them into categories, and statistically compare within and among categories. Such quantification of interview data is highly questionable and may not even be necessary for the purpose of specifying job performance.

Interviewer competencies must be considered. The interviewer needs more than the mere ability to ask questions. He or she must be able to establish the climate and maintain it, so that the respondent feels free and comfortable in providing responses. The interviewer must also be able to terminate responses that are too lengthy or not particularly helpful, without communicating a negative feeling. A great deal of nonverbal communication takes place during an interview.

It is possible for two people to share the role of interviewer. When we first experimented with this, we adopted the practice of having one person ask questions while the other one took notes. This allowed the questioner to maintain eye contact with the respondent and give his undivided attention. The notetaker assumed the responsibility of taking notes that we could review at a later time, but was also permitted to ask questions. We soon discovered that this division of labor encouraged interesting behavior from the interviewee, who would look at the questioner as he asked a question, but then quickly turned to the notetaker when responding.

After a few experiences of this kind, we reviewed our process and respective roles. What we found was that taking notes was a controlling factor in the interview. The interviewees responded to the notetaker as being more important. After all, the questioner only asked questions, but the notetaker recorded what the interviewee said and that was much more important. Our observations also indicated that the method the notetaker used could control the interview. When the notetaker stopped taking notes, the interviewee stopped talking. When the notetaker closed the notebook, that signaled that the interview was terminated and no coaxing by the questioner could encourage the interviewee to continue. We found that each of the interviewers had to develop competencies in questioning and notetaking so the roles could be switched as appropriate for each interview situation.

Evidence from other sources indicates that the behavior of interviewers can influence the flow of conversation. The interviewer must provide a steady feedback flow. This feedback can be provided by repeating, "uh-hum," "I see," "yes," and similar noncommittal utterances and other overt signals that the interviewer is interested.

In a face-to-face interview, feedback can be provided by nodding the head or other similar body language that communicates that the interviewer is involved in what the interviewee is saying. It has been noted that when the body language stops, the verbal behavior of the interviewee is influenced, and slowly the flow of oral language will ebb.

In addition to these competencies, the interviewer may use other means when collecting data. When mutually agreed upon, a tape recorder might be used. Micro tape recorders make it possible to record an interview on a small concealed device, but doing so obviously raises ethical considerations. Some interviewers start the tape recorder when the respondent enters the room, and then ask, "You don't mind this, do you? If you do, I will gladly turn off the tape recorder." This does not provide the respondent with an alternative. It puts the respondent in the position of having to request a change, with the implications that perhaps there is something to hide. If, for any reason, the respondent wants to discuss the use of the tape recorder, that discussion is already being recorded.

In using a tape recorder or similar device, the respondent should be informed, prior to the interview, that this might be a possibility and should be provided with the opportunity to merely say yes or no without having to defend the position. The respondent then will understand that the interviewer is respecting the privacy of the interview. Of course, if privacy is not a concern, there is no problem.

Technology is constantly changing, and so is methodology for gathering interview data. For example, it is even possible to use a video cassette camera. Many units are portable, easy to set up, and operate with just a flip of the switch. Using a video camera enables the interviewer to capture not only verbal responses but also nonverbal behavior. But, for some interviewees, such equipment can be perceived as even more threatening than the audio tape recorder, and the same protection of the interviewee should be provided as discussed earlier.

A most commonly used method for collecting data from an interview is still the pencil and paper. When this method is to be used, the interviewer must develop the competency for taking notes without disrupting the process. Some experienced interviewers develop skill in shorthand or some other system of speed writing, while others develop their own system of writing, which has the added benefit that nobody else can read it. Whichever approach is used, all interviewers should recognize that taking notes during an interview requires special skills. It is not easy to ask, listen, and write simultaneously. If the Designer does not have such competencies, or does not wish to acquire them, it is always possible to contract for outside professional interviewers. When outsiders are introduced into the situation, however, other issues may arise, so the Designer will have to choose from among several alternatives. If the Designer is part of a sufficiently large HRD unit, there may be people within that unit who have those interviewer competencies. If there is a great deal of interviewing to be done, contracts with external sources might prove to be a better alternative.

Meetings

The discussion here refers to meetings called by the Designer for the specific purpose of gathering data in order to specify job performance. A detailed discussion of the fine points of meetings can be found in *The Comprehensive Guide to Successful Conferences and Meetings* [79].

It is critical that the Designer run a sharply focused meeting, with identifiable results. The purpose of the meeting should be clearly stated, and that should be only to gather data about job performance. The Designer must avoid having the meeting focus on how a particular individual is performing. That issue is part of the next event in the CEM. All those who are invited to the meeting should be notified of the specific purpose and given a clear picture of the expectations of the meeting, so they can more readily prepare to participate.

As is true of most meetings, deciding who should attend is important. The Designer should consider the interdependency of the job. If possible, all those employees who are related to the job should attend. In most situations, this is not possible, as it could be too costly and disruptive. Therefore a careful selection must be made. The Designer should discuss the list of proposed participants with at least the supervisor of the job. If the supervisor disagrees with those chosen by the Designer, the Designer should discuss this further and clear up any misperceptions about the job or the extent of interdependency.

During the meeting, the Designer should consider using a chalkboard, flipchart, overhead projector, or other devices that can put the data in front of all who attend. These visual aids allow for constant revision of the data during the course of the meeting and assure that the end result will be evident to all. There need not be any other written report or minutes, for what is important is not the process, but the end result. Participants should feel free to suggest ideas and revise their ideas as the meeting progresses. An early freeze on free-flowing suggestions will bury important data.

Using meetings to collect data calls for an additional competency from the Designer. A great deal is known about small group behavior in meetings, and most Designers have probably had some prior training in this area. If that is not the case, it is essential for the Designer to develop skills in this area. A meeting to collect data on job performance cannot use *Robert's Rules of Order* or any other parliamentary approach. The Designer must seek consensus rather than agreement by voting. Complete agreement on all the specifics of job performance is not expected at the conclusion of the meeting.

Generally, the results of meetings are shared with everyone who attended, but with a meeting to collect data, that may not be appropriate. The results of this type of meeting must be added to other data. It is doubtful that a meeting will produce all the specifics needed, but it can be an important source of information.

Literature Search

The generic term *literature* refers to all forms of written sources. If the organization has a library, it can be helpful to the Designer; if there is a librarian, that is extremely fortunate. Some of the retrieval of literature requires the services of a skilled librarian, and preferably several, who have the competencies to conduct a computer search for relevant information. They know which computer services or banks are likely to have the required data. Even more crucial, they know the descriptors that are the pathways into the computer.

It is also possible to obtain such a service through external sources. For an agreed upon fee, many computer services companies will conduct the search and provide hard copy of the relevant data.

The proceedings from work-oriented conferences are also valuable sources for information. Some of these proceedings are a storehouse of viable information regarding expectations for job performance. They may not specifically mention job performance, but the information is there. Proceedings are usually in the traditional printed form and appear as hard or soft cover books. However, there is a growing tendency to provide audio cassette recordings and/or video cassette recordings of particular sessions, some of which contain information related to expected job performance.

Observation

Actually observing the job being performed would appear to be one of the best methods for collecting data on that job, but it has its limitations. When an employee is aware that performance is being scrutinized, performance will probably be altered. Very few of us will display our usual behavior while being observed. When observation is used, the employee(s) should be fully aware of the process. This requires a high level of trust and previous experience in which the results of the observation have not been used punitively.

The purpose of the observation should be made clear to all concerned and the process of observation should be discussed with the supervisor and the subordinate. Observing job performance is more than merely watching what is happening. The observer should have some competency and should know what to observe and how to do it. Checklists might be used, as well as narrative statements describing some particular actions. The observer must be unobtrusive, yet close enough to the action to make the observations valid. Periodic checkpoints should be established to determine whether the information being gathered through observation is valid and meaningful. In some situations, repeated return trips for further observation can be wasteful and disruptive.

Critical Incident

This technique asks the person performing the job to keep a log of important incidents that occur on the job. The Designer should provide the guidelines about the kinds of material that should be recorded in the log and the form the log should take. Of course, the performer should have a sufficient literacy level, though a tape recorder could be used to compensate for this shortcoming.

The critical incident is a value judgment. What the person performing the job chooses to include in the log may not actually be the crucial elements of the job performance. Criteria for inclusion should be as specific as possible, with frequent checks to assure that the material being recorded is what is wanted and can be helpful. For the manager, using the critical incident method can be useful, but it can also be disastrous. It forces the manager to look at specific performance to determine the critical elements that promote or hinder good performance. Too often, managers function under the pressure of tasks to be accomplished and consider it a luxury to stop to take a look at their own performance. The critical incident method forces the manager to take mental snapshots of specific performance, rather than looking only at results. If the manager's job is under scrutiny, the Designer may have to proceed much more cautiously than when the position is on the production line or in the office.

Trade-off Situations

As this chapter discussed, the Designer has a variety of methods to choose from to collect data of job performance. It may also be necessary, however, when selecting the appropriate method, to recognize the need for trade-offs between the desirable and the possible.

A method may be entirely appropriate, but too costly for the benefits that can be derived from collecting that information. The Designer is always working against some kind of budget and some limitation of resources. Frequently it is not possible to get the ideal job performance data. The decision must be made as to how much information can be gathered as measured against the cost, in either direct expenditures or staff time.

In this particular event of the CEM, the Designer may find that management becomes more involved than previously anticipated. New insights can evolve about what kinds of job performance are actually occurring, as contrasted with what management thought was happening. If the Designer can involve management and if the possible benefits are identified, additional financial and human resources may suddenly become available.

At the other end of the spectrum, limitations may force the Designer to use a method that involves little of what has been previously discussed. One limitation could be the lack of the resources discussed earlier. The Designer might have an insufficient budget for some of the methods that require direct financial outlays or may not have sufficient or qualified staff who can use the methods. There is an alternative. It is not highly desirable or recommended, but in some situations it may be the only alternative possible.

The Designer, using only job descriptions and similar information, can try to specify job performance. This method requires making assumptions about the job and the way it is performed that may be far from the reality, and that is why this alternative is not recommended. It is included because some situations may make it the only course open to the Designer. When the assumption route is chosen, the Designer should still try to verify the assumptions by as much direct contact with the job as the situation will allow. This direct contact could be a memo to the supervisor or those who use the output of the job. The closer the assumptions can be brought to the reality of the job, the greater the possibility that the ultimate list of job behaviors will be accurate.

EVALUATION AND FEEDBACK

As noted in the previous chapter, each event culminates in evaluation and feedback (E&FB). Following the model presented in that chapter, let us first look at the objective of this event:

To specify the performance expected of a person who is doing a designated job.

Action

The action step is what the Designer has done during this event. During this event, many variations in the expectations of job performance may have been discovered. The fact that divergent expectations exist may be the problem itself and can lead to the solution, even though the solution does not involve training. It is possible that a training program is not required, or at least, not yet. Those involved must first agree on the job performance. The Designer may have to become a consultant rather than a Designer in order to help the members of the organization reach agreements on the job and the expected performance.

Analysis

The data must now be synthesized and organized in a form that will communicate to everyone who is involved. There are many ways to do this, depending upon the nature of the job and the group that will be involved in feedback.

A common method of analysis is to list the individual steps that must be accomplished as part of job performance. The listing will be sequential, in the order required for the work to be performed. This is fairly straightforward when the job is in the area of production or where the steps must be performed in a given and fixed sequence. This list should be detailed enough to make the steps required for a particular job clear to everybody, but it will not be necessary to describe each hand motion required as part of the tasks.

Where the parts of the job are not sequential (for example, with management, supervision, or customer relations positions), the data may be organized around areas or similarity of functions. These areas might include writing, speaking, responding, questioning, or decision making. For some positions, the time of day may provide the framework for organizing the data for review. The job performance may require that the worker be doing certain tasks at specified times, and this can become the format.

Jobs in the sales area could involve both sequential and non-sequential activities. Some given steps in a sales approach make the job almost sequential. For example, a salesman would not start by writing out the invoice. However, selling involves a personal relationship that means variations should be anticipated. The data might be organized to indicate those activities that are sequential and those that are random.

Feedback

Who should be involved in feedback and why? If it appears that training is called for, usually the feedback would involve the person who will be trained or a representative, if the group is large. This, however, is not always possible, and perhaps not even desirable. If the potential trainee(s) is geographically far from where the feedback session will take place, it may be too costly to expect involvement. Also, taking the potential trainee from the work site is a cost to someone in terms of lost production. A manager may be willing to be trained, but may not be interested in being part of this feedback session. This is unfortunate, but frequently close to reality. Too few managers want to be involved in deciding on their own training, and this problem must be addressed as part of the total HRD function.

The supervisor of the potential trainee is essential for feedback. If the supervisor, at whatever level of the organization, is not prepared to be involved in the feedback, it raises the question as to whether the new learning will be used on the job. Where the proposed training is fairly obvious (a secretary moving from direct dictation to word processing), perhaps the supervisor need not be involved. But, if the concern is with job performance, the supervisor must have some degree of involvement to be able to reinforce the newly learned behaviors.

Generally, supervisors want to be involved. If conducted appropriately, feedback sessions can benefit them. It is the rare supervisor who will pass up the opportunity to be part of the feedback session. This means that the session must be carefully planned and scheduled, so it does not conflict with other responsibilities of the supervisor. As this type of feedback session will occur at each step of the CEM and will be repeated with each design task, the climate should be a positive one. This will encourage the supervisor to take part in future feedback sessions. The Designer should be sure that the session is well planned, specific, and within a limited and agreed upon period of time. After several successes, most supervisors will welcome the sessions.

Given the interdependency of jobs others might be involved in the feedback session. The group should not be so large as to become an unwieldy meeting, but sufficiently large to encompass those who are directly related to the job under scrutiny. Once again, when various people in the organization find these meetings of benefit, the Designer will not experience too much difficulty in encouraging the related people to attend.

An alternative to a meeting is to have the data and analysis shared by means of a written memo or report. This is not preferable, but may sometimes be necessary. If those involved are at different geographical locations, the written memo may be requested. If there is the possibility of significant disagreements, the Designer may arrange for a telephone conference call to enable direct communication about the disagreements.

Decisions

The E&FB final experience should address some specific questions that require decisions. This means that the decision-making people should be present, or at least involved, in the final E&FB session. Some of the decisions that need to be made are:

1. Is there still agreement on the problem?

   The problem is the one agreed upon at the conclusion of the previous event. Unless there is still substantial agreement, it is fruitless for the Designer to move to the next event of the CEM. There could be a situation, of course, where a problem has many facets, and then, only one item may be singled out for the training response. It is conceivable that agreement is reached that a problem exists, but the specific dimensions of the problem are still in dispute. Agreement could be reached that the Designer is to proceed, at least to the next event, to explore the problem further.

It may sound simplistic, but the problem should be written down as clearly as possible. Every concerned person should have a copy of the problem statement, as there will be constant reference to it during the next events.

2. Is there agreement on job performance?

   The response to this question could cover the entire spectrum from "yes" to "no" with even a strong "maybe." The desirable response, of course, is that there is agreement. If there is a lack of agreement, this too should be clearly stated. If it is possible to indicate the specific areas where there is a lack of agreement, this should be made clear to all. The Designer should not feel compelled to reconcile the disagreements, but should point out that a training program cannot be designed in the absence of agreement on expected job performance.

3. Should consideration be given to alternatives?

   This is the time to raise the issue of whether other alternatives to training, such as job redesign, reassignment of personnel, or change in procedures should be explored. After one of the alternatives has been selected, it may still be necessary to have a training program, and the Designer can pick up from that point.

4. Will time be allocated for training?

   Although the actual Conduct the Training event is still in the future, this is the time for some initial commitment on making the potential learners available. This is the time for the supervisors to recognize that it is their people who will be trained and must be made available in the future when the training is conducted.

   Depending upon what is determined during later events in the CEM, the training may take several hours a day or several days a week. If time constraints are a problem, this would be a good time for the Designer to learn about them.

If the training is to be off-the-job (at some distant site), the supervisor should agree to release the employee for the necessary time. If there is a limit as to the number of employees from any one unit who can be assigned to training at one time, this information should be shared with the Designer. The decision to assign the learner to training rests in the hands of the supervisors.

CONCLUSION

When the Designer is confident that the appropriate decisions have been made, it is possible to proceed to the next event, Identify Learner Needs.

CHAPTER 5

Identify the Needs of the Learner

This event of the CEM focuses on the specific learning needs of those who are to receive the training. As noted in the previous chapter, it is not possible to identify the needs of the learner until there is agreement about the job and how it is to be performed. In this event, the focus is on the person or people who are doing the job. (See Figure 5-1.)

Chapter 1 contained a discussion of the difference between training and education. Although it is easy to overlook the difference, this oversight can result in disaster or, at least, an inappropriate learning experience.

The objective of this event is to identify the learning needs of those who are doing the designated job. This objective will be modified for education in a later chapter of this book.

THE INDIVIDUAL

People are different, and one of the purposes of a good training program is to bridge the differences between the person and the job, so that the individual can perform in a way that meets the organizational goals. At the same time, the goals of the individual cannot be overlooked. When individual goals are in conflict with organization goals, the training can be a waste of time and money.

Values

The first step is to determine whether the individual wants to do the job as specified. There may be reasons why a person does not want to do a particular job. An example of this frequently occurs in sales. Certain sales tech-

THE CRITICAL EVENTS MODEL

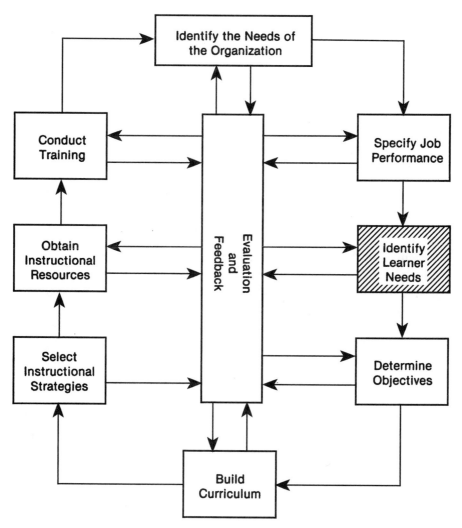

Figure 5-1. Identify the needs of the learner.

niques may conflict with the values of the individual who is selling. An individual may not perform up to expectation or may refuse to engage in some sales activities that, though perfectly legitimate, may perhaps be more "pushy" than the individual wants to be. The training program would have to deal with values like these, rather than just techniques.

When the specifics about expected job performance are known, (through the use of the previous event of the CEM) it may turn out that the individual is not suited to the job. Reassignment may be a more appropriate response than a training program.

The Designer should determine whether the job requires performance that may be counter to the values of the individual. If the individual enjoys talking to other people, serving them, and generally being helpful, a job involving customer contact would seem to be in order. For example, an individual might take a job as a bank teller because of the constant contact with customers and the opportunity to serve them. The teller finds that because of good service, customers keep coming back to the same window, and generally a personal relationship builds and develops.

In the midst of this relationship, management decides that service can be more efficient through the use of "bull pen" or ropes and stanchions strung out so that people must line up. Service is provided by the next available teller, and choice by the customer becomes extremely limited. Many of us, as customers of the bank, may prefer this arrangement, because we always seem to get into the slowest line. For other customers and tellers, the bull pen is just another obstacle to be overcome. The customers pass up available tellers while they wait for "their teller" to become available. Tellers view themselves as depersonalized and as mere extensions of the computers that swallow their output.

Additional training for tellers to show them how to work more efficiently with the bull pen method may be counter-productive, if the teller took the job for the opportunity to interact with and serve people. All that training can do is to re-emphasize the need for speed, accuracy, and avoiding long conversations with customers. Yet, that may not be the teller's value.

Needs

The term "needs" is frequently used incorrectly. As usually defined, a need is the difference between a goal (or what is expected) and what actually exists. In essence, then, a need does not exist unless someone feels a lack of some kind. That is one reason why the CEM has two events before beginning to identify the needs of the learner. First the needs of the organization, as measured against its goals, must be identified, then job performance should be specified, and finally the needs of the learner can be identified.

At this time, the focus should be only on those needs related to job performance. If other needs surface, other appropriate ways to meet them must be explored.

The Designer must also be able to distinguish between "needs" and "wants." The latter are those things individuals ask for that are not related to job performance. Wants are legitimate for the individual, but may do absolutely nothing to solve the problem.

There are three major types of needs. The first are *stated needs.* They arise directly out of the previous event. The specifics of job performance identify exactly what a person is required to do on the job.

Implied needs are not specifically stated, but arise from the situation. For a person on the existing job, an implied need can arise from a change in process, technology, or materials. An implied need can also arise when a new worker enters an existing unit. Tasks may be reassigned, requiring those already doing the job to perform differently. In a sense, some of the implied needs are really stated needs that have not been spelled out by the organization or by those introducing change into the work situation.

A very strong need, for the individual, is the *felt need.* There is almost universal agreement that learning takes place much more effectively when the learner feels the need to learn. When a person wants to perform better and the gap between performance and expectation is clear, there is a felt need.

If the Designer tries to determine employee needs without first having completed the Specify Job Performance event, he or she is more likely to get wants than needs. Wants are legitimate, but will not meet the target of improving job performance. Needs are directly related to job performance now or in the identifiable future.

GATHERING DATA

Methods for gathering data during this event are similar to those in the previous event. The difference, however, is in the actual data being gathered, and this is extremely important. Because there is a great deal of similarity, some Designers attempt to specify job performance and identify needs of the learner at the same time. "After all," they suggest, "this would mean one less trip to the job site, one less interview, and so on." The difficulty with this is that the Designer is collecting data on needs before the performance has been agreed upon.

Another problem that is encountered when these two events are not separated is that the Designer, and others, may have difficulty determining the extent to which the individual influences the job. Of course, the individual is important. To look at both at the same time, however, is to specify job performance as done by the incumbent.

Realistically the job must be done in certain ways to meet the needs of the organization. Employees put their own fingerprints on a job, and for some jobs this is not only permissible but desirable. If this is the case, it should be reflected in the latitude determined in the previous event.

Sampling

Because the Designer is designing a training program for employees currently on the job, then he or she should identify the needs of the learner as evidenced by those performing in that job slot. When this is not possible, the Designer may have to use another technique, that of sampling, or looking at only some of the potential trainees. The sample should be based on criteria that will provide the Designer with unbiased date.

In such cases, the Designer may want to consider the use of electronic data gathering by teleconferencing, computer conferencing, and other devices available in the organizations.

Still another alternative is to use a sampling technique similar to the one used in political elections. The polls conducted before an election do not include all the electorate, but focus on carefully selected individuals or areas. By polling this sample, pollsters are often able to make highly accurate predictions. It is possible to use a similar approach in this event, but it should be done cautiously.

There are criteria for drawing samples, but the Designer is not dealing with the kinds of data that require a high level of sophistication. It is possible, for example, to use this sampling approach with supervisor training programs. The number of supervisors in an organization may be quite large, but the common aspects of their job performance will have been gathered in the previous event. The Designer can develop a data-gathering instrument to identify some of the common needs that supervisors feel they have when compared with what was agreed upon under Specify Job Performance. The Designer must determine the size of the sample and the methods used to draw it. This determination should reflect the diversity of supervisors in the organization. A simple method is to list all supervisors alphabetically, and then draw a sample by taking each fifth name, depending upon the total population and the size of the sample desired.

When geography is a factor, the list can be organized to reflect that variable and the sample drawn from a proportional number from each location. Where a particular unit of the organization is significant, the lists for selecting the sample can be drawn up to reflect that factor.

Sources and Methods

This event requires many of the same sources and methods discussed in the previous chapter. This is both a positive and negative factor.

On the positive side, it means that the Designer can use some of the same competencies that were required earlier. Also, some of the relationships built in the previous event will also be useful in this event. The groundwork to identify the sources and methods will already have been done.

The negative is that the similarity may cause the Designer to make some significant mistakes. The purposes of the two events are much different, and unless this difference is constantly recognized, the data can easily become mingled and garbled.

The focus of the previous event was on the job, no matter who was performing it. Also, there was emphasis on the interdependency aspects and how that job related to others in the organization. Even the question of whether that job was necessary was raised. All of this had to be done without significant consideration for the person or persons doing the job.

In this event there is a dramatic shift in focus. Here the primary concern is people, those actually on the job at this time. The theoretical of "what should be," must be replaced by the reality of "what is!"

SOURCES

The sources of data should be as specific as possible, should include the people actually doing the job (the potential learners), and should reflect job performance.

Production/Output Records

When the program being designed is for a production job, specific production records should be available. These take many forms, and the Designer must determine what is usable and what is not. The records may report unit or group output, rather than individual output, and such a record may not be very helpful in identifying individual needs. Group performance is the result of all the employees in the group, but the needs should be individualized.

Usually when a product is produced records of quantity and quality are kept. If such records are not available, the Designer should not try to reconstruct them from other sources, but should question the reason for the absence of such data. The lack of such record keeping could indicate that the employee has not been told the criteria for effective job performance and has been given no feedback on quantity and quality. Training may not be the need, at least, not training for the producing employees. It may mean that there is a need for supervisor training to help the supervisors learn how to give instructions and feedback about expected job performance.

Where there is no measurable production, the Designer should look for other output records. These could be a log of calls completed, letters processed, or some other observable and/or quantifiable output. As noted earlier, when looking up the hierarchical ladder, such data become more elusive. The Designer may have to search for other sources of data about actual job performance in order to identify the needs.

Relative time must also be watched very closely as the data can rapidly become outdated. Some Designers prefer to obtain what is termed longitudinal data—data that is gathered over a period of time. For some purposes, this technique may have value, but where the situation is changing, that approach can be meaningless. What value is there in seeking data on prior performance, when there has been a change in process, technology, or supervision? The most recent data on performance are all that can be effectively used.

The time factor can prove to be a problem at a later point in the design process. If designing takes a long time (and long is relative), the Designer may find that the data gathered under this event is no longer relevant. Because the needs are individual, the data are meaningless if those individuals are no longer in the same jobs. The relevance is also questionable if there have been other changes in the workplace related to performance, by the time the actual training program is ready to be conducted.

Performance Appraisal

Performance appraisal is a very important source, but the process of performance appraisal reminds one of the waves and the tides. Interest in performance appraisal has had its peaks and valleys, and therefore the actual use of this technique tends to vary. Like the tides, some of it is highly predictable.

In some organizations, performance appraisal is an annual ritual, which most detest but which must be performed. It is approached with fear and trepidation, which frequently produces hostility. The actual appraisal may be more of a reflection of the supervisor than of the subordinate. If the climate in the organization is not supportive of the supervisor, the appraisal is a source, but a questionable one, for it may only be useful as an outlet for supervisor frustration.

For example, an HRD manager had a secretary who was woefully inadequate. She violated many of the actual rules and regulations which, in that organization, were extremely significant. She was unreliable and openly discussed the letters, memos, and phone calls to which she was privy, and this frequently caused embarrassment. When the time came for performance appraisal, the requisite forms were filled out and she was called in for the mandatory (and usually helpful) discussion. As might be expected, she felt that she was entirely correct in what she was doing and that everything done in the HRD office should be shared with everyone. After several discussions, it became apparent that agreement would never be reached and a negative appraisal was forwarded.

Shortly thereafter, this secretary was transferred to a different part of the organization. In her mind, and she said this for all to hear, it vindicated her performance. She had not been fired, reprimanded, nor had she lost any increment in pay. Therefore she felt she was performing satisfactorily despite her supervisor's appraisal. In a case such as this, what would happen if the Designer relied on the appraisal? Obviously it would be irrelevant, as the secretary was no longer in the same position, though she still worked for the organization as a secretary. If a need were indicated for her to learn how to respect the privacy of the material that passed over her desk, she certainly would not have had that felt need. After all, the result of the appraisal was a transfer with no implication that it was the result of any lack of performance on her part. The performance appraisal, in that instance, could not be used as a valid source.

It is also frustrating when performance appraisals are kept secret. At times this is necessary, but some organizations tend to be overcautious. In one situation, the organization had elaborate appraisal forms. The Designer, who was external, met with the CEO of that organization and listened to a lengthy and detailed description of the appraisal system. The Designer then asked to see the appraisals for the managers for whom a training program was to be designed. The response from the CEO was, "I cannot let you see them; they are confidential." The Designer explained how vital that data was, and finally the CEO agreed to digest the information, being sure that no single manager could be identified, and then share it with the Designer. The result, of course, was a long list of generalities that could not be connected to individual learning needs.

Most performance appraisals are not designed to indicate individual training needs. Frequently it is possible to tease that out of the form, but that involves a good deal of judgment on the part of people other than the potential learners. However, when performance is not up to the standard required, some training is usually needed. If the organization has this built into the performance appraisal system (not only the forms), this can be a valid source.

Supervisor

The supervisor is a basic data source. Most often the supervisor is the one who requested the training program. Therefore, the supervisor will generally have some data or information that supports the need for the individual training. By going to the supervisor, the Designer involves that person in the identification and specification of the learners' needs. Because the Designer is able to function in a variety of units at one time, he or she can determine whether various supervisors have identified similar needs for their subordinates.

To identify needs of the learner it is necessary to be as specific as possible. The Designer should seek out examples of behavior, preferably observable, which would indicate the need. The supervisor should have this information available. If the Designer is seeking the quantifiable, the supervisor should also be a source for such information.

When working with the supervisor in this event, the Designer must be cautious about another and seemingly unrelated factor that can influence the data collected. A Designer may feel under pressure to deliver—to produce a training program—and get as many learners into the program as possible. This sometimes arises when the HRD unit is evaluated based on "body count," that is, how many employees were trained, rather than on the results—on solving problems.

Likewise, the supervisor may feel that the company culture emphasizes getting as many employees trained as possible, without any direct relation to the problems or opportunities.

Therefore, when collecting data on the needs of the learner, the Designer and supervisor should be sure they are concentrating on the learning needs, and not on their own possible need to produce as many training programs or learners as possible.

Employee-learner

If a need is identified that pertains to a single employee, with no significance for other employees, designing a training program may not be the appropriate response. It would generally be too costly to design for a single individual. It is not that the individual does not have needs, but to identify needs of only one learner can be costly when compared to the possible return. One possibility is to do nothing, with the concurrence of the supervisor and the employee.

When going to the employee as the source, the Designer will automatically determine whether the employee knows what is expected in job performance. As has been said many times, the lack of performance may be due solely to not having helped the employee understand what exactly is the expected performance. When using the employee as a source, the Designer should start with the job performance expectations that were produced in the previous event, Specify Job Performance. If the employee had been involved, this statement of the job performance will not be new. The Designer may now be faced with the employee indicating that the expected performance is not possible. If the previous E&FB activities were accurate and successful, this should not happen—but it is always a possibility.

Going to the employee is necessary, but it presents a critical problem. The implication is that the employee is not working up to the level of expected performance. (This would not be the case if the training is the result of a new process or product.) The Designer is placed in the position of confronting the employee with this gap in performance. The employee may become hostile and negative. Few of us enjoy confronting our inadequacies. Going to the employee requires skill in interpersonal relationships, asking questions, and dealing with hostility.

The Designer must also consider the previous learning experiences of the employee, as well as learning style.

An employee with a fairly high level of previous training and education may be more articulate and therefore able to readily provide information to the Designer. A less articulate employee will still have needs, but may not be able to so readily indicate them to the Designer.

This may also be a good time for the Designer to begin gathering data on the learning style of the employee. A good deal of work has been done on this (see Kolb [49]), and the Designer might want to develop a method for gathering this data at this time. It will have some limited use here, but will be very important during the event, Build Curriculum.

METHODS

Meetings

Meetings are always costly, and not always cost effective. It is most desirable to include in the meetings all those to be trained, as well as their supervisors. This, however, could produce a total shutdown of the operation. Therefore some selectivity is required. The Designer should provide some criteria to the supervisor(s) as to who should be involved in the meeting. The participants should be those who are doing the job. Expectations of how the job should be done will have surfaced in the previous event. Here, the focus must be exclusively on actual performance and those persons performing in the job. The ideal would be to involve only those who have identified learning needs. But, the results may be to create a group of employees who appear to be the low performers, and consequently the meeting can become a pejorative event which could certainly block the possibilities of learning in the future. When the reasons for the meeting are made clear, this need not present a problem.

There is a question as to whether employees, at all levels, are capable of evaluating their own performance. Experience has shown that this is not only possible, but can be used effectively. For years there have been managers in the United States who have used the concept of *participative management* which includes involving employees at all levels in a variety of small meetings. This idea was picked up and used extensively by the Japanese in a process called "Quality Circles" [113A].

It is important that the agenda for meetings in which employees identify their own needs should be short and concise. The Designer should avoid discussions of elaborate concepts or generalities. The focus should specifically be on comparing the expected job performance with the actual, and identifying the learning needs of the employee participants.

Interview

When interviewing the potential learner, the Designer should endeavor to ascertain the relationship of the felt needs with those that are stated or implied. The interview should be as specific as possible.

The preferred approach is to interview all of the employees who are the potential trainees. This may not be possible because of the size of the group or their geographical location. In such instances, the Designer may have to rely on sampling, with its limitations as discussed earlier.

The Designer should avoid interviewing only those who are readily available, as they may not be representative of the group. The cautions to be observed, which were discussed in the previous chapter about where to interview, climate setting, and so on, are equally applicable here.

Observation

Observing employees actually doing the job can be extremely helpful. The supervisor is the one to identify those who will probably need the training. After the observation, the Designer may indicate those who do not need the training or those who would not benefit from the training. This latter decision is a difficult one to make, but it is sometimes necessary. There are many reasons why a particular individual may not be able to improve performance even with the best training. If the Designer can identify this and discuss it with the supervisor, it will reduce false expectations and wasteful training costs.

Observing the work actually being done presents some problems to the Designer. It may become evident that some coaching of individual employees is all that is needed to bring performance up to the agreed upon standards. Coaching, of course, is a valid learning strategy. The question is: who should do the coaching? It will be very tempting to the Designer to do the coaching while observing. This could almost appear to be cost effective, but what of the supervisor? Would the supervisor feel that the Designer has usurped the regular supervisory function? When a supervisor feels that way, that feeling could block any further observations by the Designer. The Designer must remember that the role is one of designing, not that of supervising.

Questionnaire

The questionnaire is particularly useful when the job cannot be observed and where measurement is not a factor. The questionnaire should be kept simple and relate directly to the job that the employee is performing. Too often, those who design questionnaires go on a "fishing expedition." That is, as long as time is being spent on the questionnaire, what other information can be obtained? That weakens the focus of the questionnaire, takes additional time, and raises doubts in the mind of the employee as to the purpose of the questionnaire. A serious limitation of the questionnaire when used to identify needs of the learner is that it is generally best used for obtaining data about knowledge. A carefully constructed questionnaire might elicit valid data about attitudes, but a questionnaire cannot assess skill behavior. Where skill is a factor in the possible training program, a questionnaire might not be the best method.

When measurement is to be considered, there are better methods for obtaining this information, though the Designer may still choose to use a questionnaire to obtain related information for verification. When the measurement information is available from a basic source (for example, production records), the Designer may wish to verify this by having the employee respond to a question on output. The Designer could discover that the standard production records and the employee record of output do not coincide. The Designer might discover a discrepancy in the way output is tallied and decide that training is needed in record keeping.

Tests

For a training program, pencil and paper tests are generally not helpful. The data are best obtained by interview, observation, and records. The actual job performance will yield much better and more realistic data than a test that is an artificial situation.

One testing method is a variation of the *assessment center.* The basic purpose of the assessment center is not to identify learner needs, but rather to assess the potential of an individual to do a particular job. With modifications, the assessment center has been used to identify learning needs, and that approach is not new. Before the term "assessment center" entered the literature, Designers were using a method termed *simulation.* That is, they designed a situation much like the actual work situation, but without penalties for failure. Individuals would take part in the simulation, try out new behaviors, and not be confronted by the limitation that failure would be costly. Used in this manner, assessment center/simulation is a form of testing.

For management level work, the case study method has proven very valuable in helping an individual identify how he or she might possibly behave when given a particular problem.

LISTING OF NEEDS

It is essential to make a specific list of the learning needs that have been identified. One approach is the *subtraction method* as illustrated in Figure 5-2. The *difference* between expected job performance and actual job performance is the need. This formula appears very simple, but unless the work under the previous event and this event has been done well, the differences may not be apparent enough to serve as the basis for a training program.

Sometimes a Designer may have to compromise. For example, it may not be feasible to obtain the specifics for each individual who will be a trainee. Therefore it is possible that some potential learners are already able to per-

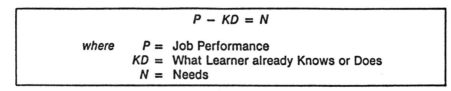

$$P - KD = N$$

where P = Job Performance
KD = What Learner already Knows or Does
N = Needs

Figure 5-2. Formula for needs

form as expected. Despite this, supervisors send those individuals to training sessions. There is little that can be done about this in the design phase, but it will be discussed further in the Conduct Training event.

Listing and Organization of Needs

The results of the differences (expected performance minus actual performance) should be indicated as specifically as possible. This can be done in various ways, but it is important for the Designer to find the form or the reporting mechanism that he or she can use most effectively to communicate with everyone involved. A Designer might make a note of some of the various forms contained in the literature or those distributed at workshops and retain them in a file to be referred to as appropriate. The Designer should not accept someone else's form without first testing its appropriateness for the situation.

Some common pitfalls can be avoided if the Designer gives adequate attention to this phase of the event. Being specific lessens the possibility of designing and training for the wrong performance. Limits are sometimes placed on how specific a Designer can be; however, that is what makes designing as much an art as a skill. Those people who have been directly involved in the job performance may have difficulty seeing the specifics, but by forcing them to do so the Designer might engender hostility and a blocking of the whole process. There is a very fine line between specificity and overkill.

The meaning of words becomes crucial. The needs should be stated in a manner that is not critical of the performer or the supervisor. Very few of us enjoy being told that we are not performing as the job demands or as well as we can. The Designer must find the words that communicate effectively and have the same meaning for all concerned. As the listing will be shared with a variety of people in the organization (and later outside of the organization), it is important that meanings be as generally accepted as possible.

One consideration about word choice is local usage. In American English, we have absorbed words into our language that we assume everyone knows. Sometimes however these words are known only to those who share the same cultural experiences, and a breakdown can occur even within cultural groups. Take the following words and ask for meanings—Kleenex, Ping-Pong, Frigidaire, and Vu-graph. All of these words are product names but are in common usage for products manufactured by a wide variety of manufacturers. The products are tissues, table-tennis, refrigerator, and overhead projector.

An experience many of us have had is to ask a new employee to "burn a copy." Do not be surprised if the result is ashes. The phrase "burn a copy" was common during the 1960s when copying machines using intense heat first came on the scene. Today, it could be equally disastrous to ask for a "Xerox" of a document, and have the employee go outside the company, since the copying machine within the company is made by another manufacturer.

These may seem like extreme examples, yet this type of miscommunication occurs within organizations and can lead to personnel problems for the supervisors who thought the subordinate was just being contrary.

Another example comes from our experience as counselors to prospective HRD graduate students. The materials describing the program are in clear written form, or so we thought. A problem arose when a prospective student asked, "What is a semester hour and how does it differ from a credit hour?" Our first reaction was that this was obvious, but then we discovered it wasn't. Actually both meant the same thing in that particular academic situation, and much of the written material used both terms. To those who used the material, the similarity was obvious. To an "outsider" it was confusing.

Most work situations have their own language, or jargon, and it is important that these be clarified on the listings of needs. Everyone involved should have clear agreement on all the terms or the design process will break down at a later event.

EVALUATION AND FEEDBACK

Having identified the needs of the learners, the Designer is now ready to implement the E&FB event before proceeding further. As noted at the outset, the objective of this event is to identify the learning needs of those who are doing the designated job.

Analysis

With the data in hand, the Designer must organize it for presentation to those who will be involved in feedback. As a start, the Designer should compare what has been gathered in this event with the listing gathered under Specify Job Performance to ascertain how the identified needs are related to job performance. If there is a discrepancy between these two listings, it may be necessary to return to Specify Job Performance. If the current event has been done effectively, there should not be any needs that do not relate to job performance. This is the point at which that check is made.

At this time, the Designer will have a list of needs. Now the list should be categorized and items that are related grouped together. For example, all the items related to "communications" might be put under one heading. However, care should be exercised that the sub items are not lost because the word "communications" may be too general and useless for design work. Under the heading of "communications," the specific items that have been identified earlier should be retained.

If there are variations due to individuals, this is also noted at this time. That is, not everybody will need all the items listed. Therefore the analysis should show which individuals have specific needs. The Designer should not make any judgments at this time as to which needs are to be met or which are most important. That will evolve in the next event.

Feedback

Most of the same people should be involved in feedback for this event as for the previous one. Here, however, it is crucial that the supervisor be directly involved. It is helpful if the potential trainee can be involved, but this will depend upon how comfortable the Designer is with the data that has been gathered during this entire event. The method of involving subordinates will be a reflection of the leadership style of the supervisor. This is another point at which the Designer must realize that the work is being done for the supervisor and the organization and that the design process should not interfere with the work situation.

If the needs have been clearly listed, it is possible to circulate the list among all those concerned and ask them to return it with comments. This is particularly appropriate when the group to be involved is either located at different sites or has different work schedules. This condition will become more prevalent as more forms of alternative work scheduling are introduced into the workplace.

A factor of privacy enters here. It may not be desirable to have everyone know the needs of all the others. One way this can be accommodated is to give the subordinates only a list of their own needs. Obviously the supervisor will have to react to the list of all the needs of all the subordinates.

Decisions

Before proceeding, the Designer must obtain specific answers to the following questions and the decisions implied in each:

1. If the needs are met, will job performance become acceptable?

   It is possible to satisfy needs and still have little or no effect on job performance. If this were to happen, the training program would have been meaningless. For example, there are times when the support by the supervisor back on the job is a crucial element. (See the chapter on "Support Systems.")

   In responding to this question, it may become apparent that the problem lies in what was indicated under "Specify Job Performance." That data may have looked good at the conclusion of the previous event but, on re-evaluation it is obvious that something on the job has to be changed.

2. If the needs are met, and the performance becomes acceptable, will the problem be solved?

   If the needs are met through training, will the problem stated at the end of "Identify the Needs for the Organization" be solved? Of course, much more must happen before the final answer to this question is evident, but at this time speculation is in order. If meeting the needs will not solve the problem, why go further?

3. How important are the needs?

   There are times when a process develops a momentum of its own. This can easily happen during the design process. It is possible to specify the needs of the learner, but the listing may not be significant enough to warrant further action. One important aspect is, of course, the financial one. Would the benefits be worth the cost? There is no easy response. Even if the benefits to be gained are below the cost to be incurred, it may still be desirable to provide the training. Cost should not be the only factor, though it may be the main one. The decision about this should rest with the supervisor and management, not with the Designer.

4. Should the job be redesigned?

   The needs may be valid, but performance might be improved through job redesign. This was raised in the previous event and becomes more significant here. Under "Specify Job Performance," the Designer was looking at the job, not the person who performed it. Now there is data on those people who are performing. Perhaps some minor redesign of the job would be more appropriate than providing training.

5. Should tasks be reallocated?

The Designer may have uncovered strengths among the subordinates that were not previously known. There could be employees who have competencies in exactly the areas needed, but who are not doing that part of the job. Rather than train, some reassignment of the tasks within the unit might improve overall job performance of that unit.

6. Should subordinates be transferred rather than trained?

This is an extension of the earlier question. Perhaps the competencies that have surfaced during this event indicate that some subordinates can make a more effective contribution to the organization and get more job satisfaction if they were in other units. The answer to this must start with the subordinate and the supervisor. Then it might require some counseling by the personnel department to identify a more appropriate placement of the subordinate within the organization. The supervisor cannot do this counseling, for even if he had counseling skills, he would not know where other jobs exist in the organization or where vacancies are anticipated. The Designer should also avoid counseling at this point for the same reason.

7. What is the availability of the learners?

If all agree on this list of needs, what are the constraints in the situation? These will have to be explored further in the other events but are included here as part of the decision-making process.

The supervisor who will assign the subordinate to the training program (away from the job site) must indicate the shortest and longest times that that person can be spared. Also, if there are any factors that make certain days or times less desirable than others, they should be noted. In an extreme case, the list may indicate a great number of needs, but the supervisor will only allocate one hour a week for three weeks. If that is the case, this suggests a different problem than the one under scrutiny. It could also mean that the supervisor is not committed to training as a response, although nothing may have been said previously.

CONCLUSION

When positive decisions have been made about these questions, the Designer can then proceed to the Determine Objectives event.

CHAPTER 6

Determine Objectives

We now come to the event (see Figure 6-1) that has caused more controversy and conflict than any other aspect of designing training programs. Before 1960, training programs used objectives that had a wide range of flexibility. Several individuals attempted to clarify the area of learning objectives. In the early 1960s, Skinner and those who followed his approach insisted on "specific behavioral objectives," and no deviation was allowed [58].

Over the years, it has become obvious that objectives are necessary, but no single method can satisfy the requirements of all people and all programs.

By the end of this event, the Designer will be able to:

- Identify the elements that must be considered in determining objectives for the program.
- Produce learning objectives related to the design under consideration.

Before proceeding further, we need to discuss some terms related to objectives.

There are scholars who try to distinguish between terms such as program and course. Generally a course is a single learning experience that stands by itself, with a determined beginning and end. A program is usually a series of courses.

Those definitions may suffice for colleges and universities, but they cannot be directly applied to the HRD field. Within the CEM, the term *program* will be used to identify the training experience being designed. Whether it will consist of more than one learning experience cannot be determined until a later event of the CEM.

THE CRITICAL EVENTS MODEL

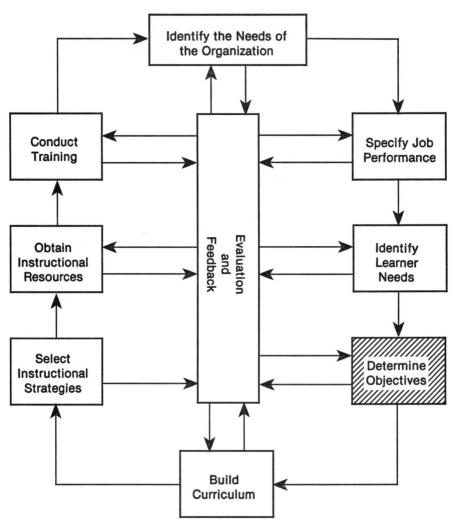

Figure 6-1. Determine objectives.

In the present event, two areas must be explored and two decisions made. The first concerns the overall program and the ways it relates to solving the problems that were identified in the Identify the Needs of the Learner event. The general objective is to have a program that will solve these problems. The second area and decision relates to the specific training experience.

WHAT ARE OBJECTIVES?

An objective is a statement of what is to be accomplished by an activity. Designing a training program does not start with objectives, but with successfully identifying the needs of the learner in the previous event. At the end of that event, it is possible to develop a list of the learner's needs. These are not objectives, but objectives will evolve from these needs.

To determine objectives it is necessary to go through a process involving people and data. It is not a straight-line process but an evolving one, with many twists and turns. The Designer should not be put in the position of having to write the objectives, and then having to defend them. Determining objectives should not be viewed as an adversary proceeding.

It is deceptively easy for the Designer to take the needs identified in the previous event and write objectives. These, however, become the Designer's objectives and not necessarily those of the organization or the learner. At a later point, the Designer must take the available data and actually write some objectives to test out understanding and seek agreement. This should not be done too early in this event, because pushing to premature closure can produce hostility that may block effective agreement on objectives.

When considering objectives, the Designer should look ahead in the CEM at the events to come and recognize that the form and content of the written objectives will dramatically influence whatever follows. Specific behavioral objectives are helpful in evaluation, but can wreak havoc with curriculum or instructional strategies. Objectives written in specific behavioral terms do not generally allow for the spontaneity some people require in a learning situation.

Decisions about the form of the written objectives must reflect a variety of factors, including the learner, the organization, the material to be learned, and the extent of the change in performance being sought. Underlying all of these are the value system and concepts of the Designer, as influenced by all those factors. There are many learning theories, and some will be considered in the next event, but the Designer should have some idea of the learning theory that would be most appropriate for this particular training program.

A major use of objectives is in evaluation. The more specific the objectives, the easier it will be to evaluate learning and performance. Indeed, the objectives should be written with evaluation in mind. The Designer must conjecture about methods to determine that the objective has been reached.

That decision will not actually have to be faced until the Conduct Training event, but it must be considered at this point.

DEVELOP PROGRAM OBJECTIVES

To develop program objectives, the Designer starts with the needs identified in the previous event. The first step is to organize these needs into a priority listing.

Priorities

Developing a list of the needs according to priorities starts with agreement on what is a priority. The Designer must know the needs of the individual and the organization in order to establish categories of priorities.

It is unlikely that all the needs that have been previously identified can be satisfied in any one program. This does not mean that the needs are not valid, but rather there are always constraints that limit the possibility of meeting all the needs.

One way of listing priorities is by *time*. The CEM started with an organizational problem for which HRD could be a response. How soon must that problem be solved? If it is in manufacturing and the problem is that defective output is being produced, time is of the essence. Unless the production line can be closed down, every item produced could be defective. It is important to provide necessary training as soon as possible so as to decrease or eliminate rejects.

Another kind of priority might be the use of *resources*. What would it take, in the way of company resources, to provide the training program? The cost-benefit aspect has been discussed previously. Here the concern is with when the resources can be made available. Each organization has its own cycle of cash flow, for example, and the need for cash for training could determine the priority classification. *Availability of personnel* could be another priority. If the proposed program is for salespeople, and they are out in the field, several of the needs might have to be delayed until those people are available.

Within any given organization, other items determine priorities. The Designer must determine those before devoting too much time to needs that could have a low priority. Rather than attempt to present specific classifications, let us generally explore other factors that could influence or determine priorities.

Another priority is *frequency,* or how often a specific performance, related to the need, is required. Although the need may be valid, the performance related to it is demonstrated only rarely or will not be required at all until some future time.

The *potential learners* could also become a priority. Earlier, availability of the learners was considered, but there is also a factor of sensitivity to consider. If, for example, a vote for a union is on the horizon, this could be the wrong time to provide some kinds of training. Also, if the company is issuing statements to the public and the press about its deteriorating market position, that could influence which needs would be best met at this time.

Factors *outside the organization* also influence priorities. If the organization is under attack from consumer groups, government agencies, or competitors, the range of needs that can be satisfied would be different from a situation where there is no such attack. The Designer must be aware of those external forces that could cause a shift in the priority of needs.

Training generally means that the learner must be away from the job. Although it is possible to have some individualized training on the job site, this is not yet common enough to be given great consideration, but it is a factor that must be explored. If the individual cannot be away from the job, the Designer might consider using individualized instruction. If so, this should be explored at this point, for it will influence the objectives as well as all the other events of the CEM that follow. Given the limitations of individualized instruction, the priorities may have to be altered.

After priorities have been determined, the needs should be listed to reflect the priorities. Note that it is not the objectives that are listed, for they have not yet been determined. First, the needs are listed. It might soon become apparent to the Designer that not all the needs can be met and that it would be wasteful to write objectives for all those needs that cannot be included in the proposed program.

In refining the needs, prioritizing and examining them, the Designer may find that some needs can be combined. This should be done carefully, so as not to weaken the priority listing. Where needs are very similar or overlapping, grouping them can be helpful in making decisions about program objectives. However, when considering training objectives, it is necessary to refer back to the original needs listing.

Process

The Designer should never determine objectives in a vacuum. It is relatively easy to work alone at one's desk, writing objectives, but this heightens the possibility of producing irrelevant statements. If the Designer works in isolation, writes the objectives and passes them around for review and reaction, he or she could cause conflict with the other members of the organization. Not all conflict is bad, but this one could be. The Designer is not the only one with a vested interest in the final objectives. Therefore others in the organization need to be involved in the process of determining and writing the objectives, not merely in evaluating them later.

The most crucial people are the supervisors. The supervisor is the one who must make the learner available, and is frequently the one who must devote some resources (usually financial) to the training. But even more important is the fact that the supervisor is the one who is directly concerned with the ultimate performance change which will result after the training.

In a sense, the same can be said for managers. They are concerned, by definition, with the performance of the supervisors in their area. If the objectives are for the purpose of changing performance, some managers will want to be involved. For training, involving the managers is important if only to make sure that the objectives are consonant with what the other managers are planning.

In one company, when the Designer reached this event, the objectives were concerned with a selling strategy to create a high demand for a particular item the company was selling. The planned training was to provide the sales staff with more skills and knowledge about the product and market. The objectives were carefully drafted with the assistance of the district sales managers as well as the sales supervisors. Fortunately, in this case, the Designer urged that the objectives be reviewed at the next higher level of the organization. This recommendation was not usually made, although the Designer had urged similar action in previous design work. This time, somebody listened. The draft objectives were sent to a higher level for review and came back with a resounding negative response. After blood pressures returned to normal, the Designer, managers, and supervisors asked for the reason. It was simple. The organization was planning to make some significant changes in market strategy. Until the higher levels of management clarified their strategy and agreed on the changes, designing and conducting the training being considered would not be appropriate.

This information had not been communicated earlier, because management did not want to risk leaks. At this time, however, management had to take action to delay the training program until their decisions were made and communicated.

At this point in determining program objectives it is not necessary to involve the potential learner, though there is no harm in doing so. Considering the possible disruption and cost incurred in any design process, the Designer should take a conservative approach. There are some benefits to involving the potential learner, but if the Designer has been checking each event carefully, involving the potential learner could be redundant.

SKILLS, KNOWLEDGE, AND ATTITUDE

There are a variety of ways to convert needs into objectives. One generally accepted pattern is to explore the skills, knowledge, and attitudes (SKA) that relate to the needs and the learning program.

The literature on educational psychology or related disciplines has provided other terms for skills, knowledge, and attitudes, such as:

skill   = psychomotor
knowledge = cognitive
attitude   = affective

Generally these terms are referred to as the three domains of learning. The Designer must recognize these three areas, watch for them in the literature, and keep them in mind when developing objectives.

Learning is the process of acquiring some new skill, attitude, or knowledge, and can be contrasted with performance, which is using the skill, attitude, or knowledge. The obvious difference is between acquisition and use. Not all learning is acquired with a use in mind, but it is probable that all learning in some way influences performance. In training situations, the concern is with the direct link between learning and performance.

Can performance change without learning? That is a difficult question to answer. Theoretically this is not possible. Individuals cannot perform what they have not learned. The problem is that there is still a lack of agreement on exactly how learning takes place, or what a person has really learned in the past. Therefore new performance may suddenly take place without an identified prior learning experience because the learning had taken place at an earlier and unidentified time.

Generally the terms behavior and performance are used interchangeably. In recent years, emphasis has been given to the word "performance," particularly as it signifies something observable. At one time, behavior was defined in that manner. Designers will find managers who say, "I don't care how the employee behaves, I am interested in performance." It would be of little use to begin a semantic argument with the manager over the use of those words. In essence, both the manager and the Designer seek the same end—the performance that the employee exhibits on the job.

The complexity of relationships is depicted in Figure 6-2. The total container represents the potential that every individual is born with. As has often been said, very few of us use a significant amount of our potential. Into this potential, flow two different kinds of learning. The first is incidental learning. It results from experience that comes from living and adapting to our environment and to the forces with which we are constantly in contact. We do not start out with needs and objectives, but we do continually learn. The second kind of learning is intentional learning. It results from the activities we undertake with the express purpose of learning.

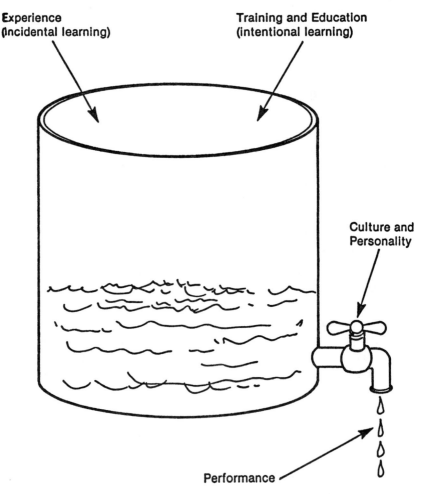

Figure 6-2. Learning and performance.

Within each individual, the two kinds of learning are continually mixing and interacting. The result is the possibility of a change in some kind of performance. Many factors influence that possibility. A major factor is the personality of the individual—those internal forces that limit what one can do or cause one to do differently. Another is the external factor, which is the culture that either encourages or discourages certain kinds of performance. Those factors act as a spigot, turning performance on and off. Therefore the individual can learn, but may still not be able to perform because of these factors.

Given that, let us look at skills, knowledge, and attitudes in terms of providing intentional learning.

Skills

Skills are sometimes thought of in relationship to blue-collar or production line workers only. That is not the case. An executive who cannot write a good letter lacks skill in letter writing. Skills are also necessary in delegating and in other duties required of executives and managers.

Learning a skill requires practice. It is impossible to learn a skill by listening to somebody talk about it, by seeing a demonstration, or reading a book. Skill, by definition, implies action of some kind.

It is easier to write learning objectives for skill-related training than for the other domains. As skills are observable, they can be stated more specifically than the other two areas of learning.

Knowledge

Most learning involves some kind of knowledge. Knowledge itself does not change performance, though it may influence it. If there was a direct relationship between knowledge and performance, it would be easy to change the latter. Merely have people learn the "right way" or the "truth," and they would all perform in an acceptable manner. Reality teaches us that such is not the case. Knowledge may be power, but it does not necessarily change performance. The Designer should not fall into the trap of assuming that "to know is to do."

That does not mean that knowledge is not important. Quite the contrary. Most of us want to know the "why" of an expected performance. We are not robots and do not want to be treated as such. There are times when we seek more knowledge than we can use. Such thirst should not be discouraged but must be balanced against the needs of the learner, the subsequent expected performance, the solving of the problem, and certainly the availability of resources. In the next event, Build Curriculum, consideration will be given to the specific question of what kind of knowledge should be included. At this event, the focus is on the way knowledge relates to the learning objective.

Attitude

This is the most controversial area of learning. There are behaviorists (Skinner, *et al.*) who insist that as attitudes cannot be observed or measured, they cannot be learned. The behavioral people, (Lewin, Rogers, *et al.*) contend that attitudes are crucial to most human performance. It is not necessary to take a fixed position on either end of this debate. If a Designer is interested in pursuing this further, there has been some interesting work done on identifying and even measuring values and attitudes (see [92B]).

Of more immediate concern is the direct relationship of attitudes to performance. The question frequently posed is "Shouldn't we change attitudes in order to change performance?"

This is one of those questions that does not have a single, simple, or direct response. There are valid and strong arguments on both sides. Some researchers insist that learning must precede any change in attitude to bring about performance change. Others contend that performance can change and people will learn to rationalize their attitudes to conform with the new performance. Both are right—to a degree! Each of us can probably cite examples to substantiate either possibility. Neither position can stand entirely on its own. When we deal with attitudes, we encounter a part of the individual that is more intrinsic than skills or knowledge.

That does not mean that the Designer should ignore attitudes. They are essential to performance, unless one adopts the position of a supervisor who says, "I don't care whether you like it or not, just do it."

When exploring the needs that relate to attitudes, the Designer must proceed cautiously. Some people react in forceful and even violent ways when their basic attitudes are scrutinized. This was evident during the decades of the 1960s and 1970s when, for the first time, minority groups were introduced into factories and offices in the U.S., which had previously never known a Black or Hispanic. Women, as a minority, can attest to some of the treatment they received when managerial positions were opened to females in greater numbers than ever before. Programs in those volatile areas could not rely only on knowledge alone. They had to address attitudes, although the objectives may have been stated in other terms. Many programs were offered as "a means of complying with the law." People were not asked to change their attitudes, but were required to change their performance to comply with the law.

DEVELOPING LEARNING OBJECTIVES

At some point, the needs must be converted into learning (training) objectives, after agreement on the broad program objectives. These must then be reduced to more usable items, frequently referred to as specific behavioral objectives. There are many sources the Designer can use in order to get help in writing such objectives. The process and thought that go into producing the learning objective are the important things; the writing is the end result.

Mediation

Learning objectives do not exist in a vacuum. The actual objective must reflect certain realities of the training situation. One aspect is the way the learning will be delivered. There are two basic means for transmitting learning: machine-mediated and instructor-mediated.

Machine-mediated instruction achieved its greatest impetus with the introduction of teaching machines in the early 1960s. At that time, in part because of the increased interest by the military, the market grew and the machines became more sophisticated. General acceptance was delayed until the development of the microprocessors, portable computer terminals, and other devices that made machine-mediated instruction more available. For the most part, we now have machines that are related to computers, although it is still possible to have free-standing learning machines.

When the learning is machine-mediated, the objectives must be very specific. One reason for this is that the machine can only do what it is programmed to do, and the program must relate to previously agreed upon objectives. Once the machine is used, there is a limit to flexibility. The more sophisticated machines can allow for branching and other alternatives, but those alternatives are limited to what has previously been entered into the machine.

Although the decision about the delivery system (that is, mediation) will not be made until later in the design process, some thought must be given to it at this point. If machines are to be used, the objectives must be as specific as language allows.

When the program is to be *instructor-mediated,* the objectives need not be quite so specific. Objectives are still necessary, of course, and they should not be poorly written, but the level of specificity is not as crucial. When the instructor is a professional, overly specific objectives might even prove to be a hindrance. The professional instructor should exercise some influence over the training situation and be allowed some flexibility in meeting the objectives.

There is one form of instructor-mediated learning that requires objectives that are more specific, though limited. This is a system referred to as *peer mediated-learning (PML).* This type of delivery uses an instructor who is not a professional, but rather, a peer of the learners. This approach has many benefits, but also some limitations. If PML is to be used, the objectives should be very specific, but also very limited, unless the intent is to try to make the peer into a professional, which defeats the reason for using peers. The Designer obviously should not expect the peer to have the flexibility of a professional instructor.

If it is possible at this point in the CEM to make a decision about the mediation approach to be used, it would facilitate the writing of the learning objectives. If such a decision is not possible at this time, the Designer must proceed to write objectives based on what appears to be the probable form of mediation. It is essential that the Designer indicate what the form of delivery is apt to be, for without identifying that aspect it is not possible to know the level of specificity required for the learning objectives.

Writing Learning Objectives

The Designer now comes to the task of actually writing the learning objectives. A useful learning objective should be stated in terms of the desired outcome, not what has to be done to achieve that outcome. The objective should not describe content or practice. For training, the learning objective must indicate the performance of the learner at the end of the training experience.

One way to focus on the end result of the training is to start the list of learning objectives with a statement such as "By the end of this learning experience, the learner will be able to . . ." This statement emphasizes that the focus is on the learner, not the instructor. It also underscores the requirement to look at the completion of the training and the performance that is expected at that time.

Three components should appear in an objective:

1. Performance
2. Condition
3. Criterion

Performance is stated in terms of what the learner will be able to do by the end of the training. It is easier to state what the instructor will do during the experience, but that is not the purpose of the learning activity. The expected outcome is the change of performance on the part of the learner, not the instructor. This does not mean that an instructor may not learn during the experience, but that is not the objective.

The objective should be stated in terms of the observable and measurable whenever possible. Because the focus is on performance, the objective should not contain any statement about content, instructional strategies, or any other factors that indicate how the learning will take place. Rather, an objective should start with a statement such as "At the end of this learning experience the learner should be able to . . ."

The second component is *condition,* which specifies the limitations or constraints under which the performance is expected to take place. Note that these are not the limitations of the training situation, but of the final performance in the training environment, before actual use on the job. This is called terminal performance. That is when a significant evaluation step must occur, as will be seen later in the CEM. If the condition statement reflects an understanding of the job, it limits the loss through transfer of training when the learner takes the new performance back to the job site. The condition should state the actual tool or tools to be used in performance. The Designer checks with the supervisor the actual condition under which the job is performed. This avoids the situation where the learner says, "Sure, if I had this tool back on the job, I could do it the way they want." It keeps the training center relevant (in tools and equipment) to the job site where the performance will take place. It also recognizes any limitations that actually exist in the job area as contrasted with what the textbooks say should be happening. A condition can be reflected in an objective by stating "At the end of this learning experience the learner should be able to . . . under . . . (conditions)."

For example, the condition for a manager might be that "the learner conducts the performance appraisal on company time in a private but informal locale." Some managers may take exception to that condition. They would prefer to take some employees out to the local bar or a restaurant after work for the appraisal conference. To take an employee away from the work situation, during hours, may be disruptive to the work. If the appraisal is done on company time, finding a private but informal locale may be difficult. Many offices use open space arrangements and other features that eliminate private space.

A Designer cannot borrow objectives, particularly those concerning conditions, from outside the organization. The condition statement must represent, as closely as possible, the conditions under which the actual performance is to take place. This may present a problem later when planning for the evaluation of the training because the training situation, by its very nature, is not the work situation. Therefore care should be exercised when actually evaluating. Without this written condition, however, evaluation becomes difficult, if not impossible.

Another factor to be considered in the condition statement is time. When the performance is time constrained, this should be reflected in the written statement. For production-related training, the time component is easy to identify and to put into writing. For service-related training, this is sometimes possible. An example of a condition statement with a time constraint is "to serve six tables during designated peak hours and nine tables in non-peak hour times." For managerial performance, time may be difficult to establish, except for some tasks. A time condition for a manager might be to be able to prepare a periodic written report "within two hours after the initial data have been provided." Time management is crucial for managers, but until there are specific standards, the condition objectives for such programs remain difficult to write.

The third component is *criterion*, or stating what is acceptable performance. With the first component the Designer looks for performance and with the second component he or she looks for the conditions under which that performance should occur. Now the Designer must look at how well the learner is expected to perform. Presumably 100 percent performance is the goal, where it is measurable. The question is whether 100 percent performance is necessary. Before asking whether the learner can produce that level of performance, other questions should be asked: Is 100 percent necessary? What is the leeway, the plus or minus, which would still be acceptable performance for the individual and the organization? It is a waste of resources to bring people up to a level of performance that is not required.

This is a difficult area to determine, even for measurable jobs. Quality manufacturing dictates a zero defect policy and for some manufacturing processes this is not only desirable, but essential. For others, a certain deviation from tolerance is permissible.

For jobs that are less measurable, such as some managerial and some service jobs, criteria are much more difficult to state. The Designer should not err by writing criteria that are not acceptable to the organization. During the design process, when working with others on criteria, the Designer may highlight a problem in the organization—the lack of existing criteria for performance of some jobs.

Criteria should include both quantity and quality. Therefore the written objective should contain both elements to the degree possible. This is the component that provides the greatest area of confrontation for some jobs. Perhaps this is the reason that some managers shy away from written objectives for training. Such objectives require a specificity that has not previously been stated. It is not unusual to find, at this point in the CEM, that the problem identified earlier can readily be solved by being specific about the quality and quantity expected on a job.

The Designer should be aware of another possible side effect. If supervisors, managers, and other personnel feel insecure about being specific about quality and quantity, hostility can arise. That hostility may take the form of opposing all HRD because the training program cannot show a cost-benefit result. In other words, the Designer cannot quantify because the supervisors and managers have not quantified. Some managers and supervisors are realistic enough to recognize that they cannot oppose training generally, but they do stay as far away from the HRD operation as possible to avoid having to be specific.

It is not a totally bleak picture. Those individuals who have not previously worked with performance criteria can be encouraged to see the benefit of stating the criteria in specific job-related terms. The situation must be approached cautiously so that it does not imply criticism of them. Some supervisors and managers will welcome the help of the HRD people in surfacing a lack of specificity of which they were not aware. For those supervisors and managers, this part of the event can prove helpful, and of course they will see the Designer and HRD as a help to management.

A useful tool for all three components is the use of verbs. The Designer will find that if each component is stated as simply as possible, but always starting with a verb, writing objectives becomes a positive activity. Figure 6-3 presents a list of some of the common verbs that can be used. Selection of the

Stimulus Responding	Motor Chaining	Verbal Chaining	Multiple Discriminating	Concepts	Principles	Problem Solving
associate	activate	cite	choose	allocate	anticipate	accommodate
gave a word for	adjust	copy	compare	arrange	calculate	adapt
grasp	aline	enumerate	contrast	assign	calibrate	administer
hold	close	letter	couple	catalog	check	adjust to
identify	copy	list	decide	categorize	compile	analyze
indicate	(dis)assemble	quote	detect	characterize	compute	compose
label	(dis)connect	recite	differentiate	classify	conclude	contrive
lift	draw	record	discern	collect	construct	correlate
locate	duplicate	reiterate	distinguish	file	convert	create
loosen	insert	repeat	divide	grade	coordinate	develop
move	load	reproduce	isolate	group	correct	devise
name	manipulate	(re)state	judge	index	deduce	diagnose
pick up	measure	transcribe	pick	inventory	define	discover
place	open	type	recognize	itemize	demonstrate	find a way
press	operate		select	match	design	invent
pull	remove			mate	determine	realize
push	replace			order	diagram	reason
recognize	stencil			rank	equate	resolve
repeat	trace			rate	estimate	study
reply	tune			reject	evaluate	synthesize
respond	turn off/on			screen	examine	think through
rotate				sort	expect	troubleshoot
say				specify	explain	
set				survey	extrapolate	
slide				tabulate	figure	
signal					foresee	
tighten					generalize	
touch					illustrate	
turn					infer	
twist					interpolate	
					interpret	
					monitor	
					organize	
					plan	
					predict	
					prescribe	
					program	
					project	
					schedule	
					solve	
					translate	
					verify	

Source: Job Analysis for Human Resource Management: A Review of Selected Research and Development. U.S. Department of Labor. Manpower Research Monograph #36, 1974, page 33, (as adapted).

Figure 6-3. Useful verb list for writing objectives.

particular verb that is acceptable to all is one way of assuring that the written objective will be useful and used.

EVALUATION AND FEEDBACK

After the objectives have been written and discussed, the E&FB event takes place. Of course, there may well have been some E&FB activities during the event, but it is important to conclude the event with specifics.

The Designer should start by reviewing the objectives of this event. By the end of this event the Designer will be able to:

- Identify the elements that must be considered in determining objectives for the program.
- Produce learning objectives related to the design under consideration.

The first objective is related to the priorities and similar factors that the Designer will have explored. The second should have produced the written objectives.

Analysis

For analysis to take place, the written objectives must be shared with at least the supervisor, perhaps the managers and, if possible, the learners. The program objectives should be stated in terms that relate to the original problem or purpose that triggered the CEM. The Designer may wish to actually restate the original problem, as agreed upon at the conclusion of Identify Needs of the Organization. Although some of the same people will still be involved, time will have passed and this particular training program may not be the high priority for others that it is for the Designer. It is also possible that there have been some changes in personnel since the initial event was concluded, so it is important that everyone is still in agreement about the original problem.

The Designer should present the learning objectives for analysis by providing written statements. One technique is to list them all, one after another, on the same page and then follow this listing with an individual, double-spaced page for each objective. Putting all the objectives on one page can appear overwhelming. The separate pages provide for the analysis and thought that is required at this part of the event. The double spacing enables the Designer to communicate that the words are not set in concrete but are subject to modification and change. The recipients of the analysis can change it by writing between the printed lines.

Learning objectives should be listed in some priority order. If possible, the Designer should ask supervisors and others to contribute to this ranking during the event. The process of ranking is time consuming, as it requires several iterations, so it is best done before reaching E&FB. If there is no other alternative and ranking could not be done earlier, it must be done here. If it was done earlier, this would be the place to have the ranking reviewed.

In the analysis, the Designer should indicate how each objective relates to what had previously been agreed upon under Identify the Needs of the Learner. Each need should have an objective or a reason indicating why no objective was written for that need. If any objectives have been written that do not relate to a specific need, and this is possible, the Designer should indicate the basis for including that objective.

The Designer may also indicate the possible result of not meeting an objective—a performance that would not change or a need that would not be met. It is unlikely that all objectives can be met, unless there are unlimited resources. Therefore the relative cost (not only in financial terms) of not meeting an objective must be considered.

Feedback

As with the E&FB in the previous events, the Designer must first consider who should be involved. The crucial person, once again, is the supervisor. The Designer may wish to provide the supervisor with the objectives and analysis for review prior to any meeting. The Designer cannot expect the supervisor to read and react immediately. The supervisor needs time to think about the objectives and perhaps even test them out. As the objectives relate specifically to how the job is done, the supervisor may prefer to review the objectives at the job site.

The supervisor may also find it helpful to review the objectives with the concerned employees. It would be more appropriate for the supervisor to do this than the Designer. Because the objectives relate to the components of performance, conditions, and criteria, they also relate to how well the employee is actually performing. This is an important supervisory concern, rather than an activity for the Designer.

If possible, managers should also be involved, but the Designer should not be overly concerned if some managers indicate a lack of interest at this point. Some managers need not, or cannot, be concerned with the specifics of job performance, for to do so would be to function on a supervisory level. Managers should however be concerned with the program objectives, as they relate to the broader implications of jobs concerned with organizational goals. For reasons of organizational politics, a Designer might choose to share the objectives with managers, but should not push for any direct response.

A complaint heard all too often is that there are too many meetings in the design process. Unfortunately the successful design experience requires meetings, but the Designer is cautioned to have them only when really necessary. At this point in the design process, it may not be necessary to have a face-to-face meeting unless there are apparent areas of disagreement on the objectives.

If more than one work unit is involved, bringing together the supervisors of the various units could be necessary. A meeting might be unavoidable, but before calling such a meeting, the Designer should determine that the benefits would outweigh the negative response that might result from having to attend another meeting. The one item that could require a meeting is the ranking of the learning objectives. The need could vary from one unit to another, depending upon a variety of factors including personnel, work schedules, production schedules, and locale. If a program involves more than one unit, the rank order of learning objectives will have to reflect a compromise that is best obtained through a face-to-face meeting.

Decisions

As a result of the E&FB some decisions can be made:

1. Are the program objectives acceptable?

   The major focus here would be on agreement that the original problem still exists and in essentially the same form as earlier stipulated. If there has been any change, of which the Designer is not aware, it must surface before proceeding further.

   When several units are involved, it is possible that the program objectives may still be valid for some but not for others. In a large organization, as the program objectives become clear, it can also become apparent that other units of the organization could also benefit from being included.

2. Are the learning objectives acceptable?

   This is a more difficult decision to reach. The Designer should avoid letting supervisors and others involved turn this decision over to the Designer. This is sometimes done by supervisors who say, "Well, the objectives are too technical and contain all kinds of jargon, so why don't we leave it to the Designer?" This must not happen. If the supervisors do not feel comfortable with the objectives, there is a problem and a land mine is being planted that could produce a crisis at a later time.

3. Have all the needs been reflected in the objectives?

   The answer to this could be negative and still be acceptable. While proceeding with this event, there could have been an earlier agreement that some of the needs were not as essential as they appeared to be. If that happened, it would have been indicated in the analysis, but should be agreed upon here.

4. Is the priority of learning objectives acceptable?

   The importance of the priority listing becomes apparent when the Designer moves to the next event, Build Curriculum. At that time, it will probably become necessary to limit the number of objectives because of time and other factors. If the priority ranking is not agreed to now, the Designer will have to do additional work in the next event.

5. Do the objectives relate to the Specify Job Performance event?

   The purpose of the training program is not only to meet needs, but to relate to job performance. Although, logically, by following the CEM, these should all be congruent, there is always the possibility that something went a bit off-track during the process. It is important to check continually. Therefore, at this time, it should be agreed that if the stated objectives are met, they will be congruent with the job performance that has been specified earlier.

6. Can the objectives best be met internally or externally?

   This is a difficult question to answer at this time, but it is one that must be asked. Once the objectives have been agreed upon, it is possible to have some general idea of the program needed. Perhaps training programs or packages already exist on the market that can meet the objectives. If so, the Designer can then move right to the Obtain Instructional Resources event. If not, the next event would be Build Curriculum. There is also the possibility of some combination.

CONCLUSION

Continuing on the assumption that the training program will essentially be designed in-house, and that the decisions about the questions listed above have been positive, the Designer can now proceed to the next event, Build Curriculum.

CHAPTER 7

Build Curriculum

The Designer is now at the point in the CEM (Figure 7-1) where the focus is on the information that is to be learned and the sequence of the learning process. This information and the sequence in which it is learned is called curriculum.

By the completion of this event, the Designer will have

- Developed a specific list of the items to be learned to meet the previously determined objectives
- Specified the order in which the learning is to take place

CLARIFYING TERMS

By defining a few terms that are crucial to the Build Curriculum event, we can improve communication and understanding.

The term *syllabus* can have several meanings. Generally, the syllabus is the listing of the content which is to be learned. It contains the main topic headings, subheadings, and may possibly go to several levels of specificity. Indeed, the syllabus is the place where the listing of content should be as specific as possible. It does not indicate how the learning is to take place, only what is to be learned. The syllabus sometimes indicates the flow of the units. In that sense, it almost becomes synonymous with curriculum, and some people do use the terms interchangeably.

Another element is the *lesson plan*. Lesson plans set forth, very specifically, how the instructor will guide the training sessions. When a lesson is learner-centered, the lesson plan indicates what the learner will do. It is the actual road map to help the instructor and learner reach the determined objectives.

Developing lesson plans is necessary for the successful completion of this event, and it will be discussed in more depth later in this chapter. The term

THE CRITICAL EVENTS MODEL

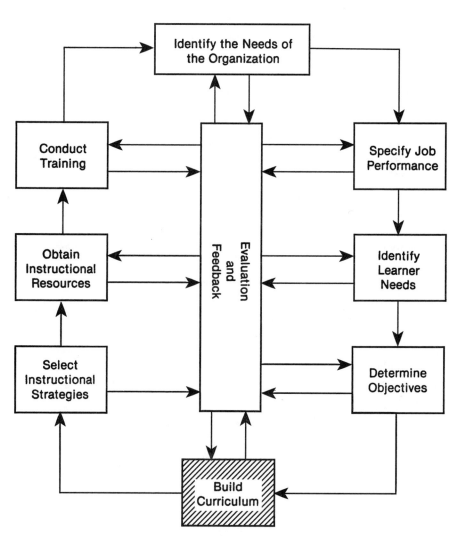

Figure 7-1. Build curriculum.

instructional strategies refers to the methods, techniques, and devices that facilitate learning. People in HRD have been accused, and rightly so, of being faddish and gimmicky. There has been a tendency demonstrated at some recent conferences and exhibits to use the latest media (or multimedia), the star speaker or presenter, or the "hot" item. There is nothing wrong with using any or all of these, but the first decision a Designer should make is "what" is to be learned. The "how" of learning can be explored later. Instructional strategies address the how. They are important, so much so that a whole event (Select Instructional Strategies) is included in the CEM, but it should not be used until the Build Curriculum event is completed.

The objectives that resulted from the previous event now make it possible for the Designer to start identifying what must be learned to reach the stated objectives. The curriculum should deal with skills, attitude, and knowledge. How this is stated is, in part, a reflection of the beliefs of the Designer and the nature of the subject matter. Some Designers prefer to list the curriculum in terms of skills, knowledge, and attitudes, while others are comfortable blending the three domains.

The objectives serve as a checklist. Each of the stated learning objectives should be readily identifiable in the curriculum. Conversely, there should not be any part of the curriculum that does not relate to an objective. The Designer can readily construct a matrix that illustrates this relationship, if needed.

Theories of Learning

The curriculum should reflect a theory of learning. Some purists insist that the entire curriculum must reflect a unified theory, while more eclectic Designers feel comfortable in using different theories at different points of the curriculum. Over time, each Designer will select those theories that appear to be most useful, and discard those that are not helpful. It is a judgment call by the Designer.

At this time, all we have are *theories* of learning. There are many ways to look at a theory, but essentially it is much like the concept of a model which was discussed in Chapter 1. A theory is a way of explaining something that is essentially abstract, but for which a plausible explanation can be built so it can be used. As such, theories are subject to change.

A Designer has few if any options. So little is still known about how people learn that it is not possible to deal with "laws of learning." At one time, what are now called theories were presented as laws, but the more researchers worked on the laws, the closer they came to replacing them with theories. Given the range of theories, how does a Designer get to understand and use them? Malcolm Knowles has been helpful in presenting "organismic" and "mechanistic" models [46].

The *organismic model* is based on the concept of the learning environment, as a living and changing element. This does not mean that there is no form, but rather that it is a constantly changing situation. The emphasis in the organismic model is on process rather than product.

A common reference point is the use of the word "behavioral" when referring to the various theories in the organismic model. Some of the theorists associated with this model are John Dewey, Kurt Lewin, and Carl Rogers.

The *mechanistic model* is characterized by the stimulus-response approach. Learning is viewed as conditioning, with a strong emphasis on the quantification of the learning. Those who follow this model are often referred to as "behaviorists." Theorists associated with this model are Edward L. Thorndike, I. P. Pavlov, and B. F. Skinner.

The field of learning theory is by no means this simple. Within the two models are many theorists who differ in emphasis and approach. Some theories do not fit readily into either category. For the Designer, the problem is one of understanding enough about the various learning theories to be able to make distinctions and to use them effectively. It is not necessary to quote or cite any of the differing theorists, but the Designer must know enough about learning theory to know what has been researched and theorized in the past. There are proponents and opponents of every learning theory that exists. The Designer may not want to choose sides, but at times must make decisions as to which learning theory is most appropriate for a specific training program.

VARIABLES TO BE CONSIDERED

A curriculum cannot be built without recognition of some significant variables. Variables are factors, some of which are difficult to stipulate specifically, that have an impact on the way the learning will be delivered. Although the ultimate delivery (Conduct Training event) is still ahead, the Designer must consider some aspects of it at this time.

One variable is the learner who has had learning experiences before the one under consideration. The Designer cannot possibly know about all those learning experiences, but should not ignore the culture or prior experiences of the learner when designing the training program.

The nature of the *instructor* must also be considered. If the Designer is considering machine-mediated instruction, it may be necessary to limit the curriculum in regard to skills and attitudes. Of course, as more experience is amassed with machine-mediated instruction, it may become evident that skills and attitudes can be included as easily as knowledge. If the instructor is a subject matter specialist, more latitude can be allowed in the curriculum than when the instructor is not as well versed in the subject matter.

At this time, the Designer can opt to include all relevant subject matter and later determine how it will effect considerations in the Obtain Instructional Resources event. The vision the Designer has of the instructor at this time influences what is to be included in the curriculum.

A third consideration is *geography,* or the relative physical distance between the instructor and the Designer. Some programs, once mounted, allow for almost no contact between the Designer and the instructor. Packaged programs usually allow no contact at all. Some programs designed by a central HRD unit and sent out to various parts of the company allow very limited contact. In the retail gasoline business, for example, central units design programs that are conducted in field offices or at the service stations themselves. In those cases, curriculum content is different, depending upon who the Designer envisions the instructor will be and how much contact the Designer and the instructor will have while the program is being conducted.

SELECTING CONTENT

This is the part of the CEM where it is recognized that the Designer is not expected to know content. Each of us has ego needs, and it is sometimes difficult to acknowledge that there are some things we do not know. This is one of those times when it is essential to make this statement loud and clear. The Designer has unique talents to bring to the design process, but knowledge of content is not that special contribution. The Designer should have an in-depth knowledge of how adults learn and how to use the CEM or other appropriate models for design.

It can become a trap for the designer when the content appears to be so generic that everybody should know it. This includes areas such as supervision or management and sub-areas such as, leadership, and delegation. It can be difficult for the Designer to communicate to some managers that content in those areas changes, and though the Designer might endeavor to keep up to date, there are others who make those areas their specialty. They are more suited to be content people.

There are infrequent instances when the person who has been hired to design may also have subject matter expertise. There are still those organizations, as in the accounting field, that prefer to select an accountant for design work. If that has been the choice and the Designer knows that the job entails competency in both design and content, there is no conflict. Such people are rare, but it is possible for an organization to identify and select such people. It is not possible to put a value judgment on such a decision, whether it is good or bad. There are too many variables that must be considered, including whether or not the organization views design as an entry point for content people who will then move into the line organization.

Designers can get caught up in the subject matter to the point where they become encouraged to become specialists in content. In one situation, we worked with an organization in Malaysia that was concerned with cultivation of oil palms. We designed appropriate training experiences, although both of us come from urban backgrounds. About six months after we returned home, we received an invitation to become members of an international consulting organization in the field of agriculture. We responded that we appreciated the invitation, but that our field was learning, not agriculture. They responded by noting that the program had received such glowing comments from those in the country, as well as from the UN and other international agricultural experts, that we must know more agricultural content than we realized. We once again wrote to express our appreciation for their kind remarks, but noted that we preferred to be known as specialists in learning design and, therefore, could not accept their invitation. It was tempting, but we felt that such membership would communicate inappropriately to potential clients.

PEOPLE INVOLVED IN CONTENT

The Designer can, and generally does, rely on others for the content area. These people are called subject matter specialists (SMS), though the term subject matter expert is also used.

There are various considerations for which the Designer can turn to an SMS. A major one is budget, which can dictate whether the Designer is restricted to internal people or can go outside the organization. Just because the Designer has the budget is no reason to go external, but it does provide the Designer with more options.

Internal People

In the earlier events of the CEM, the Designer may already have identified those people who could serve as internal SMS. Supervisors are one such group, although they may not have the time to devote to this activity. Some supervisors might designate one of their subordinates to serve as an SMS.

Other internal SMS resources could be employees who have previously been through the same or similar learning experiences. Though by no means professionals, they could serve as an SMS in relating proposed content to the actual job.

Large organizations have R&D departments and other staff resources who might provide an SMS. Small organizations might have such resources, but it is less likely. In some large organizations, an appropriate SMS might be working in another part of the organization, so arrangements are required to obtain the necessary input. A variety of arrangements are possible. If the need is minimal, the Designer can just visit with the SMS and discuss the content required in this event. Other arrangements can allow for more time for an internal SMS to work with the Designer. All the arrangements should legitimize the use of internal SMS by the Designer.

Another possibility is a *part-time assignment.* That is, the person is assigned to be an SMS for a specified number of hours or for a designated number of days. The SMS still remains with the original work unit, but meets with the Designer on an arranged schedule. When the SMS is involved in production, such an arrangement is essential, so the supervisor knows when a job must be covered and for how long. This arrangement is similar to common work assignments found in a matrix organization.

It may not be possible at the outset to know the full extent of the assignment. The Designer should negotiate with the supervisor for a minimum time allotment, with the understanding that some additional time might be necessary. Depending on how such internal assignments are handled in the organization, the Designer could be required to provide the budget to cover the loss of time or the cost of a replacement for the employee used as an SMS by the Designer.

When the SMS is a high-level person, such as a manager, the arrangement can be more fluid. The manager could agree to be an SMS, but not be prepared to allocate specific time slots. Managers, it is generally accepted, cannot control all of their time. They must be available to be responsive to problems. Planned meetings between the manager and the Designer may have to be canceled at the last moment due to a crisis or a call from the executive suite. This can be frustrating to the Designer, but if managers are used for SMS, this is part of the "price" that must be paid.

Another common arrangement is a *temporary assignment* where the SMS is released from the regular job and actually moves into the HRD unit. Such an assignment may be for several days, even several months, but usually, it is for a stated period of time. Budget can be a factor, for the HRD unit may have to consider the SMS as a temporary employee for that period, with the salary or wage being charged to the HRD unit. Some companies' policies allow for such internal transfers without any charges, but this is becoming less common. The trend is towards making each unit of an organization, particularly in large organizations, an identifiable financial center for either cost or profit.

During that temporary assignment, it should be made clear that the SMS has not been drafted into the HRD unit and this person will not remain in the HRD unit. Sometimes an SMS opts to remain in the HRD unit, if there is a place for that person. This practice must be avoided, however, or the HRD unit will develop the reputation of being a "pirate." The result will be that in the future other units of the organization will not detail their best people as

SMS for fear of losing them. The quality of SMS people will decline, with resultant damage to the design process.

External People

External people are all those outside of the organization who could be called upon to assist in selecting content. These people are frequently referred to as consultants though the more appropriate term would be "vendor" or "supplier." There are essentially two groups: those who provide services and those who provide goods. But, of course, some provide both.

If the Designer is considering purchasing a program, seeking a vendor of goods is appropriate. Some vendors have packaged programs that have been widely tested. It is possible for the Designer to get the vendor's "track record"—to share in the experience of others who have used that vendor. Vendors will be discussed later in this chapter when looking at the question of "Make or Buy?" The vendors of services can be extremely helpful at this point, for they can serve as SMS. The Designer should select those who can function as content consultants, rather than as process consultants. The content consultant should be able to provide specific content from which the Designer can select what is needed. There are various kinds of external content people who can serve as SMS. A frequently used group of people are professors from colleges and universities. Generally, those academics make a point of keeping up to date with the state of the art of their particular field. In addition, they often are required to do research of their own. This is supplemented by the research being done by their graduate students. Being in that position, the professors are an extremely important resource for content.

As with any group, generalizations can lead to error. Just because a person carries an academic title and is employed by an institution of higher learning does not mean that person is up to date on the latest in the particular field. There are academics who stop learning as soon as they get tenure or upon completion of their own doctoral dissertation. The Designer must exercise the same care in selecting an SMS from a university as from any other external source.

Personnel from vendor companies can be a valuable resource, if caution is exercised. The Designer must distinguish between the vendor organization that will provide an SMS and the specific individual who will serve as an SMS. It is not unknown that a company that provides an SMS for the Designer may also be looking for a long-range relationship, such as providing a whole training program. The Designer must exercise the usual caution of any purchaser, but should not allow this stance to deprive the design process of the rich resource that is available from vendor companies.

Many organizations provide external SMS, and many go out of business so frequently that a list here would be obsolete by the time this appears in print. There are, however, some possible sources from which the Designer can cull out the necessary external content specialists. These include professional and trade organizations who generally publish such lists in annual compilations.

There are other external people and resources but they do not generally see themselves as serving in the SMS role. Professional societies and organizations related to the specified content area sometimes provide publications as well as people who can serve as SMS or provide content. This is common in fields such as engineering and accounting where there are ongoing study groups, commissions, and other formal activities that are directed towards the content of the field.

Suppliers to an organization can also be an external resource for contributing content. When suppliers provide a machine or device (for example, computer, telephone, office equipment), they will also frequently offer training opportunities for the customer's employees. In some cases, the program they provide will eliminate the necessity for any further design work. In other situations, the Designer will still have to continue designing, but can use the content already identified by the supplier.

A source that is frequently overlooked because it is inexpensive and sometimes considered suspect, is the federal government! In the U.S., the Government Printing Office has a warehouse of materials that have been researched and published, (using tax money) and are available at ridiculously low prices. Many of these pamphlets and books contain excellent material for content in specific fields such as occupational health and safety and some of the newer technologies such as the nuclear field.

TYPES OF CONTENT

Content can be quite broad, even when it is tied to specific objectives. Here, too, as with needs and objectives, it is important to develop some priorities. It is possible to provide a model for organizing content based on priorities.

All the content, related to the objectives, can be organized under one of four categories:

1. Essential
2. Helpful
3. Peripheral
4. Unrelated

Placing the various content components into one of these categories is no easy task. The Designer will find, however, that doing this will clarify the content and even sharpen the previously agreed-upon objectives.

Essential

This category consists of the absolute minimal content that the curriculum must contain if the training program is to meet the previously stated objectives. The question to ask constantly is: Can this material be omitted? If the answer is "yes," the content can still be useful but more appropriately placed in a different category.

To identify the items to be placed in this category, the Designer can anticipate a common human behavior. It is expressed by: "When I was learning to do that job, this is what I had to learn, and look where I am now. Therefore anybody learning to do that job should be taught the same things." Of course, the statement may not be made so openly, but may just be implied or hinted. This is most evident when dealing with supervisory and managerial programs. It would be unusual for an engineer today to insist that learning how to use a slide rule is essential, though it was a basic skill a decade ago.

Helpful

The next category, *helpful,* refers to the content that supplements the essential. The content in the essential can stand by itself, but if conditions permit and there is sufficient time and other resources, the helpful content can be included. One way of identifying the helpful is to ask the question: Could the performance change without this content? If the response is "yes," it tells us at least that it is not essential, but the Designer may have to probe further to determine if it is helpful.

For example, take the case of a maintenance person who is being trained to replace fluorescent lights. The essential content will relate to positioning the ladder for safety, removing the guards (if there are any), removing the old light, putting in a new one, and so on. Each of these steps can be specified and each is important and necessary. The content related to those steps is essential. Under helpful could be items such as how fluorescent light compares to traditional incandescent light in terms of handling the bulbs, the use of the fluorescent starter, the reason for the guard or diffuser, and so on. The maintenance person can certainly replace the light knowing only the essential. The helpful provides content that is indirectly related to the performance expected, but content that will help the maintenance person understand more about the job.

Peripheral

The peripheral content can also be tested in terms of whether the performance can change even if the peripheral content is not included. It is difficult to establish a firm demarcation between helpful and peripheral. At best, it is a judgment call. Given the example discussed earlier of the maintenance person replacing a light, peripheral content might consist of some items such as the comparative lumens expected from each source, comparative costs for their operation, and advantages and disadvantages of each form of illumination.

The Designer will find that different SMS, as well as supervisors and managers, will have their own pet areas of content, which they contend must be included. Some will be essential and some may also be helpful. The Designer should not be surprised if there is also some peripheral. This stems from the concept of, "That is what I learned; therefore, that is what should be learned." The inclusion of this material may be more a political decision than a design decision.

Unrelated

One can readily question why this category should even be considered. If the content is unrelated, isn't it obvious that it should not be included? Perhaps. The unrelated content arises in various ways, but one of the most common is the tendency of someone to feel that if the content was good for somebody in another organization, it should also be included in this training program.

Unrelated content poses a problem because it will generally arise from outside the usual design process. It will be communicated by some higher level person who heard that another organization used that content, so why don't we? Unfortunately the Designer may have so much difficulty responding to that question without getting into specifics that a posture of benign acceptance is adopted. The Designer can't win them all, and there are times when compromise is necessary. One approach is to include such content, but under this category. If that content is included in the final curriculum, at least everybody will know the category and treat it accordingly.

PROCESS OF CATEGORIZING

The Designer may wonder why he or she should bother to categorize. The answer is complex, but let us explore some of the aspects. When items are written down in an outline or list form, there is a tendency to give the same weight to each item. Obviously not all the content will have the same importance to the learning or to the desired change in performance. As will be seen later, sequencing is one way to provide emphasis. Categorizing is another.

Frequently there will be more content than can be learned in the limited time available. The Designer must choose what to include and what to exclude. The omissions should be the result of a positive decision, not oversight. By categorizing and retaining this information, the Designer is able to show the wide range of content that was considered, compared to the limited content that was finally included.

Categorizing is essentially the responsibility of the Designer. This is in direct contrast to almost all of the earlier work in the CEM, where responsibility more frequently rested on the supervisor or manager. In this event, the Designer functions as a professional and must make the appropriate decisions. Of course, it is helpful to seek the advice and reactions of the supervisor, but the Designer is cautioned not to place too much of a burden on the supervisor. If the previous events have been completed successfully, the assignment into categories can be done by the Designer with the assistance of the SMS.

Categorizing will take time. There may be many iterations before the Designer and the SMS feel comfortable and confident that the content categories contain clear and defensible elements. There will be continual testing and exploration of the content items. The content must be stated so clearly and specifically that it is almost possible to instruct directly from that content. There will be the need for a transition into a teaching form (the lesson plans), but that will take place later in this event.

In previous events, the Designer had the option of using E&FB. Here it is mandatory. Before going further, the Designer should check back using questions, regarding each content item, such as:

- Will this content, if learned, meet the previously stated objectives?
- Will this content, if learned, meet the previously identified needs?
- Will this content, if learned, lead to the performance specified?
- Will this content, if learned, solve the previously identified problem of the organization?

Obviously an affirmative response is required to each of these questions, particularly for the essential material. For the other categories, the response will be a weaker affirmative, and probably a negative in the case of unrelated. If any essential content does not receive a clear affirmative response, the Designer should re-examine the content and then process it back through the actions to determine at what point a deviation occurred.

SEQUENCING

The first component of the curriculum is the content. The second is the sequence, or in what order the content should be presented to the learner. There are no absolutes, but there are some generalizations that the Designer considers when making the decision about sequencing.

One approach is the *general to the specific.* In this approach, the learner is first presented with an overview, and then the content is introduced in a way that will move toward the specific. This seems simplistic, but it reflects some assumptions about the learner and a commitment to a learning theory. In this sequence, the Designer uses the Gestalt approach, which is based on the learner needing a focus on the total learning situation before proceeding to the specifics and is considered the behavioral concept. This concept is based on the work of Lewin, Rogers *et al.*

A different approach, the *specific to the general,* is also possible. This sequence is based on the behaviorists, such as Skinner. It contends that the learner need not know the end result, but if the training program is appropriately constructed, the learner will reach the end result, the general, by going through the well-planned specifics. This sequence is important when the end performance of all the learners must be identical.

Both sequences make some assumptions about the learner. The Designer should not be misled. Some critics of the latter (behaviorist) approach contend that it dehumanizes, while critics of the former approach (behavioral) argue that it does not produce any performance changes that are observable and/or measurable. If there is any generalization that can be made it is that no one way of sequencing is best for all content and for all learners.

Sequencing should reflect the content and the learner. It has been found that learners who have high social needs (for example, interaction with others, oral communication) tend to benefit more if the sequencing is from the general to the specific. Indeed, such learners sometimes reject just the specifics and consequently have difficulty with programmed instruction. This high social need is no better or worse than a low social need, but it is different. Sequencing must consider the social need of the learner.

Another approach is from the *concrete to the abstract.* The learner starts with content that is solid, observable, or beyond dispute, and then goes on to the abstract. This is contrasted with the *abstract to the concrete* that starts with generalizations that lead to more solid specifics. This latter form of sequencing is sometimes used with content that is philosophical or based on broad generalizations. In this approach, the learner can be more crucial than the content. This sequencing must be used with extreme caution in a cross-cultural training situation.

The Designer must also explore the concept of *context,* which refers to the amount of information that is in a given communication. Perhaps this can best be seen through a language experience we had when we were learning to speak Japanese. The more polite one becomes in speaking Japanese, the more vague the statements. Often, when studying the language, we were not sure exactly what was being said because of the use of "honorifics" in the language. Our language instructor would reply with, "You have to know the context." That is, you have to know the specific situation in which the oral communication is taking place. It is a situation that could be quite ambiguous for some of us. If we come from a low-context society, we want things spelled out. We rely on laws, printed statements, contracts, and other items that are indicative of a low-context society.

A value judgment should not be placed on this, but the Designer should recognize that there are differences. We experienced this during a conference of the International Federation of Training and Development Organizations (IFTDO) in Rio de Janeiro. We had with us a group of graduate students from George Washington University who attended the IFTDO Conference with us. We were given booklets at registration that contained tickets for each evenings social function. We exchanged the tickets daily for more specific coupons for that evening's activities. Neither the tickets nor the coupons stated specifics. We (from a low-context society) wanted to know exactly what would happen that evening. Our hosts (from a high-context society) merely shrugged their shoulders and waited for the evening. Obviously a social experience is not a training experience, but the learner approaches both with the same concept of context.

There are other variations in sequencing, but they are essentially all based on some kind of dichotomy similar to those just discussed. Some examples are known to unknown, particular to the general, and observation to reasoning. In each case, the reverse can also be used as a content sequence. Before starting to sequence, the Designer must have the content clearly stated and written. Sometimes the content itself will indicate the sequence, but at other times the learner will be the governing factor. Usually sequencing tries to accommodate both.

Sequencing can also be affected by the type of delivery system to be used. The most common way of offering training in work situations is to use several days, one following after the other, or *continuous learning.* The reasons are many, but the most obvious one is that it is easy to schedule a training program in this way, and it causes less disruption to the normal work procedures than some other alternatives. When distance is a factor, the single continuous training experience is less costly, as travel costs are incurred for only one trip.

Another alternative is *spaced learning*. In this mode, the content is separated into various components, depending upon the frequency of the spaced learning. Instead of one continuous training situation, the learner returns to the job at stipulated times and then returns again to the training situation. This recycling can occur once or many times.

Why should a Designer consider spaced learning? In the more traditional mode (continuous learning), the learner leaves the job, goes to the training situation, and then returns to the job. During the entire learning time, the learner is in an artificial situation. If training is to be effective, a high-risk environment should be provided, so the learner can try out new performance without risk of negative criticism or punishment. It is a situation that allows the learner to "fail successfully." Such performance cannot be permitted at the actual job site.

When spaced learning is used, the Designer faces the challenge of planning for reentry and providing for relevance. At the conclusion of a continuous learning experience, the learner is confronted with taking the new performance and immediately applying it to the job. If the learner has a question, there is no opportunity to confront the instructor and the learning group with "I tried it the way we learned it, but it didn't work." Spaced learning provides for small learning increments, application on the job, and feedback or relearning in the training situation.

When the Designer has alternatives, spaced learning can be considered. There are several variations. One that is relatively easy to provide for can be used when all the learners are in the same physical facility or when travel time and cost are not a consideration. Group instruction is conducted for a specified number of hours during the day, perhaps two hours, over a period of several days. At the end of each two-hour period, the learners return to their regular jobs. A variation of this method is to conduct the sessions for a specific period of time, usually two hours, for only one day a week, over several weeks, with the learners returning to their regular jobs after each session.

Another variation, not as commonly used, is to set aside a block of perhaps three training days (the actual days will depend upon objectives and content), and allow the learner to return to the job for a stipulated period of time after the training experience and then return to training.

We used this sequencing in a program of "Creative Thinking for Managers." Spaced learning was used because managers were asked for performance that was much different than was previously the case. Generally managers are rewarded for results, not for trying, while creative thinking does not promise results, but emphasizes the attempt. Executive approval, in this case, was obtained for the program to use spaced learning. The managerial group came together for three days, during which the learners engaged in various exercises and experiences to help them focus on thinking creatively. The last afternoon of the third day was devoted to planning for back home application during the interim between the two spaced learning situations. The learners then returned to their regular jobs for a month.

During that time, they were to try to use the material at least once and more often if possible. They were not to create artificial situations, but rather use the creative learning techniques in some real situations during that back-on-the-job period of the spaced learning. When the learning group reconvened, the first activity was to explore what happened when they tried to use creative thinking in real work situations back on the job. After that, additional material was presented, based on the feedback, as well as some material used earlier for this unit. Obviously the sequence of presenting the material is different for spaced learning than for a continuous program. The content will still be the same though, because the objectives are identical for both continuous and spaced learning.

With the content determined and the sequence selected, the Designer can soon proceed to the next step of converting that material into lesson plans. Before that activity, the Designer pauses for another important decision.

MAKE OR BUY?

The Designer can proceed with the CEM and make a program internally or consider purchasing an appropriate program that already exists and buy externally. Some Designers tend to continue in the design process without exploring an apparent and reasonable alternative. If possible, Designers should at least consider purchasing. As the HRD market expands, an increasing number of specialized companies are offering various forms of packaged programs for sale.

The exploration of packaged programs should not take place until the content and sequence have been determined. If packaged programs are considered at an earlier event of the CEM, the content and sequence probably will be distorted to relate to the package rather than to the previously developed data in the earlier stages of the CEM. This does not mean that the Designer should not consider trade-offs in revising curriculum and sequence if the appropriate external package is identified. Rather, the process proceeds as described up to this point, and now the Designer can look at packages.

Packages are only one part of the total resources available to the Designer from outside the organization. There are modules, units, and components, all of which could be coupled with the internal resources to make a total program. There is nothing wrong with a Designer buying some external resources as a way of supplementing the internal capability.

The Designer might opt to buy the whole program from an external resource. When the need is a general one in the workforce, such programs are frequently developed. The external vendor seldom devotes the necessary resources to develop a program that will have only a limited market. Programs of a general nature are available, for example, for training supervisors and managers. Some non-HRD companies, Dupont for example, found a market for its packaged programs on maintenance. An expanding product that is becoming available in many forms of packaged programs is training programs related to computers.

When the Designer identifies an external program that is closely related to the desired content and sequence, the first step is to determine availability and restrictions and the conditions that come with the package. The Designer should ask questions such as:

- Can the program be bought outright?
- Are there any restrictions on the use of the material?
- Must subsequent use be authorized by the vendor?
- What is the cost for subsequent use?
- Can the learning materials be reproduced by the Designer or must supplies continually be purchased from the vendor?

Some programs can be "purchased," but the Designer is required to use only "certified" instructors. When this is the case, the vendor may supply the certified instructors or conduct a parallel program that certifies the instructors.

It is unusual that the material purchased on the open market will meet the needs of each Designer without modification. There are two approaches to handle this situation. The Designer can purchase the material and modify it to be consistent with the content and sequence previously determined. (This reemphasizes the reason the content-sequence task should be completed before exploring purchasing.) Such modification may not be as easy to make as it sounds. If the vendor has done a good job, the content and sequence should represent what the vendor believes are general needs in the purchasing public. It is not likely that these needs will be the same for each individual purchaser. Modification can easily destroy the content and certainly do damage to the sequence. Despite this, modification is possible and is sometimes more satisfactory than the Designer writing the entire training program.

Another approach is to take the previously determined content-sequence and modify it to be consistent with the material to be purchased. At first, this appears to be a distortion, but it is a realistic and even beneficial procedure. If the program is readily available, the cost can be much less than proceeding with the CEM, when such factors as staff time and the cost of development of instructional materials are considered. The Designer might select from the content-sequence the material that can be immediately satisfied by the purchase of the available training program. Then, the remaining content-sequence can become a separate training experience.

This alternative is easy to state, but not as easy to accomplish. Dividing the content is difficult, and the sequence may have to be severely altered. The Designer must make a professional judgment in this situation. In some instances, there may be pressure on the Designer to use some well-advertised or generally accepted external resource. This may require even more work than just continuing internally, but it may be politic for the Designer to purchase from the vendor and then make the necessary adaptations.

A question frequently asked is "Which approach is less expensive?" This is an extremely difficult question to answer. It also depends upon when it is asked. All too often the Designer is confronted by this question immediately after the Identify the Needs of the Organization event. At that early point, it is not possible for the Designer to do more than provide a loose approximation. As the CEM proceeds, the Designer is better able to provide comparative cost data. At this event of the CEM, the Designer must be able to justify the relative cost of proceeding internally (that is, make) as contrasted with external purchase (that is, buy). Even at this point, all the cost data will not be absolutely determinable if the decision is made to proceed internally. As the Designer continues to deal with a variety of people, he or she has little control over the exact amount of time the completed design will take.

On the buy side, the costs can be determined fairly accurately. That is, the purchase price can be calculated. If the Designer is concerned about "cost per learner," that amount may be more difficult to determine because the final decision as to the total number of learners has probably not yet been made. At this time, the Designer must once again estimate.

Because many HRD units are understaffed (or at least consider themselves to be in that position), Designers frequently opt to purchase because that requires financial resources rather than human resources. The Designer frequently finds it easier to obtain funds than staff. Therefore the temptation is to purchase and not to use staff to continue with this event or the next event of the CEM. The Designer can skip to the Obtain Instructional Resources event because in this case, the resource is the money. Most Designers, for a variety of sound reasons, will still opt to continue the internal design, so we will proceed with the CEM.

LESSON PLANS

Before writing lesson plans, the Designer is advised to do some E&FB. There is no point in using time to write the lesson plans if there has not been agreement on content and sequence. The evaluation, at this time, will not be in depth, but should determine if the content is relevant to the data gathered during the previous elements. This will be checked again during the final E&FB for this event.

The lesson plan translates the content and sequence into a form that is useful for the training situation. The lesson plan does not include the method for delivering training. That will be discussed in the next event, Selecting Instructional Strategies. The reasons for this distinction will become apparent during the discussion in this chapter and the following chapter.

The Users

The actual form of the lesson plan will be influenced by various factors. A major factor is *past history*. The Designer should not merely repeat what has been done in the past, but if the organization (that is, the HRD unit) has an agreed-upon lesson plan form that has been used frequently, the Designer is advised to first examine that form. There can be many good reasons the form evolved and became generally accepted. The Designer can recommend changes, but should recognize that changes can produce resistance. Is it worth the effort to try to change the form? Is there a very good reason?

Another important factor is the *instructor*. If during the process of designing a suggestion is made that the instructors will come from the line, the lesson plan will have to be very different than if instruction is to be provided by people from the HRD unit. A nonprofessional instructor needs a different lesson plan than a professional one.

In a program we designed for line people, the lesson plan was limited to four directions to the instructors:

- Ask. We wrote the specific question the instructors were to use.
- Tell. We wrote the specific instruction.
- Distribute. Handouts were keyed into the lesson plan with specific instructions for distribution.
- Notes. We made comments to the nonprofessional instructor in terms of answers that could be expected and details of classroom management situations.

If the instructors had been professionals, the fact that the material was so explicit could have been considered an insult. It certainly would conflict with the self-image of a professional instructor. The nonprofessionals, however, were eager for such material and responded very favorably to that kind of lesson plan.

Even nonprofessionals might offer resistance to the preceding detailed lesson plan if they had been given a prior training program to familiarize them with the lesson plans. Indeed, there would probably not be a need for such detail if the training program for instructors was carefully designed.

When the Designer cannot determine exactly who will be doing the instruction, it is wise to err on the side of more detail rather than less. Obviously it is easier for the instructor to use only parts of the lesson plan than to be forced to construct a lesson plan. Not all instructors have that competency, nor should they be expected to have it.

JIT

One form of lesson plan is the famous *Job Instruction Training (JIT),* which first emerged during World War I and became generally accepted during World War II. It was designed to provide nonprofessional instructors, usually line personnel, with a quick and easy formula for providing instruction at the job site. It is still used today. It is so simple that at first it seems naive, yet it contains the necessary elements for a successful training situation. The steps are:

- Preparation
- Presentation
- Application
- Verification

Some people use different words for the four steps, but the steps are generally accepted.

Preparation is what the instructor must do to get ready for the training situation. This includes becoming familiar and comfortable with the lesson plan or other material provided. It also means checking out the physical facility, the equipment necessary for the particular session, and the required materials. There should also be provision for preparing the learner. This includes making sure that the learner has been informed of the time and place of the training and that adequate provisions have been made for work coverage while the learner is in training. This is necessary even if the instruction takes place adjacent to or on the job site. For the period of instruction, no matter how brief, the learner is not expected to perform the regular tasks of the job or produce the expected output.

The next step is *presentation,* which includes those activities that are the initial part of the training process. It can include several instructional strategies and is concerned with the initial learning. It does not mean only lecture. It usually means, when used in production performance, a demonstration of the correct method or procedure. It also includes questions, discussion, and a variety of other presentation possibilities. The emphasis is on the activities of the instructor.

Presentation is followed by *application,* which occurs when the learner uses what has been learned during the presentation. In the area of psychomotor skills, where JIT is used most extensively, application means that the learner actually performs the task or that part of the task which has been presented. It can also include a role play, simulation, or any other learning strategy that provides an opportunity for the learner to actually use the material learned while still in the training situation.

JIT concludes with *verification,* which today is more commonly called evaluation. In actual practice, some verification will take place during application, because before the learner can conclude the training he or she should be able to produce or perform at the acceptable level. In verification, the instructor and learner agree that the learner has the necessary level of performance to be qualified to work alone on the job.

JIT is one way to organize a lesson plan, but it is more applicable to the psychomotor area and omits some of the factors an instructor must provide for and which the Designer has the responsibility for building into this stage of the design process and lesson plans.

GENERAL FORM FOR A LESSON PLAN

There is no one best form for a lesson plan. Rather, a lesson plan must reflect the interaction of content, sequence, type of instructor, type of learner, and the norms in the organization. It is possible, however, to indicate some of the general items that should appear in a lesson plan, as shown in Figure 7-2.

A lesson plan is prepared for each unit or segment of the training program. The units can be stated in hours or in one whole day. Generally, when the experience is for more than one day, a separate lesson plan is prepared for each day to link material from one day to the next. The lesson plan should not be immutable, but should depend on the learning concepts built into the plan and on the experience of the instructor. The Designer is obligated to set forth, in a general description of the training program, the degree of latitude that should be exercised to enable the learner to meet the objectives through the training program.

Objectives

The objectives contained in the lesson plan are those that were developed as a result of the previous event. If the Designer finds it necessary to change the objectives in any substantive way, the writing of the lesson plan should

Program Title: _____

Objectives of this lesson:

Preparation:
   1. Physical environment
   2. Equipment and materials
   3. Instructor
   4. Learner

Time	Major Topics	Instructor Activity	Learner Activity	Strategies

Figure 7-2. Lesson plan.

be delayed until there has been a recycling, through E&FB, back to the previous event.

The objectives, as indicated earlier, are stated in terms of the factors of performance, conditions, and criteria. By this time, the objectives should be so clear that an instructor can pick them up from the lesson plan and immediately understand them. Indeed, there are times when the instructor must do exactly that for the instructor may not have had any prior training and the Designer may not be available to explain the objectives. Of course, well-written objectives do not need any explanation.

Preparation

Some instructors must do all the preparation themselves, while others can rely upon aides or personnel whose sole function is to prepare the learning setting. No matter how it is done, the lesson plan should have clear and unambiguous directions to prepare for the learning experience.

Four factors should be considered. The first is the preparation of the *physical environment*. This includes the availability of the room, its condition, the set-up (when a special arrangement is required), and control (to reduce external interference).

The second factor is *equipment and materials*. It is not possible for this part of the lesson plan to be completed during this event, as the specific learning strategies have not yet been selected. At this time, the Designer can only note a heading such as "equipment and materials" so that they will not be overlooked later. Upon completion of the next event (Select Instructional Strategies), it will be possible to complete this part of the lesson plan.

The third factor is the *instructor*. The preparation will vary, but it is expected that every instructor will have access to and will study the lesson plan prior to the start of the actual instruction. This part of the lesson plan should indicate which specific activities need to be implemented by the instructor prior to meeting the learner.

For example, a program was developed for the Metropolitan Police Department of the District of Columbia, and the instructors were all from an external organization. The lesson plans were developed in detail and specified that each instructor was required to ride a shift in a police car before instructing. By no means did this experience make the instructor an expert on police work generally and not even on just what was involved in riding in a patrol car in an urban area. It did however help the instructors understand something of the work life of the learners they would be instructing as well as how the police viewed people from outside their organization.

The fourth factor is the *preparation of the learner*. It should not be expected that an individual can be withdrawn from the regular work situation, thrust into a learning environment with little or no notice, and still retain a level of trust and interest.

All of these factors will be addressed again in some of the following events. Particular attention will be paid to these factors when we reach the Conduct Training event.

Time

The lesson plan lists the *expected duration* of each element of the lesson. The Designer realizes, of course, that individual differences in the instructor and the learners, as well as other factors, will influence the exact time devoted to any element of the lesson plan. The times indicated are only guidelines, but time must be indicated. It is unfair to require the instructor to determine the duration of the various units, when the instructor was probably not involved in the CEM. The time suggested for each unit communicates to the instructor something about the emphasis to be given to that part of the curriculum.

The listing of time should also communicate to the instructor something about flexibility. Time should never be listed in units of less than five minutes. It is unrealistic to make the time allocation that specific unless the entire lesson is scripted and everything is written out and has been timed beforehand. Such lessons are less frequently used than they were years ago, but occasionally one still finds a lesson plan with time gradation of two and three minutes! At the other extreme, a single unit within the lesson plan should not take more than one hour.

When projected visuals are used (for example, video cassettes) it is rare for one to last more than 30 minutes. Indeed, a longer period than that is questionable, from a learning viewpoint, unless there is some kind of intervention by the instructor and reaction by the learners.

Within those general parameters (no fewer than 5 minutes, no more than 60 minutes) the Designer indicates how much time each unit might take. The way the listing is written should be a reflection of the organizational culture or norms. In a military organization or in organizations located in some countries outside the United States, the 24-hour clock is the accepted norm. Therefore the time on the lesson plan should be in similar notations. It would not list 9:00 a.m. as the starting time, but 0900 hours. This becomes confusing to those outside the organization, when after noon, 1:00 p.m. becomes 1300 hours. If the instructor comes from within such an organization, the time listing must obviously reflect that organization's normal use of clock hours. When the instructor is from outside, it is a good idea to inform the instructor in advance how the listing will appear on the lesson plan.

Some lesson plans do not give a specific clock hour, for the experience may be conducted at different times in different parts of the organization. The lesson plan will generally start with 00:00 signifying the start of the clock no matter what the actual time of day or night. If the first unit is for ten minutes, the next listing would be 00:10. If the unit goes beyond one hour, there would be a listing of 01:20 which designates that this would be one hour and twenty minutes after the start of the program.

Provision is also made for planned breaks for refreshment, lunch, and so on. The lesson plan should indicate the length of the break. Of course, the actual break given by the instructor in the training program can vary, but it is the responsibility of the Designer to indicate in the lesson plan what provision has been made for the breaks.

It may seem insignificant to pay this much attention to time. If the Designer is also going to be the instructor, it is unnecessary to be this detailed. When the instructor will have little or no contact with the Designer, it is essential to indicate the time in sufficient clarity so the instructor does not have to improvise more than is required in any learning situation.

Main Topic

This column on the lesson plan has several purposes. For the Designer, it is a direct link back to this event of the CEM. The major headings in this column reflect the content and sequence that have been agreed upon earlier. The column serves as a checkpoint for the Designer.

For the instructor, this column provides an overview of the flow of the lesson. The major topic headings indicate the overall content that will be covered and the sequence. Because the instructor has probably not been included in the CEM, this column communicates the curriculum directly to the instructor. It is possible to put subtopics under the main topic, but they should be kept to a minimum. They should only be included if it is necessary to provide the instructor with more specifics about the content that will be covered.

Instructor Activity

This column lists what the instructor will do during the lesson. The detail will, once again, depend upon the qualifications of the instructor. Professional instructors might resent too much detail, while nonprofessional instructors might require all the detail that could be of help to them.

At this point in the development of the lesson plan, not all the specifics can be written down. This will have to wait until the next event, though it is possible to include some specific material such as questions. If the instructor is expected to ask questions, this is indicated in the appropriate part of the lesson plan. Asking questions is much more difficult and sophisticated than many instructors realize. Therefore the Designer can opt to actually write out carefully developed questions rather than just indicating that this is the point in the lesson where questions will be asked.

The Designer has to anticipate all the other tasks required of the instructor, and tasks do tend to change throughout any given lesson. Instructor activity also relates directly to Strategies, which will be discussed later. When the instructor has options, the Designer lists them and the possible outcomes that can result from one option as compared to others. The options might relate to the competency and experience of the instructor, the nature and experience of the learner, the availability of materials and equipment, or the physical environment where the learning might take place.

Learner Activity

Learning should be a very active situation, and it is important that the learner and the instructor both be active. Even a lecture, essentially a one-way communication, has active components (for example, taking notes, phrasing questions).

It can be difficult for the Designer to indicate specifically some of the learner activities, because they will depend in a large part on the actual learners. The Designer can only identify and list some of the possibilities of learner activity. Activities will be in direct relationship to the objectives, the curriculum, and the potential and expected performance. The learner should at least respond and be encouraged to be pro-active and to initiate some activities (for example, develop a learning contract, relate the lesson to actual job situations). To encourage the learner to merely respond is to seek only reactive behavior, which for many adults can be defeating in a learning situation.

Strategies

Learning strategies apply to both the instructor and the learner, but for convenience the term *instructional strategies* is used. The variety of such strategies is extensive, as will be seen in the next chapter. The actual selection will be made during the next event. Until this entire event is concluded, it is not possible to indicate which might be the most desirable instructional strategies.

At this point in the development of the lesson plan, the Designer can make suggestions. For example, he or she might suggest that a case study is desirable at a certain point. The exact case study will not be selected or written until the next event. Right now, all that is required is the suggestion in the lesson plan that a case study be provided at this point. These suggestions are important, and the Designer should not wait until the next event to write them down. There are times, of course, when the Designer can be very specific, even though this is less desirable. For example, the Designer may know that a video is available that is directly relevant to a particular topic in the lesson plan. It could be helpful if the Designer, at this point, makes a note of that on the lesson plan, but also reserves the right to make changes during the next event if another video appears to be more appropriate. Here, too, the Designer should reserve the right to change even the suggestion about a video when the lesson plan is reviewed in the next event.

Evaluating

There is no specific column in the lesson plan for evaluation, for it is a pervasive activity that should take place at many points during each lesson. Evaluation should not be left until the completion of a session or unit, although those are points at which there must be specific evaluation.

When discussing evaluation, the Designer always starts with objectives. It is not possible to evaluate if one does not have objectives. In the suggested lesson plan, note that objectives is the first heading. The Designer indicates *what* is to be evaluated, and then *how*. Obviously the "what" will refer to the objectives, but they may have to be restated for purposes of evaluation. When evaluating, the Designer should seek those factors that are at least *observable,* and when possible, *measurable.*

Some researchers contend that if there is no measurement there can be no evaluation. Perhaps they have a point, but they should ask the question, "If there was no measurement before the learning, how can there be any after?" If the performance does not presently have any measurable criteria, the Designer can encourage management to introduce quantification of performance. If management will not do that, the Designer cannot build in an evaluation using measurement. Of course, the Designer can build in a quantification of the learning that has taken place as a result of the lesson, but this cannot be extended to indicate that the measurement applies to performance.

Evaluation is generally equated with tests. In most situations, this is unquestionably the relationship, but it is also possible to evaluate by other means. Let us start, however, with tests.

There are two major types of tests. One is the *standardized test* that can be purchased from an outside source. There are companies that specialize in constructing tests, and they will be able to provide the protocol regarding their tests. That protocol indicates the important factors of standardization, reliability, and validity. Given the data on these factors, the Designer can determine if the standardized test is appropriate for the objectives.

When a training package is purchased from an external source, as discussed earlier under "make or buy," the Designer should also request the test that should accompany the package. Rarely however can the Designer actually find such tests. Much more has to be done to encourage vendors of packaged training programs to provide tests that have an established protocol. As the consumers (that is, the Designers) do not usually demand this, the producers/vendors are not encouraged to supply the tests and protocol.

The second major source of tests is the Designer. Sometimes, it may be the instructor, but this has many pitfalls. Generally, an instructor is not required to have an ability to develop tests. This is particularly true when instructional personnel come from line operations. Designing test instruments is a sophisticated activity that requires more than being able to phrase questions. The Designer has the responsibility for providing the appropriate tests to the instructor. This means that the Designer must be able to develop tests, have someone on the HRD staff with this competency, or bring in an external resource to develop tests that are related to specific objectives.

Analyzing test results is an equally difficult task. When a test is constructed by a professional, it will likely be organized in such a way that the results are immediately available and usable by the instructor and the learners. This does not exclude the use of statistical manipulation to better understand the results, but such analysis must either be made explicit and simple, or the material should be left to the professional in the HRD unit for analysis.

An all too frequently repeated cliche is "If the learner hasn't learned, the teacher has not taught." This is unfair and dangerous. From a general viewpoint, it puts the burden of responsibility on the instructor, rather than on the learner. If this view is accepted as policy, it forces the instructor to "teach to the test," that is, to provide only the instruction that is directly related to the items on the test.

On the theoretical level, because the test should be a reflection of the objectives, it should mean that the instructor is "teaching to the objectives." This is valid only if the test has been so carefully constructed that an exact relationship exists between the test and the objectives. For some psychomotor (skill) activities, this can be done. For knowledge and attitudes, it is much more difficult if not impractical.

Tests are not limited to the traditional written form. There are other ways to test. All tests should be based on some criteria, however once one moves away from the written or performance test, this becomes more difficult.

A simulation can be used not only for training, but for evaluation. In a simulation, the learner is asked to perform in an artificial situation that is as closely related to reality as possible. The resultant performance can be below standard in a simulation without undue cost to the learner, the organization, or peers.

The assessment center technique can be used for evaluating learning. Even case studies and role plays can be used for evaluation, but the analysis of those activities must be different from the analysis made when those strategies are used for learning. Similarly, other learning strategies can often be used for evaluation.

An important question is *when* to evaluate. The general rule is frequently. Evaluation should be made throughout a lesson, particularly at crucial points or times in the lesson when a main topic has been completed or when a full understanding of a main topic must be ascertained before proceeding. These times are sometimes referred to as *formative evaluation points,* because evaluation is conducted while the training is in process and the formation of new ideas and performance is emerging. The results of a formative evaluation allows the instructor to choose several alternatives. When formative evaluation is designed into a lesson plan, the Designer is required to indicate possible alternatives and provide appropriate material. Formative evaluations can be offered at several points during a lesson and are expected to influence the remainder of the training program.

At the end of a lesson or program, a *summative evaluation* should be made. Generally such an evaluation will not have any direct effect on what has already taken place in the lesson just completed. It can, however, serve as an indicator to the instructor to proceed to the next lesson or to review and repeat some of the prior training. Once again, the Designer builds in some appropriate alternatives concerning the summative evaluation. One alternative may merely be that when learners fall below a given point on the summative evaluation, the instructor calls for help from the HRD unit.

At this point, the preliminary lesson plan is complete, but before proceeding to the next event, the Designer must cycle through the E&FB event that is performed at the conclusion of each event of the CEM.

EVALUATION AND FEEDBACK

The Designer must now ascertain whether the event was completed successfully. The objectives for this event were that, by completion, the Designer would be able to:

- Develop a specific list of the items to be learned in order to meet the previously determined objectives.
- List the order in which the training is to take place.

The end product of this event is the lesson plans that are written to reflect the stated objectives. The Designer, however, must explore the alternative of whether to use just the lesson plans or both the listing of content, and sequence, and the lesson plans.

Analysis

The Designer must determine which approach to analysis would prove most helpful. That decision is influenced by the nature of the content and the form of the lesson plans. The Designer should consider which approach will communicate better to the people who will be involved in the feedback. Another option, of course, is to offer both (content and lesson plan), but this may require more time for review than is available.

If time and personnel allow, the Designer follows the pattern used in developing the lesson plans; that is, the Designer starts with the content and indicates how each element within the content relates to the previously determined objectives. This is relatively easy when there is a direct relationship. For some content, further explanation may be required to justify its inclusion.

The sequence also can be stated. The reasons for sequencing may be more difficult to set forth, and because the Designer relied on some particular learning theory there can be a temptation to discuss learning theory in the analysis. The problem is that most of the readers of the analysis are not concerned with learning theory, and indeed, need not be. That is the reason they called on the Designer, who is the professional in the field of learning theory.

There is a way to bridge this gap in the analysis. The Designer can state specifically the assumptions that have been made about the nature of the subject matter and the kinds of learners expected. This latter, particularly, will elicit the opinions of the supervisors and managers concerning the employees they intend to send to the training program. The supervisor and managers also have some assumptions about the learners, and it is important that these be compared with those stated by the Designer in the analysis.

Bringing together the content, sequence, and assumptions about the learner (the application of learning theory) is extremely important. These three elements should be consistent. There will be a temptation for the Designer to write lengthy documentation about the relationship of these three elements, but restraint must be exercised. Only as much information should be included in the analysis as will be helpful and will facilitate the decision making that is the concluding activity in the event. This relationship should be set forth clearly, and possible alternatives should be indicated.

One alternative relates to time. The analysis should indicate content elements that might be dropped if the total time must be decreased. Until now, the Designer could not indicate exactly how much time the training program would require. Now the Designer can be specific. When faced with the time requirements, the decision makers may express satisfaction with the curriculum but ask that the training be done in less time.

A reduction in time must mean a reduction in content. Time constraints should not be met by "asking the instructor to move faster." The Designer should indicate in the analysis how decisions about time will effect the main topics of the lesson plan or content areas. These decisions may require that some topics must be dropped from this training program, but the Designer can suggest that they be included in a different training experience to be offered at a later time.

During feedback, a suggestion may be made that more time is required, particularly when skill development is concerned. The Designer does not have to indicate that possibility in the analysis, and probably cannot. But the Designer should be aware that this can happen after the analysis has been reviewed and feedback has been received.

The Designer should indicate in the analysis whether a make-or-buy decision has been made and specifically state the basis for that decision. Although the appropriate people may have been involved in the earlier decision, they may want another chance to review what happened now that the larger part of the training program is observable through lesson plans.

It may be discouraging to the Designer, after complying with an earlier decision and developing the lesson plans, to find that at this point these same people now suggest a buy option. This decision may not be a reflection on the competency of the Designer, but rather an indication that once the specifics are available (through the lesson plans) the same people may have a different point of view.

Something similar can happen when the decision is to buy. When the Designer brings the purchased program into the analysis for feedback, there may be some second thoughts. Of course, this can be even more expensive than recanting the previous decision, but the important question is at this time, what is the appropriate decision about make or buy?

Feedback

As before, the criteria should be used to select those people who can be helpful at this stage of the CEM. If potential learners were involved in the previous events, they may not however be necessary here. The decision to include potential learners may be based more on the politics and culture of the organization than on learning theory.

Supervisors should be included. If supervisors do not have an opportunity to be involved in feedback, the success of the program can be in jeopardy. Another apparent reason for such involvement is that a major decision must be made concerning the time allowed for training. Time is a crucial factor for supervisors who are asked to send producing employees away from their jobs. The feedback session may almost be the point at which the supervisors make the commitments that will enable the Designer to have some feeling of confidence in the ultimate success of the training program. If the supervisors react negatively, compromise may be in order.

Managers may be involved at this time primarily because additional resources may be needed. The managers will very likely not want to be concerned with the content, sequence, or lesson plans. These are operational factors that they traditionally leave to others. The decision about time or other resources can be a managerial decision, so managerial involvement would be helpful. In most situations, however, there is room for negotiation.

It is appropriate to consider involving the SMS, particularly if they are internal people. Doing this provides for further verification by the Designer that the input from the SMS have been understood and used. It is not necessary that every bit of their input should have been included, and it is not necessary that every SMS be involved in the feedback. Certainly it is appropriate that provision be made for some communication with some of the previously involved SMS people.

Decisions

The event should conclude with some specific decisions by those involved in the feedback, relating to the following questions:

1. Does the content meet the previously determined objectives?

   The objectives were stated specifically at the conclusion of the previous event. In the interim, a variety of people made contributions to the content. All of these people were familiar with the objectives, but they may have a variety of interpretations. During discussions and arguments, it is possible that the objectives become obscured. Now is the time to return and verify that the content is related to the objectives.

2. Will that content satisfy the identified needs of the learners?

   This is much the same as the previous question but reflects the common problem with communications and the use of words. The content should relate directly to the needs, specifically those that were selected for further consideration. Another way to ask this is "If the content is mastered, will the need of the individual learner be met?"

3. Does the content relate to performance?

   Following the same line of inquiry, the Designer seeks to decide if the content is really what the job is all about. A direct match must exist between content and specified job performance. If it does not, the differences should be explained or rationalized. Ultimately this question must receive a positive response.

4. Does the content relate to the previously identified need of the organization?

As noted earlier, the need of the organization for the training program was to solve a problem. The content may not have a direct relationship to the problem, but at the same time, the content should not create additional problems. When it is readily discernible that the content can solve the problem, there will be no hesitation in receiving a positive response to this question. When the relationship is not so obvious, additional discussion may be required before a positive response can be made.

5. Is there agreement on the make-or-buy decision?

This point should have been settled earlier, but it can always come up again. The Designer forestalls the possibility of this happening by including this question in decision making at this time. If there is still any strong feeling against the decision made earlier, this is the time for it to surface. Indeed, the Designer would want it to surface before going further. The purpose of this question is to seek reaffirmation, not to continue a previous discussion. If it provokes discussion here, perhaps the previous decision was not as binding as it appeared to be.

6. Will potential learners be made available for the period indicated?

This is where the supervisors must reach agreement. At this point, it will be possible for the supervisors to begin planning for coverage during the time when the training program is implemented. If there might be any difficulties, these should be voiced when making this decision.

CONCLUSION

If the final decision is to buy a packaged training program, the Designer does not have to become involved in the next event, Select Instructional Strategies, as these should be part of the purchased program. Depending upon the specific package purchased, it might even obviate the necessity for the Obtain Instructional Resources event, and the Designer can proceed to the final event, Conduct Training.

Assuming, however, that all of the preceding decisions have been in the affirmative and the decision is still to continue in-house development of the training program, the Designer now moves to the Select Instructional Strategies event.

CHAPTER 8

Select Instructional Strategies

The previous chapter suggested that the selection of instructional strategies be delayed until after the curriculum had been built. The objectives of this event (see Figure 8-1) are that the Designer will be able to:

- Select instructional strategies that are appropriate for the curriculum, the learner, the method of instruction, and the organization.
- Revise the lessons plans, as needed, to reflect the decisions about instructional strategies.

We will explore some general guidelines, but there are so many variations that it is generally impossible to link a particular element of the curriculum with a particular instructional strategy. (For a list of Instructional Strategies, see Appendix.)

NOMENCLATURE

Complicating the situation further, is the virtual explosion of instructional strategies. Some of this is due to the increased use of technology, but some of it is also due to the fact that people from disciplines other than education have come into the field of HRD. It is easy, therefore, to become embroiled in semantic confusion.

Many articles have been written concerning terminology for instructional strategies. Among the terms suggested are methods, technique, devices, media, material, and equipment. We have chosen to describe all such activities as *instructional strategies*. This is done for two reasons.

First, there is no evidence that producing categories will be helpful.

THE CRITICAL EVENTS MODEL

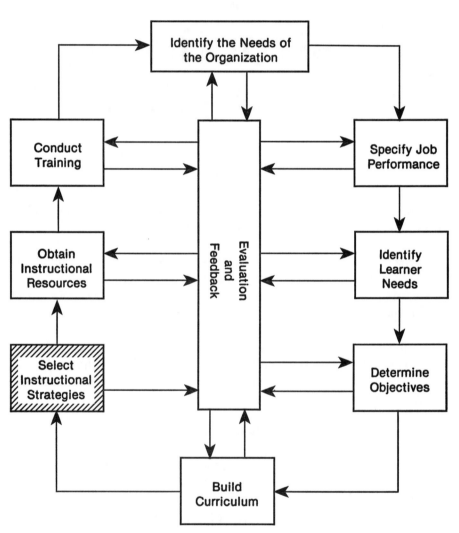

Figure 8-1. Select instructional strategies.

Second, the word "strategies" reinforces the idea that any learning situation involves the use of a combination of methods, techniques, devices, and so on. It also communicates that a strategy is a method of reaching some objective, but it is not the objective itself.

The history of HRD is replete with examples of strategies that have gotten out of hand because they took on a life of their own. In the early 1950s, brainstorming was introduced through the work of Alex Osborne and others, and rapidly gained acceptance. In some of the highly developed programs using brainstorming, Designers used learning aids, including whistles, lights, reinforcement cards, critical cards, and other supplementary materials. In one instance, with which we are personally familiar, a Designer developed a program using supporting materials and brainstorming that was truly magnificent. As a result, however, this Designer's behavior became highly predictable. No matter what the training program (the Designer was internal in the organization), there was always a curriculum piece that required brainstorming. Obviously, after many years, this became laughable. Unfortunately, the Designer held a position of power and no one felt they could give the necessary feedback to that Designer. The HRD unit suffered, however, simply because managers began to seek external design assistance rather than have another brainstorming session.

A similar experience can be recounted with "sensitivity training." Perhaps our biases should be set forth so the reader does not misunderstand. One of the co-authors became involved in that type of learning quite early and subsequently became a member of the National Training Laboratories (NTL), the leading exponents of that form of learning. We conducted labs, T-groups, and similar related learning experiences. Unfortunately, since its development in 1948, some of its proponents saw sensitivity training as the response for all the problems of human behavior and designed it into virtually every training program. Today, such limited response is no longer the vogue.

Programmed instruction (PI) is another example. It had its major initial impact in the early 1960s and was touted by its proponents as being the way to learn until it was soundly criticized. Obviously there are many more examples, but the point is no single strategy suffices for all learning situations.

The terms teaching, learning, and instruction must also be defined. Generally the term *teaching* is used to designate the activities of the person who directs the learning experience. This can be a teacher, professor, instructor, group leader, facilitator—the list can go on. *Learning* is used to signify the activities of the learner in the situation, who can be a trainee, student, pupil, or participant.

Note that such a division suggests a gulf between the teacher and the learner. It negates an often used approach in which roles may be reversed for a brief period. It overemphasizes one-way communication from the teacher to the learner.

In discussing the CEM, we use the term *instruction* to refer to the process that occurs during a learning experience, in this case a training program. Therefore, the reference to *instructional strategies* encompasses all the various teaching and learning activities as well as the supporting mechanisms that are used by all involved in the experience. These can also be called learning strategies.

FACTORS INVOLVED IN SELECTION

The selection of appropriate instructional strategies becomes more challenging with each passing year. The availability of sources is rapidly increasing as the market for HRD continues to expand. New producers continually enter the field. That is good, for it provides more possibilities, but it complicates what the Designer has to do during the selection process.

The continuing impact of new technology must also be considered. There are now many technologies that are both threatening and challenging, depending upon the competency and experience of the Designer. The field has expanded to the point where the Designer may not be the appropriate person to make a decision about a specific instructional strategy, but instead must call upon a specialist who has a wide range of experience with a variety of instructional strategies.

There is an inherent trap that the Designer must endeavor to avoid when using an expert in the field of instructional strategies. One organization, for example, developed instructional programs that required numerous slides. It was a large, multi-site, multinational organization, and the need for the slides was directly related to programs that were produced in a packaged form, and sent all over the United States and the world. It seemed logical, at the time, to hire an instructional strategies person who had competency with slides. The organization did this, but within months discovered that they needed two people and more equipment!

As their slide operation grew, it soon became evident to some in the organization that they had experienced that not unusual phenomenon, "If you give a person a hammer, soon everything in sight must be hammered!" Everything in the organization was reduced to slides. The HRD director actually had to dismantle this part of the operation before Designers could begin to explore alternative learning strategies.

Often Designers want to know what criteria to use to select an appropriate instructional strategy. A mixture of variables must be considered (as listed in Figure 8-2). The Designer must identify where a particular unit of a program exists on the scale between any two factors.

```
┌─────────────────────────────────────────────────────────────┐
│            Considerations for Selecting Instructional Strategies            │
│                                                                 │
│  instructor centered _____ learner centered     │
│                                                                 │
│  individual_____group            │
│                                                                 │
│  abstract subject matter_____concrete subject matter        │
│                                                                 │
│  self instructional _____ group learning     │
│                                                                 │
│  didactic_____experiential    │
│                                                                 │
│  low learner experience _____ high learner experience      │
│                                                                 │
│  short time to apply_____long time to apply      │
│                                                                 │
│  long time for learning _____ short time for learning    │
│                                                                 │
│  low instructor competence _____ high instructor competence      │
│                                                                 │
│  low student motivation_____high student motivation  │
│                                                                 │
└─────────────────────────────────────────────────────────────┘
```

Figure 8-2. Considerations for selecting instructional strategies.

For example, the Designer must decide whether the particular instructional unit (part of a lesson plan) will be individual or group. When the Designer can identify this criterion, he or she can focus on the appropriate instructional strategy. Obviously individual or group is not the only factor that must be considered, so the Designer will have to use most of the list in making selections.

Although doing this is time-consuming, the end product is certainly worth the effort. As a Designer develops a level of competency in using the list, the task becomes easier, but by no means should it be ignored or overlooked.

Final selection of an appropriate learning strategy is based on a combination of factors, and some require much more insight than just checking a list—any list. For example, factors such as learning psychology, administration, culture, the instructor, and the learners must also be considered.

Concepts of Learning Psychology

The Designer can study learning psychology to determine what various experts have to say about selecting the appropriate instructional strategy for a given objective. One common method is the cone of experiences. The cone represents a continuum from the simple to the complex, from direct experience to wholly vicarious, or any other continuum selected. The difficulty with this approach is that it assumes that there is a continuum, and that concept is debatable. It also puts selection on a one-dimensional plane that excludes the variables of the subject matter, the previous experience of the learner, and the style of the learner. It usually completely ignores two other factors that will be discussed later in this section.

The cones have some worth, for they organize the instructional strategies into usable patterns. The problem is with the Designer who seeks the answer from the cones or continuums despite the complexity of the variables. A single instrument will not permit the luxury of a quick and easy selection.

Administrative Practices

Overriding almost any other administrative considerations is the one of *budget*. When the HRD Designer is working with a limited budget, the possibility of selection is curtailed, for many strategies require a financial expenditure for materials. When equipment becomes a consideration (for example, video cassette recorders), a significant budget may be required.

Often the problem is not that the organizations will not make funds available, although in some situations that might be that case. More often the difficulty is one of timing. When budgets are being prepared, it is not always possible to forecast probable future expenditures for equipment related to a program that has not yet been designed. The HRD director will try to make provisions for some expenditures in that category when preparing the annual budget. The difficulty is that some HRD directors do not have control over their own budgets. Even when they do, it is difficult to sell a budget item when the need is not apparent. This leads the HRD director to trying to stockpile when economic conditions are favorable, but the items that may have been stockpiled frequently do not meet the needs of the program being designed.

Selection reflects administrative budgeting practices. The Designer should not take a negative stance. Just because they have not been budgeted for does not mean that materials and equipment for instructional strategies cannot be obtained, because every budget process provides for some flexibility. If the Designer can demonstrate the need strongly enough, funds might still be made available.

Another aspect of budget is timing. Every organization has a cash flow sequence. There are certain times of the year, a particular month or week, when cash is more or less available. The HRD director must remain sensitive to this when seeking funds for unbudgeted instructional strategy items.

When the HRD manager and the Designer are the same person, this sensitivity will be obvious. However, as HRD units become more active and grow in size, a gulf can develop between the HRD manager and the Designer. In that situation, it is the responsibility of the Designer to keep the manager informed. Unfortunately it may not be until this event in the CEM that the Designer can identify the budget requirements for a particular instructional strategy.

Much the same can be said about *facilities*. There are some instructional strategies that require special facilities. These can be as basic as a room that can be darkened if slides are to be used. The facilities can be more sophisticated if technology, such as closed-circuit TV, or group-oriented strategies requiring appropriate space for small break-out groups are involved. There is a growing tendency among large corporations to build or lease their own facilities. Generally they are not labeled HRD facilities, but rather "conference center." In some cases the company will actually build a center. There are many facilities in the northeast United States that cater specifically to HRD activities. The Sunbelt can claim a growing number of such facilities that were built primarily to provide an appropriate learning environment.

Companies frequently use hotels and motels for some of their HRD activities. Some of the facilities have very sophisticated equipment, while others provide only chairs, tables, and bare walls [79].

The Designer must know what is available or possible in the way of facilities when selecting an instructional strategy. The HRD director must be involved, if the budget and facilities are different from what had been provided previously. Although it may not be possible to obtain an additional budget or different facilities this year, the HRD director might want to anticipate the budget and facility needs for next year.

Culture of the Organization

Culture is always a difficult dimension to determine for it is "what everybody believes," but is not actually stated. When procedures are written in a manual, directive, or similar document, they become legal or administrative practices. This does not mean that everybody follows them, but at least everybody knows about them. Culture, on the other hand, is not written, but generally represents accepted behavior in the organization. As such, it is not always possible to tell when one has acted against the culture until penalized by the people or the system.

The most frequently repeated phrases when one encounters cultural practice are "We have always done it that way" or, "Everybody knows that is not done in this organization." An example comes from the Marine Corps, who at one time used sensitivity training as an instructional strategy (see Appendix). After a time, sensitivity training fell into disrepute in that organization. The cultural norm developed that sensitivity training was not to be used in the Marine Corps. No edict or dictum was issued, but the message was loud and clear. However, sensitivity was still needed to reach stated objectives of some of the Marine Corps training, and it became an example of "old wines in new goat skins." The strategy was renamed and continued to be used as needed, but with the new title it was no longer considered counter-cultural.

In many organizations it is generally assumed (cultural behavior) that executives and managers should be sent to external training programs rather than to those provided internally. These programs could be conducted by other organizations or, at the very least, conducted off the regular work site. There may not be a written policy or statement to that effect (that takes it out of cultural behavior), but many organizations we worked with made it a requirement when designing a program for that level of personnel.

History within an organization creates cultural norms. In one large oil company we worked with, the managers from all over the United States and frequently from overseas were brought together twice a year for training. The training was coupled with home office consultation. We had not been told about the various rituals that accompanied this activity. In a later discussion, the in-house HRD person remarked that there did not appear to be any need to tell us about the pre-session activities because those would be taken care of.

Unfortunately, those pre-session activities (cultural behavior) involved some interesting rituals. For one, newcomers to the group were not introduced. It was later explained that fighting one's way into the group was one indication of being able to survive at management level. The week-long session started with a "social." Actually it was what college students would call a "beer bust." The intent was to visibly consume as much liquor, not beer, as possible while still maintaining one's balance and composure. This "social" started before the opening evening session, continued for several hours, and was then interrupted for a content session. After the completion of that session, the participants were expected to once again join in the libation and festivities. The "evaluation" of cultural acceptance was the ability to engage in this activity the first evening and still be prompt for breakfast at 7:00 a.m. the next morning and participate in the first day's session. Consequently, these activities had a significant impact on the training program. Obviously, they were not built into the design.

Generally, cultural behaviors relate to dress, times of day that are used or must be avoided, and even times of the year that are more or less desirable. There may even be a "requirement" that each training session start with a predetermined ritual or event. The list of cultural behaviors can be quite lengthy, but understanding it is crucial in determining how a session can be organized and which instructional strategies are appropriate.

The internal Designer is expected to know these cultural requirements. Generally, however, only members of the particular group know the appropriate cultural behaviors. If the Designer is not a member of that group, study and open communication are required to identify the cultural factors that influence the selection of instructional strategies.

If the Designer or the instructional strategies developer is external to the organization, skills are needed to identify and provide for the cultural factors. This is not easily done, for by definition, cultural behavior is not written. This emphasizes how important it is for an external person to have a reliable internal counterpart.

Instructor

If the program is intended to be entirely machine-mediated, with no live person in attendance, the emphasis is on the technology, not the person. The Designer need only consider who will deliver the learning program in physical terms, such as setup, arrangements, and so on. This will be discussed further in the event Conduct Training.

Even when a learning experience is essentially machine or technology oriented, there may still be a person in attendance who can be called an instructor although the person will function more as a coach. As a result, much different behaviors are required than when that person serves as the traditional, "stand-up" instructor.

The more prevalent mode in most training programs is the use of an instructor who uses some of the various strategies that are listed at the end of this chapter. The learning experience is under the "control" of the instructor, even though self-directed or learner-directed strategies are used.

It is essential that the Designer have at least an idea of who that instructor might be. (There is also the obvious consideration that most training programs require more than one instructor.) Even more to the point, the Designer is in a better position to select effective strategy when he or she knows the instructor and the competencies that instructor will bring to the learning situation.

If the instructor is a professional, the range of possible instructional strategies available is much broader than when a nonprofessional is being used. This should not be read as being disparaging to the nonprofessional, because such instructors are extremely significant when knowledge of the subject matter is important or peer learning is significant. The nonprofessional can also be more effective when an objective calls for a leading company figure, such as the chief executive officer or a vice-president. Those nonprofessionals may feel uncomfortable with some of the technology available (including something as comparatively simple as slides), but the presence of that high level nonprofessional may be essential to meeting the objectives of the training program. For example, it may be that the culture of the organization requires the involvement of people at those high levels.

Another nonprofessional instructor is the line person who is also a peer. Since 1954 we have used supervisors to train other supervisors. Training sessions conducted by one of their own can have a stronger learning impact on learners than sessions conducted by a professional who may be comfortable with the instructional strategies but has never walked in the shoes of the learner.

Some professionals feel more competent with one instructional strategy than another. A professional instructor may have no problem with using projected materials (for example, slides or overheads), but might balk when required to use the video cassette recorder. It may be necessary to conduct training programs for the professionals in the use of a new technology or an old method (for example, role playing), but if the instructor does not feel comfortable with that particular strategy, it may be necessary for the Designer to make modifications.

When the Designer has selected a particular instructional strategy, but thinks that there may be some resistance or discomfort on the part of the instructor (professional or nonprofessional), there is another alternative. The next step of the CEM, Obtain Instructional Resources, contains provisions for meeting this possible need. It includes training of instructors as one component, so discussion of this alternative will be deferred until the next chapter.

Learner

If the learner rejects or fights a particular instructional strategy, the Designer may consider selecting an alternate one. This does not mean, however, that the instructional strategies be limited only to those that are familiar and/or comfortable for the learner. There are times when discomfort is a part of learning. Discomfort can even create a need to learn, but if the discomfort level is too high, the learner is apt to block, fight, withdraw, or call upon a variety of other psychological mechanisms rather than learn.

The Designer can consider "bridges," which are learning experiences that are used to prepare the learner for the next learning experience. If the learner has never engaged in role playing, the Designer can build into the lesson plans some warm-up experiences that will allow the learner to experience a low-risk example of role playing before using this strategy with the content of the particular session. For example, a scripted role play might serve to make the bridge to the unscripted role play.

als may feel uncomfortable with some of the technology available (including something as comparatively simple as slides), but the presence of that high level nonprofessional may be essential to meeting the objectives of the training program. For example, it may be that the culture of the organization requires the involvement of people at those high levels.

Another nonprofessional instructor is the line person who is also a peer. Since 1954 we have used supervisors to train other supervisors. Training sessions conducted by one of their own can have a stronger learning impact on learners than sessions conducted by a professional who may be comfortable with the instructional strategies but has never walked in the shoes of the learner.

Some professionals feel more competent with one instructional strategy than another. A professional instructor may have no problem with using projected materials (for example, slides or overheads), but might balk when required to use the video cassette recorder. It may be necessary to conduct training programs for the professionals in the use of a new technology or an old method (for example, role playing), but if the instructor does not feel comfortable with that particular strategy, it may be necessary for the Designer to make modifications.

When the Designer has selected a particular instructional strategy, but thinks that there may be some resistance or discomfort on the part of the instructor (professional or nonprofessional), there is another alternative. The next step of the CEM, Obtain Instructional Resources, contains provisions for meeting this possible need. It includes training of instructors as one component, so discussion of this alternative will be deferred until the next chapter.

Learner

If the learner rejects or fights a particular instructional strategy, the Designer may consider selecting an alternate one. This does not mean, however, that the instructional strategies be limited only to those that are familiar and/or comfortable for the learner. There are times when discomfort is a part of learning. Discomfort can even create a need to learn, but if the discomfort level is too high, the learner is apt to block, fight, withdraw, or call upon a variety of other psychological mechanisms rather than learn.

The Designer can consider "bridges," which are learning experiences that are used to prepare the learner for the next learning experience. If the learner has never engaged in role playing, the Designer can build into the lesson plans some warm-up experiences that will allow the learner to experience a low-risk example of role playing before using this strategy with the content of the particular session. For example, a scripted role play might serve to make the bridge to the unscripted role play.

The Designer should not underestimate the learners. Even though to the best of the Designer's knowledge the learners may never have experienced a particular strategy, they may have had that experience outside of the work situation. Many community organizations (churches and so on) use some of the more sophisticated instructional strategies that formerly were almost the sole property of profit-making organizations. The impact of technology, particularly on some of the younger people in the workforce, has provided learners with some experience that is beyond the ken of the Designer. The use of computers for learning is a prime example.

Learning styles are an important consideration in selecting an instructional strategy. We still have much to learn about learning styles so it is not possible to provide exact listings that indicate the instructional strategy for a particular learner. Also, when learning is done in group settings, the instructional strategies must reflect the group rather than a single individual.

Back to the Lesson Plans

Considering all the variables just discussed, the Designer now returns to the lesson plans and selects instructional strategies. The selection process may indicate that some of the curriculum elements will have to be offered in a fashion different than originally contemplated.

The factors just discussed can require a significant alteration in a lesson plan, and the Designer may have to backtrack through the CEM. Taking into account the requirements imposed by a particular strategy, the Designer must decide whether elements of the content or the sequence must be changed. Frequently there will be no changes, but the Designer should explore this possibility as part of this event.

EVALUATION AND FEEDBACK

Once again the Designer must consider E&FB, but the emphasis is much different here than in previous events. The objectives of this event were to:

• Select instructional strategies that are appropriate for the curriculum, the learner, the instructor, and the organization.
• Revise the lesson plans to reflect the decisions about instructional strategies.

Analysis

The differences in the analysis for this event reflect, in part, that the E&FB may not include learners as has been done previously, and the Designer can opt to use external people to react to what has been accomplished.

There are many ways to prepare the analysis. Under certain conditions, the Designer can list each instructional strategy and the reason for its selection. By no means is this an easy task, but it can serve to highlight the assumptions upon which selections were based and the reasons one was chosen rather than another alternative. At a more specific level, the Designer can also indicate, for example, why one particular video was chosen over another. The more detail the Designer can provide in this analysis, the clearer will be the completed lesson plan that is the ultimate result.

At this point, the Designer highlights what material is readily available and what must be made or bought. This includes rentals or other temporary procurement. Although no final decision can be made at this time, such information will be required during the next event, Obtain Instructional Resources. If the analysis contains sufficient data for decision making for the current event, it will also provide the basis for the next event. A lesson plan has been produced that reflects the type of instructor who will be expected to use it. Although instructors have not yet been selected, and the actual selections will not be made until the next event, the Designer can indicate the profile of the prospective instructors.

There are times when several instructional strategies may be equally appropriate, and the Designer should provide alternative lesson plans with the same content and sequence but with different proposed strategies.

Feedback

The groups to be involved in feedback in this event will differ somewhat from those involved earlier in the CEM. The Designer provides an appropriate link so that those involved for the first time are not made to feel inadequate, which would hinder feedback.

The Designer may wish to share the lesson plans with others in the HRD unit, if the Designer is fortunate enough to have available peers. As an alternative, some Designers develop networks of peers outside their own organizations with whom they can exchange lesson plans for feedback.

When the content is not familiar to the Designer, the lesson plans can be shared with the subject matter specialists who were involved in earlier events of the CEM.

It may be desirable to involve the supervisor in feedback. Of course, the supervisor is not expected to be an expert on instructional strategies, but it is possible for supervisors to provide insight into how their people might react to the instructional strategies selected for the training program.

Because the instructors are expected to use the lesson plan, it is logical to involve them in the feedback in this event. Unfortunately it may not be possible at this point to specifically identify the instructors. If the instructors will be from within the organization but have not yet been identified, the Designer can ask that some potential instructors provide feedback on the lesson plans. The focus of the feedback should be on the instructional strategies, not on the curriculum, but it is important that the instructors feel comfortable with the fit between the curriculum and the instructional strategies.

There is another group who have not been part of the CEM up to this point who might be involved. These are the budget and finance people. If there is the possibility of funding problems, this is the time to involve these people. Of course, if the Designer has determined that no special financial resources will be needed, involving the budget and finance people is superfluous.

The budget and finance people are not particularly interested in all the details of the training program, but they frequently want to get something more than a formal request. They want to have some feeling for what they are expected to fund. They should not be overwhelmed with the lesson plans, but the analysis should be marked carefully to indicate those areas in which the budget and finance department can be expected to have some concern.

Decisions

Many of the decisions the Designer has to make for this event are of a technical nature and relate to learning and instructional strategies, which are areas in which the Designer is expected to have competence. However, other people are still to be involved because their input to the process is essential. The following are the questions that must be asked:

1. Do the instructional strategies implement the curriculum?

   There is no other purpose for the learning strategies than to implement the curriculum that has been previously agreed upon. If there is an inconsistency between a particular instructional strategy and the curriculum, reexamination of the curriculum may be required. Generally the curriculum should not be changed to satisfy the selection of a particular strategy; it should be the other way around.

2. If the lesson plans are implemented, will the objectives be reached?

   The lesson plans should be based on the objectives previously agreed upon. It sometimes happens, though not too frequently, that the final version of the lesson plans contains some alterations in the previously stated objectives. This is the place for a check on the agreement of the objectives in the final lesson plan and the objectives determined by the earlier event of the CEM.

3. Do the lesson plans reflect the identified learning needs?

   This too is a checkpoint question. It should not be difficult to determine whether the lesson plans are directly related to the identified needs. It is equally important to verify that the needs have not changed. Needs could have changed because there has been a time lapse between the event that focused on identifying the needs of the learner and the completion of this event. It is also possible that the potential learners have changed because of job reassignment, attrition, and so on. If that is the case, learning needs may have changed and therefore may not be correctly reflected in the lesson plans.

The Designer should not be defensive about changes that occurred as a result of time lapse, but should recognize that all organizations are in a constant state of flux and change. The Designer may choose to ignore this natural phenomenon but only at the risk of producing a training program that is outdated before it is offered.

4. If the lesson plans are used, will they relate to current job performance? This question has been carefully developed to encourage the Designer to relate to the job as it is now expected to be performed. As with the previous question, the time lapse factor is significant. The rapid impact of technology, managerial decisions, and new equipment are only a few of the factors that cause rapid changes in job performance requirements. The lesson plans should be compared to job performance, as it exists at this time, to determine if there are any changes that require further examination of needs, objectives, or curriculum.

5. If the training is conducted using these lesson plans, will the problem be solved?

CHAPTER 9

Obtain Instructional Resources

The Designer who has followed the Critical Events Model to this point will find that this event (see Figure 9-1) brings together all the work of the earlier events.

The objective of this event is to assure that all the necessary resources will be made available for the program that has been designed.

VARIETY OF RESOURCES NEEDED

In an organization with a large HRD unit, the Designer will probably involve the supervisor of programs or a similar management person because Designers are not required to have the skills needed to implement this event.

In large organizations, coordinating the necessary resources may be seen as a management function, and the Designer is generally not considered part of management. In a small HRD unit, the Designer likely will also be required to function as a manager, particularly during this event of the CEM. In this event the Designer may have to work very closely with an HRD manager.

The variety of resources needed is not unusual and falls within the traditional categories of physical, financial, and human.

Physical Resources

The Designer can now identify the specific *equipment* that is required. Equipment refers to those items that are expected to have a life beyond a single use, such as audio visual items including VCR, projectors, and slides.

The rationale for including video cassettes, slides, and similar items in this category is that they are generally used for more than one program and must

172

THE CRITICAL EVENTS MODEL

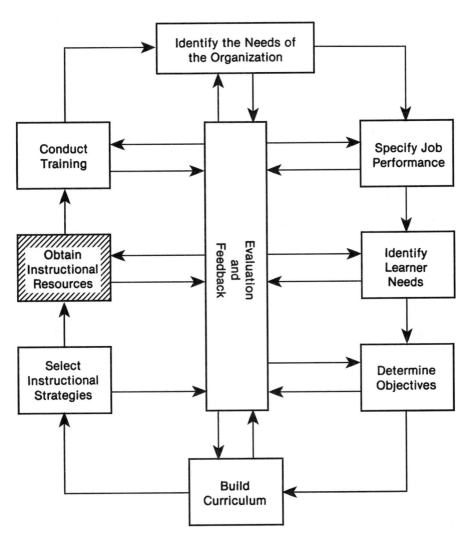

Figure 9-1. Obtain instructional resources.

be accounted for and inventoried. Even video cassettes that are rented for a single program may be included in this category because they must be accounted for and returned.

The Designer must first identify the exact equipment that is required to implement the lesson plans and then determine availability. If training programs are conducted within the organization facility, there is probably a depository that contains the equipment and a unit that controls its use. In general, the equipment should be in the hands of the HRD unit, but this is not always the case. In some organizations, such equipment is under the control of some other part of the organization, and the HRD unit must initiate requests when the equipment is needed.

In either event, the Designer must see that the necessary equipment is on hand and available at the times needed. When an organization conducts many training programs at the same time, careful scheduling is required. In organizations with many programs, a specialist is usually responsible for the scheduling and maintenance of the equipment, and the Designer works with that specialist to coordinate the particular equipment needed for a specific lesson. If there is no specialist, the Designer may have to determine whether the equipment is in working order. The obvious problem is that the Designer can check this out before the program begins only to find at a later time that the equipment has been used in the interim and is no longer working. This is an important problem, for it discourages some Designers from including equipment in their lesson plans.

When an off-site facility is being used, the equipment situation is different. There are three possible ways to provide equipment for off-site programs. The first is for the organization to provide its own equipment. Depending upon the size and type of equipment, this may not always be practical. Technology has reduced the size of much of the equipment used in training programs, but there are still some programs that require special equipment or a labor squad to bring the equipment to the site.

A second possibility is to rent the equipment from the facility. A facility that has been built as a "conference site" can be expected to have the basic equipment of projectors, easels, and so on. This cannot be taken for granted, however. At one major hotel in New York City, one that describes itself as having a conference facility, we had blocked 16 rooms for small group work. The hotel information stated that each room came with an easel. Later, in the negotiations, we discovered that the hotel had only one easel and the others would have to be rented and charged to our account.

The third alternative is to rent from companies that specialize in renting equipment of the kind used in training programs. There are many such companies, and if rental is the policy of the organization, the Designer should maintain a list of companies, the kinds of equipment, their rates, and previous experience with delivery and condition of the equipment. Some hotels and motels that offer facilities for training programs advertise that equipment is available. They may even provide a lengthy list with prices and conditions. However, the supplier may not be the hotel, but an outside firm that has an arrangement and even space in the hotel/motel. The Designer will have to determine if the facility requires that the supplier be used, or if the Designer is allowed to rent from another organization, for delivery to the hotel/motel.

Renting either from the conference site or from an external supplier has many advantages. The Designer's organization does not have to maintain an inventory of the variety of equipment that may be needed and have funds tied up in equipment that may be used only infrequently. A rental company has the responsibility for maintenance of the equipment and for any repairs that are necessary. A good rental company will be able to provide a wide range of equipment and will change the equipment as technology changes.

Materials are defined as expendable items that are used in a training program. An inventory need not be maintained, and neither the instructor nor the Designer is held accountable for the materials made available to a program.

Some materials are fairly obvious, such as writing implements, note pads, and even chalk. A difference of opinion can arise when we talk of items such as felt tip markers, masking tape, and clear transparencies. Some organizations actually inventory these items and the instructor must account for them. If a cost analysis were done, it would probably determine that it is more expensive to maintain records and to take the time to assign accountability than the cost that lost materials warrants. The Designer will have to conform to the practice within the organization, but should try to influence it so that such items are not considered equipment. If instructors have to account for each marker (turning in dried out ones) or clear transparencies (even though misused with a permanent marker), the tendency will be for the instructor to avoid using such materials even though they are stipulated in the lesson plan.

Some materials must be controlled, but in a different way. If a training program requires the use of a workbook, it is expendable and therefore classified as material. The learner will use the workbook and either discard it or retain it to refer to at the work site. In either event, it is not to be returned, and therefore falls within the classification of a material. Confusion may arise from the need to print numerous copies of the workbook. This requires inventory control to assure that there are enough copies when the need arises. The instructor is not expected to return any workbooks.

It is the Designer's responsibility to plan for the materials that will be needed. Even if they are commonly available materials such as pencils, the Designer must provide sufficient notice to whoever provides them from within the unit so that stocks are not depleted. If there is more than one Designer/Manager, this becomes even more crucial. Designers know what they will need, but there may be an inordinate demand that cannot be met if all the Designers do not funnel their material requests through one channel.

The final physical element concerns *facilities*. This is generally thought of as classroom space or conference space, depending upon the organization. The Designer must be cautious about the use of these words because they can communicate something different from what is intended. The word "facilities" is a more encompassing and neutral term.

When an organization has numerous programs, space may be assigned to the HRD unit in which to conduct those training programs. The ideal model is to have this space controlled by the HRD unit, so that scheduling does not become a problem. When control of space is not in the purview of the HRD unit, the Designer will have to request space much earlier in the CEM, even before the event to select strategies determines the kind of space that will be required.

Financial Resources

It is now possible for the Designer to prepare a specific budget for this program. The exact process will depend upon whether the HRD unit is funded as a budget center, a cost center, or a profit center (see [80]). No matter what the form, it is still desirable to cost out each program, and this is the time for it to be done.

Indeed, some costs may already have been incurred such as payments to subject matter specialists from outside the organization. Some calculations will have been made in relation to instructional strategies or make-or-buy decisions. Now is the time to bring all of this together.

Unfortunately, a common error made by Designers is to propose the program at the lowest cost. Of course, the Designer should not be extravagant, but cost is relative. Does your family want a small mobile home or a big multi-room house with grass and trees? It is not possible to give a single or simple answer to that question. You would probably respond that it depends on need, financial resources, future movement of the family, location, and other related factors. Similar thinking is required when costing out a training program. The Designer first identifies the variables and then develops alternative cost plans.

The Designer should not assume that the organization wants the cheapest program. It may want the best, but cheapest and best are neither the same or mutually exclusive. The Designer estimates the most desirable program and the comparable cost. A basic reason for this approach is that the organization relies on the Designer to propose the appropriate program. If the Designer tries to trim it down to the lowest cost under the assumption that cost is the only factor, a disservice is being done to the organization.

If there has been a history of low-cost programs, the Designer can anticipate some resistance when costs go up. The Designer must be able to justify
the cost in terms of the marketplace and the results.

Because costs are measurable, the Designer must recognize the need to
show financial results for a training program. This is not always possible, but
the closer the Designer comes to showing results, the less difficulty he or she
will experience in obtaining the requested financial resources.

In some cases, the final evaluation of the training program can be reported in financial terms. The Designer, or someone in the HRD unit, must be
able to think in the financial terms of the organization. Concepts must be
explored and understood, such as return on investment (ROI), profit, bottom
line, and cost effectiveness. Despite the general literature in the field, the
Designer will find that each organization has its own formula or way of looking at the financial expenditures and the measurement of return or results.
The Designer will probably turn to the HRD manager for assistance at this
phase of the event.

Budget alone is not enough, *cash* outlay is also important. The budget only
says that the organization plans to have the money earmarked for that item;
it does not say the money can actually be spent. The Designer may be surprised to find that cultural behaviors relate to the budget. For example, in one
organization where we worked "everybody knew" (remember cultural
behavior?) that a department head was expected to spend only up to 90 percent of the budget without higher level approval. Generally only 80 percent
would ever be spent, so the higher levels could show the results of their
efforts in cost cutting and savings. A Designer who planned to spend the total
budgeted amount would not remain long with that organization.

Some items may be purchased from other parts of the organization or may
be charged to other parts of the organization. Although these are only internal book transfers, the Designer must determine the appropriate procedure
and build this into the budget. It is necessary for the Designer or the HRD
manager to ascertain the specific guidelines for what is to be costed or
charged either internally or externally.

A training program has many costs that can be anticipated, but for which
there is little general agreement with regard to accounting. For example, consider the salary or wage of a learner while in training. How should this be
costed? There are many possible variations and each organization has its
own way of handling situations like this. They might decide to charge the
"lost production" to the cost of training or to ignore the whole thing and take
no note of this personnel cost. Similarly, the costs of travel may have to be
considered in the training budget. They may be absorbed by the learner's
unit or may even appear in someone else's budget.

The Designer should determine how all the items are presently handled in the organization. This requires that the Designer (or someone in the HRD unit) devote the necessary time to identify all the anticipated costs. Then the items can be specified and decisions can be made as to what will be charged and how. When the Designer does this unilaterally, there are bound to be problems. The financial people in the organization must be involved so that funds can be made available and appropriate accounting procedures are followed.

An item that is frequently overlooked is the need for repairs and replacements. All equipment, at some time, will require some repair. If the HRD unit relies on equipment rented from the outside, provision for the repair cost will not be necessary, but the rental costs must be considered. When the HRD unit has its own equipment, the HRD manager must be familiar with the way depreciation is handled in the organization, and the Designer must be sure that this accounting procedure is included in the cost estimate for the training program.

It is understandable that a Designer and some HRD managers would prefer not to become involved in the financial aspects. However, if the HRD manager is a general manager type who is only temporarily in the HRD unit, this individual would probably be knowledgeable about the financial procedures in the organization. If the HRD manager does not have that background, someone on the HRD staff who is conversant with the financial procedures in the organization should be employed. The least desirable solution is to have someone outside the HRD unit responsible for drafting the budget for the training program.

The Designer should also know when to request funds. The budget cycle varies from organization to organization, but it is there. In some organizations, it is specifically stated in manuals and procedure handbooks. Many organizations do not specify all the elements in the cycle, because they are "known" only by those in power. If the HRD unit is not in the power structure, good training programs can be deprived of part of the budget or may not receive funds when they are needed.

Human Resources

Training programs require human resources. Even if the decision is to provide a totally machine-mediated program, people are still necessary at some point.

A training program must have a program facilitator who is generally not the Designer. The titles used for the program facilitator vary greatly, and one is the *supervisor of HRD programs*. That person functions much as any supervisor, in that the work is accomplished through the efforts of others.

The supervisor of programs should not be the instructor, although this can happen, particularly in very small organizations. Perhaps it cannot be avoided in those situations, but it should be whenever possible. In an HRD unit in a large organization, it is possible for a person to be a supervisor of programs for one program, while being an instructor in another. It is even possible for the Designer to be a supervisor of programs, but these two positions require much different competencies.

The supervisor of programs must come from within the HRD unit because that supervisor is responsible for many activities, which will take place in the next event. Therefore, when obtaining instructional resources, the Designer indicates the need for the supervisor and even recommends who within the HRD unit would be the best supervisor for this program. The supervisor can be designated much earlier in the CEM. Whenever possible, the Supervisor should work with the Designer from the first event. Generally this does not happen, but the earlier the supervisor can be involved, the more familiarity there will be with the program that results from the CEM. Too often the Designer completes the work up to this point, and during this event the supervisor and Designer work together, but after that the Designer is out of the picture. This is the reality, even if it is not the best thing. However, the Designer must work within the limitations imposed by the organization while still seeking the best use of the resources available.

Another important human resource is the *instructor* who is the individual responsible for delivering the training. Even a totally machine-mediated program needs an instructor to function as a counselor or coach. In all learning programs, at least one person must be designated as the instructor to whom the learner can relate.

There are many kinds of instructors. In this event, the Designer identifies the kind of instructor needed for the specific program being designed. In some situations, the instructor may have been tentatively identified at an earlier event. Now is the time to designate the requested instructor by name (or names when there are more than one instructor).

The instructor may come from within the organization or be external to the organization. The instructor might come from the HRD unit within the organization, although many organizations are finding that it is unproductive to maintain large instructional staffs. In some unique situations, such as in the military, internal instructional staffs are preferable. In company-owned learning centers, instructional staff can be assigned from within the company for specified limited periods of time. Many organizations conduct courses in supervision and management with instruction by HRD staff.

If HRD staff are to be used as instructors, the Designer should determine during this event whether the required staff will be available. Seeing that the staff is available is usually the responsibility of the HRD manager, but the manager should rely on the Designer for recommendations.

The external instructor may come from a variety of sources. An external SMS who had been consulted during the design phase of the program might be recruited to instruct. Universities have also become an important source of external instructors for some programs. Consulting companies, or vendors, also provide instructional services.

It is important that some explicit agreement, perhaps even in writing, be made with the external resource. This is particularly important when using a company rather than an individual. There are many instances when an HRD manager expected to get a particular instructor from the vendor only to be told at the last minute that a substitution would be made. This is most likely to happen when the vendor has an outstanding star or two who are in constant demand. It is wise to determine exactly who will be doing the instruction.

Earlier in the CEM, a decision to "buy" may have been made. Some packaged programs include instructional assistance. If instruction is part of the total packaged program, little has to be done at this time except to determine that the financial resources have been provided.

Whether staffed from internal or external resources, there could be the need for what is commonly referred to as "training of trainers" or preparing an individual to serve as an instructor. The term "instructor of instructors" has not gained general usage, although it is more descriptive. The learning program for instructors is by no means a set and established program, but varies depending upon need.

When the instructor already knows the subject matter, all that may be required is a training program to develop the instructor's competencies to instruct that program. This is essential when the lesson plans call for instructional strategies that may be beyond the current competency of the identified instructors.

It is also possible that the instructor may know the strategies, but needs instruction on the subject matter. This, of course, raises that perennial question as to whether the organization should select instructors for their competence in content or in process. Naturally the answer is it depends. There are too many variables in any such situation to give a definitive response. If instructor training is required, additional resources and time will also be required. Preparing instructors can delay the start of the final event of the CEM, but such a delay is preferable to providing an instructor who is not prepared.

The final, but obvious human resources are the *participants*. It can be argued that they are not a resource in the usual sense, though they are certainly essential to the program. At this point, the list of potential learners should be made firm. Specific rosters should be developed so that exact quantities of needed materials can be specified, dates and times can be scheduled, and all the myriad tasks related to delivering the program to a specific group can be taken care of. In some organizations, particularly those using the budget center approach, the HRD unit may be given only the number of attendees, and not the specific names. Sometimes this is sufficient, but not if pre-course work is required or if screening of participants is necessary to provide for either homogeneity or heterogeneity.

The Designer must now determine if the potential learners whose needs were identified earlier in the CEM are still the same learners who are scheduled to attend the program. If they are, then the program is on target. If there have been changes, the Designer must determine the extent of those changes and whether any modification of the program and the lesson plans are required.

Ignoring this step can produce a great deal of conflict. The Designer can follow all the events and design an excellent program only to discover that the participants who arrive for training are much different from those previously identified in the CEM. It does no good to find out who was wrong, because no one was in error during the earlier design work. If time lapsed from the earlier event to the present, some personnel changes can be expected. Although it is time consuming at this point, the Designer must determine the effect of any personnel changes on the program that is ready for delivery.

A personnel change among the supervisors who were involved in the earlier events can also be significant. By no means do all supervisors behave in the same manner, yet there is a tendency to think that the job makes the person. Of course, the job influences behavior, but each person brings different competencies, values, and beliefs to a job. If the supervisors are not the same supervisors who were involved in the earlier events, the Designer can anticipate some difficulty unless there is a plan to involve the current supervisors before the program actually starts.

CHECKLIST OF INSTRUCTIONAL RESOURCES NEEDED

The following checklist brings together the variety of instructional resources required by the lesson plans.

Scheduling

- Will the learners be available?

  The focus of the program is on the learners. This is the point at which the Designer (or the HRD manager or supervisor) determines whether the learners will be available. The actual notification will not occur until the next event, but here the Designer seeks agreement from the supervisors that the learners will be able to attend the program.

- Will the necessary facilities be available?

The specific facilities were identified earlier. Now, it must be determined if they will be available when needed for the actual program.

- Who will actually instruct?

This is the time when the instructors should be designated specifically by name.

- Will the designated instructors be available when needed?

The dates of the program are required so that instructors can be assigned. If the instructors are internal, they may have to be released from their present work assignment for the instructional period and be allowed adequate time for preparation. If they are external, specific contracts or letters of agreement may have to be drafted and perhaps signed before there is certainty that the external instructors will be available.

- Will the instructors require any prior instruction before beginning their duties?

If the instructors are internal and are subject matter specialists, they may need some form of "training of instructors" before they begin instruction. If the instructors come from the HRD unit, they may still require some kind of preparation for the specific program before meeting with the participants.

When the instructors are external, preparation may also be required. A frequent error on the part of HRD people is to assume that an external instructor is ready to "park the car and start instructing." In some cases, that may be true. When it is not, and no provision has been made for some preparation, there should be no surprise if the external person is less than adequate. If the external instructor uses a packaged program, very little internal preparation is required. If the external instructor provides material, the internal HRD staff should ascertain that the material is appropriate for the total program. If the external instructor is expected to use the lesson plans designed internally, provision should be made for preparation and review with the internal Designer.

Equipment and Materials

- If they are to be purchased, is there a specific list of the items?

It is now possible to list specifically what has to be purchased and the amount of money that will be requested. It may, however, be necessary for the Designer to revise the list after budget decisions have been made. A complication can arise when the HRD unit requires open or competitive bidding for equipment. (This is less frequently done for materials.)

The bidding process may take considerable time and slow down the schedule, but the Designer has several alternatives. If a "crash" training program is being considered, it may be necessary to request the equipment needed for the program at a much earlier event in the CEM. The obvious problem is, that as the design process proceeds, the Designer loses options to make changes in the instructional strategies reflected by that equipment.

If time is available, it is proper to make the decision to purchase at this point. Whenever the decision is made, a specific list is required. It should relate directly to the lesson plans previously produced.

• If the materials are to be produced in-house, is there a specific list of items?

This applies more to materials than equipment. It is unusual to produce in-house equipment, although this is possible if mock-ups or similar strategies are to be used when the equipment is not available on the open market.

The list of materials will come directly from the lesson plans. Each item should be listed, even down to pencils and paper, which are generally provided through internal requisition. If they are not, such materials should have been listed earlier under purchase.

It is not always possible in the case of materials to indicate the exact number that will be required. This is most apparent with items like flipchart paper (also called newsprint) or various writing implements. The Designer will probably have to provide more items than appears to be required so as not to impede a lesson because of a shortage of materials.

When materials are produced in-house, the HRD unit may have to rely on other elements of the organization for the production. In many large organizations, a graphic arts unit serves the entire company. HRD is only one of their clients and must wait in line with the others for such service. The Designer should check with the graphic arts unit, if there is one, as to the lead time required for the variety of materials that will be needed. It may be that because of time or other factors, the Designer will have to rely on purchase (buy) rather than in-house procurement (make). Therefore an item that starts on this list may have to be moved to the purchase list.

If the Designer intends to use material reproduced from another source, the constantly changing copyright laws must be checked very carefully. In 1979 and 1980, the U.S. copyright laws were vastly changed. (International copyright laws are even more complicated.) As newer technology makes reproduction from almost any source possible, it can be anticipated that the copyright laws will keep changing. The Designer has an ethical and legal obligation to explore those laws before reproducing the work of others.

- If equipment is to be rented, is there a specific list of items?

This will almost always apply to equipment, not to materials. The borderline becomes unclear when one looks at flipcharts or easels. They usually come with paper, markers, and so on, but the Designer (or supervisor) should be sure that such materials are available. If the lesson plan calls for a rented video tape, it should be listed. In some organizations, even rented equipment must go through a bid process. If this is the case, the cautions indicated earlier under external purchase also apply here.

- For all equipment and material, have delivery schedules been prepared?

Some equipment and material have to be available at the opening of the learning program. Others are not needed until some later date. The Designer should prepare a schedule indicating when the equipment and material should be confirmed by the HRD unit and when they should be available at the learning site.

Budget

In this event, a formal budget submission may be required. Even if no formal step is required, the budget should be explicitly stated here and retained in the files for future reference.

- Have there been previous budget estimates?

During the Determine Objectives and Build Curriculum events, reference was made to preparing budget estimates. If that was done, this is the time to review and update them based on decisions made during the intervening events.

- What is included in the budget?

It would be helpful to answer this question with specifics, but the response usually is it all depends. Agreement on which items should be included in the training budget is difficult to reach. Direct costs such as purchasing and renting are obvious. In-house costs may be determined when an organization has an accounting system that charges between departments or units. Some organizations include the cost of the salaries and/or wages of the participants. If this is done in the organization, the Designer is expected to comply with it. If this is not the case, it may not be possible or necessary to include these costs in the budget.

Obviously, the Designer should determine the budget items that must be included and to be sure they are listed. If the organization specifically excludes certain items from the budget, the Designer should not include them. When there are items that do not fall neatly into either category, the

Designer should consult with the budget people who will be reviewing the cost figures to avoid surprises for anyone involved in the training program. Above all, the Designer should be consistent. If travel is included in one budget, it should appear in all budgets. When it is excluded for any reason, the reason should be stated, so it is seen as a policy decision rather than an oversight.

- Will the training be cost-effective?

This is a frequently asked question, and rightly so. The response, however, is not possible until this event. Now that the learning program has been designed, it is possible for the Designer to determine the cost. The Designer can compare the cost information with the probable "savings" that might result from changed performance. It is then possible for the Designer to respond to the cost-benefit question.

If the problem that generated the training request does not have a cost figure on it, the Designer cannot use that budget information to determine whether a savings will result. For example, if the problem was the volume of customer complaints and the training is designed to change performance in order to reduce complaints, the training can solve the problem, but a specific cost-benefit ratio is not possible (unless the organization has developed a cost index on complaints). At a later time, when performance has changed, perhaps the individuals who identified the problem can report how much less time is required to handle customer complaints. The cost of the program then can be compared to the results. Another way to measure the results of the program in this situation is to estimate how many fewer complaints will result. It is then possible for the Designer to compare that change with the cost. However, it is possible that as a result of the training program customer complaints increase. As the employees become more proficient and the word gets out to the consumer or customer, customers may bring in complaints they previously would not have bothered with. Of course, the result could be increased sales because these formerly dissatisfied customers receive better service and therefore make more purchases! It is difficult for a Designer to produce a cost-benefit ratio that can show these factors.

- Who will be charged for the training?

This depends in part on whether the organization has organized HRD unit as a budget center, cost center, or profit center. No matter how it is organized, the Designer will have to determine specifically who can authorize charges and whose budget must pay for those charges. This should be made clear at this point, if it has not been done earlier.

• Have alternative budgets been prepared?

The Designer wants to provide the best training program possible. But what if the organization will not pay for the "best" program? One approach can be to make it "either this training program or nothing," but that can be self-defeating. Managers prefer to be given alternatives, and that can be done with the budget for a training program. The Designer must be able to show the effect of different budgets on the training situation.

The Designer should be prepared to respond to questions such as, "What would happen if your budget for this training program was reduced by 10 percent?" How can the Designer provide 10 percent less training? The Designer's response to a suggested cut should be to indicate those objectives that would have to be deleted, requiring fewer lesson plans, less time, and even a lower cost for instructional strategies.

The Designer must be able to identify those budget items that reflect the alternatives. For example, let us look at using an external facility. Should the participants be taken to a local motel or to a conference center? The cost may be significantly different; however, the cost factor is complex. The conference center may include some equipment in the cost, while the motel may charge extra for equipment. On the other hand, the motel may be able to provide food service at a lower cost than the conference center.

The number of participants who might attend a training program is another variable with budget implications. Increasing the number of participants can lower unit cost, if that budget figure is of concern. It can also mean that some people may attend who have no real need for the training. In a large organization, where many programs can be appropriate for large numbers of employees, a budget that shows relative cost based on the numbers participating can be important.

The Designer needs alternative budgets with decision points explicitly shown so the supervisors and managers involved are able to make decisions. However, that does not mean that the Designer should only present the lowest figure or provide a high figure with hidden "padding." Rather, the Designer should provide a range with clear statements as to what is gained or lost at each budget level.

EVALUATION AND FEEDBACK

The objective of this event was to assure that all the necessary resources will be available for the program that has been designed.

As the Designer moves through this event, it becomes clear that this is the point where trade-offs may be necessary, compromises can be explored, and decisions must be made. This event requires involvement of many people from the organization other than the Designer and supervisors who have been involved in earlier events.

Analysis

For this event, the analysis will contain the specifics, such as the listing of resources, schedules, and budgets. The analysis consists of much material that goes beyond the earlier emphasis on learning, and the Designer is well advised to seek the professional help of others in preparing the appropriate analysis.

The analysis includes the lesson plans as backup material, and those plans will be referred to as needed. The objectives, curriculum, and lesson plans may need to be reviewed for limitations on the resources being requested. One way the Designer can prepare is to take each lesson plan and indicate specifically which resources are needed to implement that lesson plan.

If it is determined that resources must be limited, the lesson plan should be altered to reflect this. Reduction in the number of lesson plans is actually the last step in the process, but for some people that may be the place to start.

When resources are limited, the Designer can ask the decision makers to indicate which lessons should be cut. The Designer can then review the process with them and indicate that by reducing some of the curriculum, some objectives would have to be eliminated and some needs will not be met. Too few people see the interaction among these items, and the Designer should indicate this in the analysis as necessary. The availability of resources influence the program, and this can be shown in the analysis.

Scheduling, selection of participants, and identification and preparation of instructors should all be included in the analysis. To the degree possible, people should be listed by name. When the decision is made to start the program, the analysis becomes the basic document that can be used immediately.

Feedback

Because of the wide ranging implications of this event in the organization, many people should receive the analysis and should be involved in the feedback discussions. The specific individuals will depend on how a particular company is organized, so it is up to each Designer to indicate the kinds of people who should receive the analysis and should be involved in the feedback.

The prime person to be involved is still the supervisor(s) of the potential learners. The Designer must never lose sight of the focus of the training, which is to solve a problem. The problem rests in the realm of the supervisor and therefore that person is crucial. Also, the potential learners must be sent by the supervisor. Unless the supervisor can see a benefit from the training program, it is unlikely that he or she will release employees from the work situation.

Budget people are crucial to this event. The Designer must determine who has control of the budget for this particular training program. If the funding is to come from the supervisor's budget, this is another item to be considered by the supervisor during feedback. If the budget is controlled by people other than the supervisor or the HRD manager, these people must also be involved in the feedback on this event. Such people will probably not have been involved earlier, and therefore may need some special material or analysis to understand what prompted the need for the program and the problem that the program has been designed to solve.

At some of the previous events, *managers* (as different from supervisors) have been involved. In the feedback on this event, it is important to once again involve the managers. Because managers are involved in planning, they need to know about this program and how it is likely to relate to their planning or expectations. Managers generally have more control over resources than supervisors do. Because this event is concerned with resources, it is obvious that the involvement of managers is important.

If the program contains heavy demands for instructional resources, the instructional strategies developer should be involved in the feedback. During the discussions, suggestions as to alternative learning approaches will be made, and the instructional materials developer is in a position to react to the implications of these suggestions. That person can also indicate the financial implications of any suggestions that are made. If internal production is required, the presence of the instructional materials developer is mandatory. If purchase is required, the presence of the instructional strategies developer will depend on the kind of involvement he or she has in the purchasing process.

Decisions

Most of the decisions to be made at the termination of this event are made by people other than the Designer. The Designer should provide sufficient information and a number of alternatives so that decisions can be made by others. The Designer will have spent a great deal of time, energy, and professional expertise in designing the program. The people who react to it are more concerned with finances and scheduling. It is very important for the Designer to maintain a perspective and not to overreact to their decisions.

1. Is the cost acceptable?

    Answers to this question will vary depending on who is responding. The budget people might have one answer, while the supervisor another. The final cost figure may represent trade-offs among the various individuals who make the fiscal decisions. During the event, and particularly during feedback, alternative budgets will have been discussed. Trade-offs, revisions, and variations will have been explored. Confusion can be expected, but it should not be allowed to remain. The Designer must be sure that by the end of this event there is no ambiguity about the budget, and that the cost is agreed to by those with the decision-making authority.

2. Will the required physical resources be available when needed?

This relates to budget as well as scheduling. The response to this question must come from all those who would be involved in providing the physical resources, both internally and externally. It seems like the proverbial "Catch 22" or chicken-and-egg dilemma. Which comes first, and what happens next? It may not be possible to finalize the physical arrangements such as the training site without the budget commitment. Yet, without some firm figure from the site people, probably reinforced by a deposit or contract, it may be impossible to provide the budget information required.

When impasses occurs, it is best for the Designer to discuss them so that appropriate and timely decisions can be made. During a time of rapidly rising inflation, delays can cost an unusual amount of money. For some physical resources, the time of year can be a cost factor. All of these things should be discussed so that a timely and appropriate decision can be made.

3. Is there a list of potential learners?

This event should culminate with a list of agreed-upon learners for this program. Realistically this seldom happens. Unfortunately, the final decision as to the actual learners comes just before the program begins. At this point, the Designer has the responsibility to inform all who should know that the closer they can come to a specific listing of learners, the greater the possibility of a successful program.

Quotas for various units may be established and the Designer should be informed of how many people will be sent from each unit. Numbers alone are not sufficient because they do not tell the Designer about the specific needs of the learners. Despite this, the Designer may have to settle for the barest information. If such is the case, the Designer may have to produce an additional introductory learning unit to ascertain whether the needs of those who come to the training are similar to the needs determined in the earlier phase of the CEM. Another alternative is to introduce a pretest to validate the need for the various lessons that have been designed. Of course, this requires a professional instructor who is capable of making the necessary modifications if the need is indicated.

4. Can specific instructors be assigned?

If the instructors are internal, their supervisors should be able to make a firm commitment as to their availability. The need for some "training of instructors" should be evaluated. The Designer should schedule and plan for such learning. Some additional lesson plans may be required for the instructor training program.

When using external instructors, there must be some assurance that qualified individuals will be available. The Designer or the appropriate person in the HRD unit must ascertain whether the identified external instructors will be available and are in agreement with the fiscal arrangements. If the external instructors will need some briefing, or other preparation, a decision should be made about who will do it, how and when. If at all possible, these decisions should be made now. Postponing them will mean additional work at the very outset of the next event.

5. Will the training program, with modification, solve the problem?

The qualifier, "with modification," refers to any changes that may have been made during this event. These changes may require the Designer to backtrack through the entire CEM to the Specify Job Performance event to be sure that the changes do not make the program irrelevant.

Finally, if the program is conducted, will the problem for which it was originally designed be solved? There can be many reasons why a Designer of a well-designed program may still have to respond negatively to this question. For one, there may no longer be a problem. Other factors may have intervened that significantly alter the situation. A common occurrence is a change in personnel, either subordinate or supervisor, and the problem can either change or no longer be a problem. Additional factors may be changes in materials, equipment, regulations, customer mix, and other relevant factors.

In essence, the Designer is once again validating that there is a problem and that the final version of the training program is likely to solve that problem. If that is the case, the program should be conducted.

CONCLUSION

In one sense, this event can be the last for the Designer. From here the program is often handled by someone else, usually the supervisor of HRD programs. The Designer should still be involved in order to obtain feedback on how the design is working. This can be helpful in improving the present program and in using the CEM to design future programs.

In the next event, Conduct Training, the focus will be on how the program is implemented.

CHAPTER 10

Conduct Training

This is the payoff! (See Figure 10-1.) All the work that has previously been done now culminates in the training experience. It is still possible for the Designer to make variations in the design, but most of it should remain as designed to this point.

The objective of this event is to conduct the training program previously designed.

For some programs no variations from the design and lesson plans will be permitted, while for others the lesson plans are expected to serve only as general guidelines with modifications by the instructor in the actual learning situation. As was noted in the previous event, the Designer may now be replaced by a supervisor of programs from the HRD Unit. However, it also possible for the Designer to continue with the program, but his or her activities will change from designing to supervising. The designation of Designer will continue to be used for the person who has responsibility for this event.

If a new person takes over from the previous Designer, they should coordinate their activities. The new person should become familiar with the documentation of the program, including the analysis reports, as well as the decisions made at the completion of each event of the CEM. This may suggest that the Designer should continue on as the supervisor even though the two positions require somewhat different competencies.

Whenever possible, the entire CEM should be double staffed, with the Designer taking the lead and the HRD supervisor being one of the people involved. When that is possible, the transition to this event can be accomplished with little loss in momentum and no loss of the history of the design process of the particular program. Double staffing may be considered a luxury, and therefore has not been included in previous discussions.

191

THE CRITICAL EVENTS MODEL

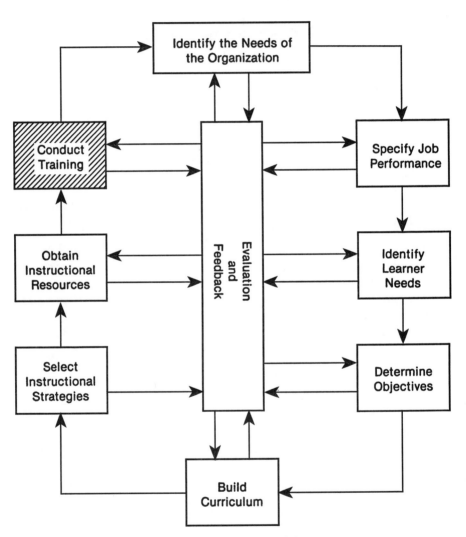

Figure 10-1. Conduct training.

THE PARTICIPANTS

The participants (the potential learners) are crucial to the entire design process. The main reason for providing the training program is to change the performance of the participants in order to solve a problem.

Up to this time, various terms have been used to designate this group, such as subordinates, potential learners, employees, and so on. For this event, the term *participants* will be used.

Selection

The decision about who will be a participant should be made by the supervisor. This may not always happen, but first let us explore the desirable and most common method and then look at the variations.

Because training is problem focused and the supervisor wants to solve problems, the ideal participant group consists of those employees *sent by the supervisor.* In that situation, the supervisor has identified those who need the training in order to solve the problem. This approach appears simple, straightforward, and direct. Hidden within the decision are a number of problems.

If the supervisor sends only those employees who need performance change, training can be viewed as punitive. If the participant comes to the learning situation as a form of punishment, the instructor can expect some form of resistance and even hostility. It can be assumed that the supervisor has explored alternative ways of improving performance, as discussed in earlier events of the CEM, and is finally convinced that training is the appropriate response. One approach is to confirm that the participants accept that decision and are interested in improving their performance.

The selection process is not an isolated incident but a part of the supervisor's total style and the climate of the workplace. If the supervisor has been using a style of participative management, it follows that the participants will be involved in the selection process. However, even with participative management, it is the supervisor who must make the final decision and allocate the necessary resources. Considering the possible punitive aspect of selection, a supervisor might opt to send people who do not necessarily need the training. This is not cost-effective, because those employees who do not need the training cannot be expected to improve their performance.

On the positive side, sending several people from the same work unit to the same training program reinforces performance norms. When several people experience the same learning, they will usually agree upon the performance expected. For the workers with the real need, training can mean a significant change in performance, while for the others it would provide reinforcement. Even for the latter group, there could be some improvement in performance, but it cannot be expected to be significant.

In some training programs the participants are self-selected. That is, participants are allowed to choose programs labeled as "training," although they might be education or development programs. In any event, these programs exist even though the objective for the self-selected participant is not always clear.

Some of these program are frequently offered on the participant's time. They are sometimes labeled as "voluntary" although that term is more closely associated with the broad field of adult education than it is with HRD. Self-selection is apparent when the HRD unit issues bulletins listing course offerings and produces what looks like a college catalogue with predesigned programs that are available to everyone. The process is usually similar to a university situation in which the participants enroll in courses.

Why should a supervisor support this type of program? From the supervisor's viewpoint it is certainly not problem-centered. However, for the supervisor to withhold cooperation can promote the impression that the supervisor is not interested in improving the performance of the subordinates. No supervisor wants to be seen in that light, so the supervisor may sign off on "training requests" even though the program will really be education or development with no direct benefit to the work unit.

The voluntary type of program is not completely negative. If the subordinate feels a need for more learning, the supervisor should recognize this and explore this need further. There are voluntary programs that could improve job performance.

Voluntary programs offered by employers can be beneficial, but they are generally not problem focused and not training oriented. When the program is offered off company time, the participant may not even need the approval of the supervisor. It is completely voluntary and not expected to be training. Some companies still offer training off company time but that practice is not widespread. Some companies offer tuition refund or reimbursement to employees for learning programs taken off company time and offered by outside institutions. This is a desirable practice, but very seldom is it training. This does not mean that companies should not continue and expand the practice of tuition refund. It does mean that they should not expect that practice to solve problems.

Whether sent by the supervisor or self-selected, the participant must know the objectives of the program and the *criteria for being in the learning group*. When sent by the supervisor, the participant should be able to focus on the problem that the training program is expected to solve. If this is not known, the participant has little indication of how the training program is expected to influence or change behavior. Without this mindset, the learning will be less effective.

Needs

When there is a specific list of participants, the Designer should compare those names with those who were involved in the Identify Learner Needs event. If they are the same people, the assumption can be made that the needs are still valid. Because of possible changes, a quick check is desirable. Checking also alerts the participants to the fact that their former responses have influenced the program they are now going to experience, and as a result they are more likely to participate actively.

It may be that those who were involved in the earlier event are not the same as the participants who are actually assigned to the training program. The same needs may still exist, but the Designer should check this out with the supervisor before implementing the program. What makes a real difference is finding that the same problem no longer exists. If that is the situation, then this information should have come to the attention of the Designer before this point. In any case, the program should not start until the Designer is sure the problem still exists and has not significantly changed. This can avoid having the right program for the wrong reasons.

On the other hand, the problem may have been exacerbated since the start of the CEM and may be even more important. There might be an urgency now to improve performance, which did not exist at the outset. In such a case, the need may be the same, but stronger.

Notification of Participants

Although the supervisor may have presented a list of participants, there is no assurance that the participants themselves have received any notification. Unless the procedure, including verification of assignment to training, is well established, participants can receive little or no notice of the training program for which they have been selected. This borders on the ridiculous, but it happens all too often.

There are too many instances when participants arrive for work on a Monday morning and are told to report to the training site. This happens more often when the training site is located some place within the work site than it does when the participant must travel to some off-site location. The responsibility for the notification procedure may rest with the supervisor, but the HRD unit should be involved so the short notice problem is reduced, if not eliminated.

Why should the Designer be concerned about prior notification? One reason is that the absence of one or more people from a work unit is disruptive. It requires shifting assignments, changing work schedules, or even obtaining replacements. The participant may have made some prior appointments (as with salespeople) or may be part of a car pool that is disrupted by a member being assigned to training with different hours or location.

Another reason is there can be the need to prepare oneself for this experience. If the adult learner has had prior negative learning experiences, some counseling or other pretraining activity could be extremely helpful in reducing the fear of failure during learning.

For a supervisor, manager, or executive to be a participant in a training program requires a significant shift in behavior. Those managerial groups are accustomed to having some control over what they do during working hours. Being a participant in a learning group deprives them of this control. Managers are not accustomed to being so constrained and need the opportunity to make the psychological adjustment required by the new constraints. Even the best self-directed learning, with high participant involvement, carries with it some constraints that the manager does not face during the working day. Therefore, prior preparation is important, if not absolutely necessary.

Also, managers have an even greater need to provide backups and alternatives. Managers are generally not as easily replaced as employees at lower levels in the organization.

Good notification procedures are extremely helpful when the participant has to make necessary arrangements. For some people, mere notification can induce anxiety, and prior notification allows time for some of this to subside. It is a good idea, as part of the notification procedure, to provide the participant with a phone number to call or a person to contact who can respond to questions about arrangements and other items that tend to feed the anxiety fire.

The notification procedure should contain a feedback loop, for it is not enough to merely send a notice to the participant. It is important to receive something back from the participant to show that the notice has been received, understood, and that the participant will attend. Also, it legitimizes the participant contacting the appropriate person in the HRD unit to ask questions or to seek help. The person in the HRD unit who is on the receiving end should be more than a clerk who just checks off that a participant called. That call is the first step in establishing the learning climate, which will be discussed later.

Some learning programs require precourse reading or other work. This is a good instructional strategy that makes effective use of the time available for training. The notification procedure should specify the particular assignment as well as provide the materials required by the precourse assignment. If there are any questions, the participant should be able to call on a designated professional in the HRD unit to seek assistance.

FACILITIES, EQUIPMENT, AND MATERIALS

In the previous event, the Designer identified the specific facilities, equipment, and materials that would be needed. At this time, a check should be made to assure that what was previously identified is actually available and, for some items, that they are physically on-site.

A liaison person must be clearly identified. Depending upon the nature and location of the program, this person could be any one of a several individuals including designer, supervisor, program director, aide, or assistant. The last two job titles can provide significant growth opportunities for non-professionals or paraprofessionals.

By effective use of these positions, the HRD unit can provide a career ladder for people who are interested in the field, but who lack experience or academic preparation. Caution should be exercised, however, for in some organizations the person in this position can become the "professional," not as the result of a planned developmental program but as a result of survival. As the professional people move on to other positions or other organizations, the aide remains and eventually through seniority moves into a professional position. The result, predictably, downgrades the HRD unit. It is not that aides cannot become professionals in the HRD field, but this should result from more than mere survival or longevity. However, having responsibility for facilities, equipment, and materials can be a good place to start.

The instructor should know the person assigned as backup for this particular program. If the instructor is experienced and professional, less backup is required than when the instructor is a subject matter specialist with little experience in instruction. The HRD manager must carefully match the backup (program director, and so on) with the particular program and instructor.

It is helpful to develop a checklist of those items to be reviewed. No checklist is provided in this chapter because it is important for each HRD unit to develop its own checklist, which reflects the types of programs, the specific organization, and the other variables of the training program. Books with checklists are listed in the bibliography at the end of this book. Using them as guidelines, the HRD unit should develop its own checklist. Even the process of developing the checklist is important because it can bring to light differing perceptions among the HRD staff. The checklists should not be permanent, but should be reviewed and modified as experience and a particular program dictate.

OPENING THE PROGRAM

The activities related to opening a program are frequently overlooked. The participants have been notified and begin trickling in. The instructor is either in the wings or entering the room, and all is ready to begin—almost. There is no one way to open a program. In some situations, it is appropriate to start immediately with the first lesson. In other situations, some activities should precede the instruction. The pre-instruction activities should be clearly identified before the program begins. Some organizations have a standard opening for all programs, while others provide a guideline and leave it to the individual instructor.

Climate Setting

Now, at the start of the program, climate setting is crucial. It consists of those activities that communicate an attitude conducive to effective learning. More than just taking care of logistics is involved, although by no means is that to be ignored. The purpose of the opening activities is to put the participants at ease and to communicate the specific learning and performance objectives of the program and the nature of the learning activities. Attention is also paid to the physical needs of the learner, such as indicating when breaks will occur, meal times, and similar related matters. Provision is made for responding to the questions and concerns of the participants.

There can be a *formal opening,* but it should not be too lengthy because it can slow down the development of a positive climate for learning. Long speeches should be avoided, although some speeches may be necessary and even desirable. Technology can be used. One large organization uses a video taped message from the president of the corporation. It lasts less than five minutes and a new one is recorded each month to provide an update and to eliminate the possibility that a participant will sit and mutter, "Oh, not again! I've heard this speech five times!" By retaping at least once a month, the tape is always pertinent and communicates the interest of the CEO or other high level official in the training. It also serves to keep that person informed about training programs.

There are other kinds of formal openings, and the specific one to be used should be planned beforehand and selected for its appropriateness to the particular learning situation. It is possible, for example, to open a program with statements from the relevant supervisors about their expectations of performance change as a result of the program.

Some programs are best started by an *informal opening,* which may include a social gathering the evening before the learning program starts. This is desirable when the participants come from different locations and have spent time traveling. The social on the evening before the start of the program provides time for relaxation after travel and increases the possibility that the participants will be alert the following morning. Of course, this means that the social should be limited in alcoholic beverages and that the participants should be encouraged to end the social evening at a reasonable hour.

Another type of informal opening starts on the morning of the initial session of the program with some form of registration. Generally this does not have to be a formal session, but one in which the participants get their materials, name tags (if appropriate), and are provided with refreshments to help in climate setting. This session usually includes coffee and donuts or some similar morning food. Because more and more people are watching their diets and wellness is a corporate as well as an individual goal, the food service can be juice, yogurt, or other identified health foods. This may seem like a small matter, but it sets the climate. However, if there are people who need coffee for a "wake-me-up," or who have ritualized their morning food (they eat exactly the same kind of food each morning), do not try to break the norm.

The decision to have such an informal climate setting experience depends to a good degree on the cultural behavior in the organization. Such an opening may be appropriate for certain levels in the organization and not for others. This may not seem democratic, but violating a cultural norm will not help to produce a successful learning experience. When the pre-session social, as described earlier, is chosen as the climate setting experience, there should be a sensitivity to the cultural norm regarding liquor. Some organizations forbid liquor on the premises. If that is the case, the Designer may find that this restriction persists even with off-premise company sponsored activity.

One opening activity that can be either formal or informal is the dinner the night before the opening. Once again, this activity is used more frequently for managerial levels, and particularly when the participants come from a variety of locations. The dinner can be a banquet where higher level officials of the organization join the participants for the opening experience only. It can also be a gathering in the coffee shop with participants ordering from the menu.

Whatever the opening activities may be, it is important that the Designer make provision for them in the budget. They are legitimate and necessary expenses connected with the training.

When the learning program starts, a member of the HRD unit or the instructor should give the participants some essential information. This information on logistical matter such as parking, emergency telephone numbers, and expense reimbursement forms can be supplemented by handouts. It is preferable that these administrative matters be taken care of before instruction starts.

Starting a session with these logistic items can set a tone that is rigid and bureaucratic. For this reason it is preferable for someone other than the instructor to provide this information. If possible, the information should be given to the participants with other handouts, but they should be given time to read the material. Some participants are not ready to learn until they have some information about expenses, telephone numbers, and similar items. Sending the information out with the program notification, discussed earlier, is one way of getting it to the participants without interfering with the start of the session. If a participant has questions, pre-session distribution limits the opportunity to obtain answers. One way to handle this is to devote the first half hour to these items and follow that with a short break just to change the climate before starting the training.

The design of the learning program influences the opening. Early in the session, if not at the very beginning, participants need to know at least three important items. The first one is the *objectives* of the program, or the desired result of the training. Each lesson will have its own objectives, but at this point the participants should be given the program objectives identified during the Determine Objectives events. They should also be told what performance change is expected.

The second item the participants should know is the *requirements* of the course. The participants should know what is expected in terms of attendance, participation, outside learning assignments, and any other requirements that are either specified or implied by the lesson plans.

The last item the participants should know is the *mutual expectations*. What does the instructor expect of the learner, and what can the learner expect of the instructor? Mutual expectations establish that the learning is a participative activity, with all parties having mutual responsibilities and expectations. The more these can be identified early in the program, the greater the possibility from the outset for positive learning.

OPERATING THE PROGRAM

Once the program actually starts, the instructor should not be left to flounder if any problems arise. Indeed, problems are always a possibility. The oft repeated Murphy's Law "If anything can go wrong, it will" applies to training programs as well as to many other aspects of life. But to the original maxim should be added, "And, it will probably be worse than you thought!" This statement is not meant to be pessimistic or to cast aspersions on the instructor. Things can go wrong, and the instructor may have little or nothing to do with the causes. It is not important during the program to determine blame. It is necessary to keep the program going at the optimum level, and then later to analyze the situation so that breakdowns will not be repeated.

The Instructor

The instructor is only human and there are many things that can happen. At the outset, the instructor may not show up. The reason should be determined, but not while the participants are waiting for the program to begin.

There should always be a backup position, particularly for the first session of the program. Someone should be present from the HRD staff to be sure the program starts properly. After that, the participants should be notified about whom to contact if there are any problems, including the no-show of an instructor. Of course, the instructor should also have this information and has the responsibility to notify the HRD unit if there is the possibility of a "no-show." This is not always possible. If the instructor is on the road and has a flat tire, and no phone in the car, there is very little chance to notify the HRD unit. There must be a contingency plan for such events.

Other situations can prevent the instructor from continuing the program. The first obligation of the HRD unit is to see that a satisfactory substitute is available. The second is to determine whether the reason for the absence is sufficient cause to request that the instructor not be used again.

An infrequent but possible occurrence is that an instructor becomes ill during the program. As long as *human instructors* are used, this is always a possibility. The instructor should know whom to notify, but the HRD unit should have alternatives available. For some programs, the illness or absence of the instructor can be handled by rescheduling or by using an alternative learning unit of the training program, but in some cases, the lack of an instructor requires canceling the session. If the HRD unit knows this early enough, it might be possible to notify the participants.

Canceling the session should be the last alternative. Once it is done, it will influence the attendance of the participants for the remainder of the program. If the instructor can be absent, why not the participants?

Materials and Equipment

Despite all the plans, something can always go wrong in the area of materials and equipment. Some of the common problems follow.

• Wrong materials

The material arrives in packages and is not opened until the program begins. Then, it is found that the package label does not agree with the contents and it is not what is required for the lesson. The packages should be checked out prior to the start of the program, but that may not always be possible. The instructor should be advised to check before the start of the session and to notify the HRD unit immediately if the materials are not what is needed.

• Insufficient copies

As a general rule, the instructor should request extras of materials. If there are 25 participants, it is customary to have more than 25 copies of materials. This allows for any damaged, incorrectly assembled, or otherwise unusable materials. Despite this planning, the instructor may find that there are not enough copies. Years ago this was considered a tragedy or panic situation. Currently, with copying facilities so readily available, this is not quite so critical. The instructor should be able to call the HRD unit for more copies and get them quickly. As a follow-up, the HRD staff should determine the reason for the shortage, so as to minimize the possibility of a recurrence.

• Equipment not functioning

It is generally acknowledged that it is necessary to have spare bulbs for projectors, but despite the constant warning, it is not uncommon to find equipment without a spare. Some of the newer overhead projectors have been designed with a spare bulb built into the machine, which is activated by a mere flick of a switch.

For other equipment, such as the VCR, malfunctioning equipment is a more difficult problem and may require the services of a skilled, or at least an experienced, individual. All equipment should be checked beforehand by the HRD staff and it is helpful to provide instructors with at least some minimal training in dealing with anticipated malfunctions.

Other equipment problems can be more serious, and the instructor should be advised when to call the HRD unit rather than to attempt on-the-spot repair work. The damage done to equipment at that point may render it totally useless and consume valuable session time. The instructor, generally, is not expected to be able to repair equipment.

The Program Director

As indicated earlier, each training program should have one person from the HRD unit who is responsible for that program. Although the Designer may still be involved, the action shifts to the program director. The instructor and the participants should be informed who that individual is, where to call or to find that individual, and what the responsibilities of that person are.

The program director should make periodic visits to the learning site, not to supervise, but to determine personally that things are progressing as planned. These visits provide the instructor with a direct and constant link and indicate to the participants the continuing interest of the HRD staff.

In some situations, the program director and the Designer are the same person. Generally this is an ineffective way to use the competencies required of the Designer. However, when they are not the same person, the program director should be in contact with the Designer. The program director should communicate problems to the Designer, rather than merely complain or be critical of what appear to be inadequacies in program design. If this is not done, there should be no surprise when some of the same problems persist in future programs. A program director usually is responsible for many programs and should have a system for keeping a record of visits and of suggestions for improvement. These suggestions will generally be about physical problems because training will be reviewed through evaluation and other mechanisms.

When an external facility is being used, the program director is probably the person who negotiated and made the arrangements. It would, therefore, be the responsibility of the program director to see that the facility met the agreed-upon specifications.

The Participant

The program director should do everything possible to assure that participants are not diverted from the learning. If a participant is concerned about factors related to the job, family conditions, or other problems, it is more difficult to learn. The program director is not required to know all the problems of the participant, but he or she should be aware of those that can influence the learning situation. The program director should avoid having the learning program add additional problems.

One problem of participants is receiving messages while in a training session. This may seem like an unimportant factor until a person has been in a training session and could not be reached. It is not unrealistic for a participant to wonder whether someone is trying to get in touch. Time spent worrying about messages is time taken from the learning situation.

As technology changes so does this potential problem. It is important that all beepers and personal phones be kept inactive during a training session. This can only be enforced if alternatives are built into the management of the program. There are many ways to handle messages and the least desirable is to put a participant in a position of being "incommunicado." That can make training seem like punishment and deprivation of rights. Almost all executives and managers expect to be constantly accessible by phone no matter how loudly they complain about intrusion.

A message board should be positioned so each participant can see it when leaving the room for a break or meals. Dire emergencies still require a more immediate response, but most participants do not experience too many such emergencies in the course of their daily lives.

Participants can also become ill. They should not be made to suffer or feel inadequate. If the training is away from the work site, the participant should be informed of provisions for dealing with illness. With more artificial medical devices in general use (from contact lenses to pacemakers), program directors should provide for emergencies related to those items.

EVALUATING THE PROGRAM

The Build Curriculum event, noted that the Designer constructs the necessary evaluation instruments to be used during the conduct of the program. Evaluation should be conducted at several points in the program and this type of *formative* evaluation allows the instructor to determine whether the appropriate learning is taking place.

At the end of the program, the *summative* evaluation should take place. Its results cannot be used to alter the program already conducted, but are very useful for future programs. The data collected by the summative and formative evaluation are crucial particularly if the present program is to be repeated with other participants.

Pretests and *posttests* may also be used. The pretest may have been conducted before the participant arrived at the program as part of the precourse work. The more common practice, however, is to administer the pretest at the opening of the program. This must be handled carefully because it can conflict with the climate setting and produce a negative effect. During the program other tests can be given, but the most crucial is the posttest. This is akin to the final examination.

The posttest can provide evaluation only of the learning, not of job performance. A good posttest should be as close to the expected job performance as possible, but it is still possible to evaluate only learning. Job performance cannot be evaluated until the participant returns to the job and is asked to perform. At that time, the evaluation is made by the supervisor, although the supervisor should be encouraged to share this evaluation with HRD staff.

Ethical considerations are involved in evaluating the programs we have been discussing. The participants in training situations are usually not voluntary, and they are sent to a training program to achieve a specific goal related to their work in the organization.

Even if voluntary, what the participants learn relates directly to their present job (training) or to a future job for which they are preparing (education) within a company. Because the company pays the bill, is the company entitled to know what they received for their money? Of course, but the company is not a disembodied ethereal being. The company is made up of flesh and blood people with whom the participant works. Generally in this situation "company" means the supervisor who is directly concerned with training. Naturally the supervisor wants to be able to justify the use of the physical and financial resources that have been made available to the participant through the HRD activity.

There is nothing wrong with reporting test scores or other evaluation to the supervisor and/or manager. If this is to be done, however, the participant should know this before the program begins. The instructor also needs to know of this requirement and it should be clearly stated when taking the assignment. If the instructor has any ethical reservations, feels it violates confidentiality, or will get in the way of the learning, he or she should note that before accepting the assignment.

Of course, the Designer should have determined this at some earlier event. The type of evaluation, the form of the tests, and the manner of feedback will all be influenced by the need to report these data to the supervisors and managers. The evaluation data, in whatever way it is gathered, is an essential part of the E&FB process.

CLOSING THE PROGRAM

The closing is as important, particularly for climate setting, as the opening was. The program should not be allowed to wind down slowly and end with confusion. This often happens when an evaluation is administered, with the instruction to "leave when you are finished." The result is that people go out one at a time, whisper to the instructor or other participants and try to leave with the least amount of noise. The result is depressing and leaves a negative last image with the participants.

The closing should be well planned and include some closing activity. It is not always necessary to have a banquet or elaborate ceremony, but there should be an identifiable activity that denotes the successful culmination of this learning experience. The impression should be conveyed that the next step is the anticipated change in performance.

Recognition for Participants

Most people seek recognition. There is nothing wrong with that, and it should be part of a learning program and handled with taste and foresight. No one form of recognition is appropriate for all programs and participants. Rather, the form of recognition that is preferable is one that is consistent with the organization and observable to all who need to know.

One of the most common practices is to award *certificates*. If the Designer has graduated from a university, particularly with an advanced degree, he or she may have a tendency to scoff at certificates. A Designer may already have more of certificates than can possibly be put up on the walls. However, such is not the case for everyone.

For some people, a certificate is important. A study done several years ago found that participants often framed certificates and hung them on the walls. At that time, training was not as common as it is today. It would be interesting to determine how many participants of previous programs have retained their certificates and what they did with them. The Designer can never go wrong in awarding a certificate, even if the participant chooses to do no more than file it away. Even if the participant throws it away, after leaving the training site, the Designer will still have fulfilled this responsibility of awarding the participant the certificate.

If a formal certificate is inappropriate, some other *written document* may still be used. This could be a letter from a high-level company official or other written notice that the participant has successfully completed the program. It is necessary that "successfully" be defined so that certificates and other documents are not given to participants who did not meet at least some specified minimum requirements. Attendance is one of the common criteria for successful completion.

The certificate should not merely be distributed at the last session of the program, but some appropriate *ceremony* should accompany the distribution. It need not be elaborate, and making it a big affair could be ludicrous. The ceremony should be appropriate to the organization, the nature of the program, and the level of the participants.

Supervisors and managers should be involved. Those who will look for performance change should be involved in the closing ceremony. Such attendance encourages the participants to take the training back to the job and to try to produce the desired performance change.

Recognition for Instructors

Too often the instructor is ignored in the recognition activity. If the instructor is *external,* perhaps the major form of recognition is payment. It is doubtful if people become instructors only for the financial rewards. Being a good instructor requires more time, effort, and creative energy than can usually be reflected merely in financial return. Instructors have ego needs, and generally, seek psychological return.

Recognition for the external instructor is usually best given outside the regular closing ceremony because it can detract from the recognition for the participants. A letter of appreciation from the HRD manager is certainly appropriate. If there is an instructor evaluation instrument, and there should be, the results of this should be shared with the external instructor.

When the instructor is *internal,* but not part of the HRD unit, specific recognition is extremely crucial. Those instructors generally do not receive any additional compensation. They may even have to make sacrifices in their regular assignments in order to successfully instruct in the program. Recognition for them should include a report sent to their supervisors particularly when the final evaluation by the participants includes laudatory comments.

Some organizations find it useful to recognize internal instructors through an annual ceremony, usually coupled with a luncheon, banquet, or similar function. At that time, high-level company officials should be present and one of the psychological benefits for the instructors is the opportunity to mix with people at those levels.

For both internal and external instructors, certificates are sometimes awarded. They are not the same as those given to the participants, but are specially prepared for instructors. Those certificates may be less meaningful to the external instructor than to the internal person. The external person generally has already received those kinds of paper recognition. The internal instructor, particularly if he or she is a non-professional who is not in the HRD unit, will appreciate the recognition. In addition, the certificate can signify an additional competency for the recipient as well as recognition for having contributed to the success of the organization.

Accountability for Equipment and Supplies

Unfortunately, there is no ceremony or certificate for being accountable for equipment and supplies. It is just part of the job. It is usually the program director or someone assigned by the HRD manager who must take charge before the participants and the instructor depart. This could be the same person who has the responsibility for the closing ceremonies and the preparation of the appropriate certificates. There must be at least one person with those specific responsibilities.

That person checks all the equipment to verify that it is returned to the proper storage or rental facility. The unused materials may be retrieved, particularly if they represent a significant expense item. The training facility is checked to make sure that the participants have not left anything behind. All this may seem mundane, but if the details are not covered, the result can be much wasted effort at a later time and even panic when equipment and materials disappear.

This closing activity should be carefully organized so as not to interfere with the climate set during the closing and should be handled as a normal occurrence without undue activity. Effective preparation for this as part of program design will enable the program director to terminate the program on a positive and successful note.

EVALUATION AND FEEDBACK

The objective of this event is to conduct the training program previously designed.

Although the program that was designed has now been conducted, evaluation and feedback are still necessary. It is possible that the actual conduct of the training program was mainly the responsibility of a supervisor of programs or a program director, but now the Designer must once again become active.

Analysis

The analysis of this event must be carefully planned because it survives as the written record of the training program. Some Designers choose to have the analysis contain a brief historical record of what happened in the design process and at each event of the CEM and also include some of the decisions that were made as the culmination of those events. There is no doubt that this is useful, but it may be of no interest to those who are concerned only with the end result of the training—the job performance.

If the historical data are important, the Designer is advised to present this either as an appendix to the analysis or as a separate document to be made available to those who have an interest or a need to know.

The most important part of the analysis is *What have the learners learned?* This information can be reported in a variety of ways and usually involves some statistical presentations. The Designer should avoid using the analysis reports as a way of indicating a competency in statistics. What is most important is that those who are expected to read the analysis should clearly understand what took place. If statistics are necessary, and they may be, they should be presented in clear terms, with accompanying definitions as required. The end result of the learning should be stated clearly, so that the reader does not have to wonder about the meaning of a particular number or table.

The evaluation may only be of the learning, although the basic purpose of training is change in job performance. At a later time, the HRD unit should be invited or at least allowed to follow up the learners on the job. At that time, a supplemental report could be written. At the completion of the training program, however, the Designer can only report on how the level of learning achieved is likely to affect job performance.

The analysis should also contain any recommendations for improving the training program if it is to be offered again. Those recommendations should not be limited only to the lesson plans and instructional strategies, but should reflect each event of the CEM. For example, the objectives may be changed or the curriculum content modified in some way. Such recommendations should be made at this time so they can be reviewed and be available for future offerings of this program. This is particularly crucial if the first offering was specifically done as a pilot.

It is also helpful to use this opportunity to review the use of the CEM. The Designer may include recommendations for using the CEM when designing future programs. For example, the Designer may recommend the levels of personnel who should be involved in E&FB in future design efforts. Or, the Designer may recommend how the Identify Learner Needs event could be improved. The analysis report provides the Designer with a mechanism for having the organization look at the design process, as reflected in the CEM, as well as at a specific program.

Feedback

The feedback report should be shared as widely as company policy and individual privacy permit. If the evaluation proves to be negative, that is, insufficient learning took place, it could be detrimental to provide for an extensive distribution. It is not that the Designer need be ashamed, but it could prove embarrassing to participants, supervisors, instructors, and even be considered a violation of implied trust in the training situation. Negative results should not be ignored, but the distribution of those results must be handled with great care.

Even for a successful program, one in which the learning objectives were met completely as indicated by the evaluation, there could be some hesitancy about a wide distribution. The supervisors involved, for example, may not want others to know of their problems. The participants, particularly those who may have done less well than others, may consider such information a violation of their privacy. If negative feelings are engendered by the feedback of the analysis report, the Designer can anticipate less cooperation in future design efforts.

To avoid these kind of complications, the Designer should ascertain during the design process if the results of the training are to be made public. If not, there is virtually no problem. If they are to be made public, this should be known to the participants before the program begins and they may even be given the option not to attend such a program. Of course, that option could lead to various kinds of implications. It is a touchy question and should be explored in detail prior to this event.

Decisions

Although there are few actual decisions to be made at this point, some questions should be asked.

1. Does it appear that the results of the program solved the initial problem?

   At this time, at the conclusion of the training program, this answer can only be based on conjecture and projection. The final answer cannot be known until the participants have returned to their jobs and are given the opportunity to apply the learning. It is possible, however, to ask supervisors and others for their perceptions of the success of the program as compared to the purpose for which it was designed.

2. Is there a need to repeat this program?

   This question should asked when this has been a pilot program for one group and is being considered for use with other groups of employees with similar needs. It may also be necessary to repeat a program because not all employees with the needs could be accommodated in one program. It is also possible, particularly when the program has been successful, to find that other supervisors now feel that such a program would be of benefit to their people.

3. If the program is repeated, are modifications required?

   The same training program used with another group of participants may require some modifications. It should not be necessary, of course, to repeat the entire CEM for a new group, but some of the events may have to be reworked.

   The problems of a new group may be similar but not identical, and some minor design modifications (objectives, curriculum, instructional strategies) of this program could be appropriate for others in the organization. Because it is a different group of learners, particular attention may have to be paid to identifying learner needs. A mistake made too often is to take a successful program for one group of learners, conduct it for a different group, and then find that the differences in the learners was extremely significant.

CONCLUSION

The Designer is now at the end of the CEM, or at least at the end of the use of the CEM for this particular design project.

It should be recognized that the design process has been presented as if the Designer works on one design project at a time. In reality, most Designers have many projects in the works at the same time. When that is the situation, a Designer may find it helpful to use the CEM diagram as a flowchart or a status board. Each separate program can be listed and tracked on a different CEM chart that enables the Designer and others to know the exact status of each program being designed.

As a Designer becomes more competent in using the CEM, it is expected that the Designer will find short cuts and helpful ways of working with the model. That is not unusual. Indeed, it is expected when one uses an open model. The Designer should feel free to make variations and changes in nomenclature, decision questions, and other elements of the CEM to more appropriately reflect the particular organization.

As each of us grows professionally, we tend to change. Using models enables us to see how we are changing and where we need to develop additional competencies.

This is the last chapter to deal directly with the CEM for training.

Chapter 11

Support Systems for Training

The CEM is complete and the training experience designed and delivered. It might be assumed that the work of the Designer is also complete, and in one sense it is, because a training program has been successfully designed. However, the Designer is also concerned with solving the original problem and that requires something beyond the design process discussed so far. It includes some other activities that will involve different parts of the organization in the design, delivery, and application of the training program.

Allow us a small digression at this point, to share how the concept discussed in this chapter evolved. We believe that it will be helpful, and perhaps serve to encourage others to engage in similar explorations and application of ideas as they emerge.

During the 1950s and 1960s in the U.S., there was concern within the HRD community about the apparent lack of success of some training programs. Although they were well-designed and well-conducted, the programs seemed to have little effect on the work situation. One response to this problem was the emergence of "organization development" (OD) which owed some of its underpinnings to community development. Proponents of this concept found that an individual with new behaviors would be unable to use them if the community did not accept those new behaviors. Translated into the workplace, it meant that an employee could learn new behaviors in a training program, but unless the work environment supported those new behaviors, no change in performance would occur.

The early attempts in OD focused on the "critical mass" approach, which assumed that if a sufficient number of employees went through a training program, the possibility for performance change was more likely. The critical mass approach was sometimes useful, but it was also extremely costly. It encouraged sending employees to training programs that were not related to their individual needs. It attempted to create a climate of change through mass numbers rather than specific actions.

Since those early days, OD has changed in many ways. The problem, however, still appeared to be with us in the 1960s. During that decade, the U.S. government mounted several national programs to help the disadvantaged enter the work force. Towards the end of that decade, the *Harvard Business Review* asked us to do a study to see if we could identify which company practices contributed to the success of those programs [76]. Although we studied mostly educational programs rather than training, a pattern began to emerge. We pursued this further in training programs with a variety of different populations and objectives, and it was from that that we developed a concept and a model that we labeled *Support Systems*. We do not claim that we were the first or only HRD group to identify this aspect of organizational behavior. Unfortunately, however, too little research and writing has been done on the specific actions an organization should take to support its training programs.

The model we developed and modified over the years is presented in Figure 11-1. By constantly using the model and teaching about it, we have gained more experience and have slightly changed the model from its original form. Subsequent research by others [6] has also strengthened the basic model.

Underlying the Support Systems model is the difference between *commitment* and *involvement*.

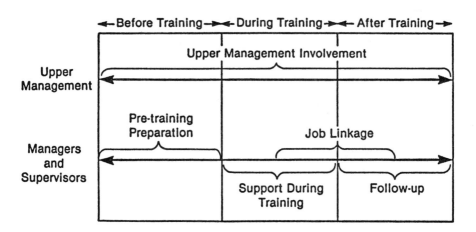

Source: Broad, Mary. "Identification of Management Actions to Support Utilization of Training on the Job." Unpublished Ed.D. dissertation. School of Education and Human Development, The George Washington University, 1980. Reprinted with permission.

Figure 11-1. Support systems model.

Commitment is a promise. It is generally a statement, a speech, or some other verbal activity frequently made when someone in upper management talks about training. Although a commitment is good to hear, it is far from sufficient—it is talk, not action. It is a start, but until a commitment moves to the next level it is only a good intention.

Involvement is action that consists of some kind of observable behavior related to a particular topic or goal. Involvement takes the promise of commitment and makes it a reality.

The difference between commitment and involvement can frequently be seen when a nonprofit organization holds a drive and asks for donations. The organization receives many promises (commitments), but it does not always get an equivalent amount of money (involvement). Of course, commitment does not pay the bills—good intentions are fine, but not enough.

The actions discussed in this chapter focus on observable behavior that should take place to support a training program. They will, of course, vary from one organization to another. The model presented is based on five action areas with specific actions for each area. It is up to the Designer to determine which of those actions are appropriate for the particular training program and to add others that are not included here.

UPPER MANAGEMENT INVOLVEMENT

It is always difficult to be specific about levels of management. In a *hierarchal* organization, it is possible to draw a line someplace on the organization charts and be specific. In a *flat* organization that has few levels of management or a *matrix* organization that draws from various parts of the organization for tasks and projects, upper management can be more difficult to identify. Many other forms of organization exist and new ones are constantly emerging.

In this model, upper level management starts with the CEO and stops somewhere around what is generally termed "middle management." The Designer will have to make that determination for the particular organization.

Upper management is not concerned with the day-to-day operations of the organization and this includes training programs. However, there are several important steps that upper management should take to support training programs in the organization. These actions follow.

Name appropriate personnel to the training design committee

In some organizations the Designer works alone, however, the CEM emphasizes the need for the Designer to work with others. A specific small Design Committee would be extremely helpful in the design process. When upper management asks that a Design Committee be formed, they indicate their involvement in the training program.

The people appointed to this committee should be carefully selected, and their appointments should be announced publicly. There should be no doubt about who is on that committee and that they have been appointed by upper management. When the appointment comes from upper management, it signifies that the committee members will be provided with the time and resources they need to participate in the design activity.

Participate in a preview of training programs

Although upper level managers are not directly involved in most training programs, they should make some time available to participate in reviewing some programs, particularly some of the E&FB activities.

Upper management is not expected to be involved in all the EF&B in any particular program or even a single E&FB event in every training program. But the Designer should look for those training programs where upper management might be encouraged to participate.

Another way the Designer can get such involvement is to arrange for briefing sessions in which the major elements of several training programs can be discussed, with emphasis on the ways those programs can solve organizational problems.

As will be seen later in this model, a pre-training phase occurs when managers and supervisors (lower levels of management) are provided with specifics on selected training programs. The Designer should encourage those lower level managers to invite their own upper level managers to this pre-training..

Issue statements on new performance levels expected following training

Because training is concerned with performance, changes in performance are expected as a result of the training. The Designer, working with others, will have identified the desirable performance changes during the CEM. It would be helpful to have upper management confirm some of those performance changes.

For example, if upper management is concerned with quality, then the Designer should endeavor to have them confirm the quality standards that will result from the training program. Statements from upper management will merely confirm what has already been determined, but the source of the message can do a great deal to assure that performance change takes place.

Require attendance at training for certain categories of employees

Too few organizations have policy statements regarding HRD in general and training specifically. The intent of this upper management action is to reinforce the idea that training opportunities should be made available, as needed, to all employees in the organization and, once an employee has been selected, attendance is required and expected by upper management.

Authorize release time or change working hours to allow participation in training

One component of HRD is to establish a definite period of time. This action statement for upper management underscores the need for time to be specifically allocated for training.

Most training programs take place within the organization and a specific policy is needed and it should be backed up by the necessary resources. Employees must be released from their regular duties to participate in a training program. When shifts are involved or alternative work scheduling (for example, flex-time), upper management should make sure that provision has been made for those employees to participate in training.

The actual schedule for training should be worked out by the HRD unit, including the Designer and the supervisors. The authorization from upper management is an important part of that negotiation.

Provide appropriate physical facilities for training programs

Upper management has a responsibility to see that the financial resources are made available so that the necessary physical facilities for training are obtainable. "Appropriate physical facilities" is purposely non-specific because upper management should not be concerned with the specifics. That is the task of the HRD manager, who should receive suggestions from the Designer.

If upper management does not make the necessary provision, this can communicate a lack of involvement in training to the entire organization. Providing for physical facilities does more than just support the training programs, it indicates upper management's support for training programs.

Provide for written notification for selection for training

The selection of an employee for training is generally within the purview of the individual supervisor. However, upper management can show support for this action, and that support can communicate several things to the individual who is selected as well as to the whole organization.

First, it communicates that upper management is aware of and supports the decision to provide training. Further, it conveys to everyone that upper management has an interest in their employees. The tone and content of the written communication should indicate that perspective. Such a communication reinforces the decision of the supervisor to provide training and indicates that upper management is aware of the involvement of the supervisor in training programs.

Approve the use of confidential organizational data as resources for training

This action is not designed to indiscriminately open organization files, but it should keep the Designer and the training program from being stymied by bureaucracy. Recall the incident in an earlier chapter in which the organization had an extensive and well-developed performance appraisal system, but the data could not be shared with the Designer. This upper management action addresses that problem.

The Designer should not be given access to the entire performance appraisal of a potential learner, but should certainly be authorized to see the part that relates to learner needs. Upper management should approve the release of such data so the Designer is not forced to fight the system.

Another reason for this action occurs when upper management has plans that will cause changes in jobs and performance. As discussed earlier in this book, those changes frequently generate training needs. Accordingly, some parts of that confidential data should be made available to the Designer early enough in the CEM to enable the Designer to produce the appropriate training program. That data can also have an impact on training programs the Designer is currently working on.

Participate in one or more training sessions

The involvement of upper management can be evidenced by physical presence. Everyone knows that upper management are busy people, but attendance at carefully selected sessions of training programs will communicate involvement. If possible, their presence should be for more than a two-minute talk or a visit to the back of the training room.

The Designer and upper management can identify those training programs in which upper management participation is not only desirable but essential. A specific role can be identified for upper management and they can be given an appropriate briefing on the participation expected from them.

Not all programs require the direct participation of upper management, but these managers can be involved in climate setting and in the closing ceremonies. If the climate setting includes an informal social, the presence of upper management will certainly communicate their interest. At closing ceremonies, someone from upper management might distribute the certificates or make appropriate closing remarks.

Meet with HRD unit to discuss ways to apply new performance

Just as upper management should participate in selected sessions, they should also participate in selected activities in the CEM. Frequently, these sessions will occur during E&FB. By meeting with the Designer and other HRD staff, upper management can gain a better grasp of some of the training programs and indicate their own thinking about expected performance. The HRD manager should also encourage upper management to include some managers/supervisors in those meetings. It will reinforce the involvement of upper management in training.

Provide for salary increase on return to the job after a successful training program

This action can be controversial. Although it can reinforce the benefits of training, it can also communicate some other factors. For example, if the training program was needed because of poor performance, then it is not helpful to reward learners for doing what they should have been doing before the training. When, however, the training contributes significantly to an increase in quality and/or quantity above what is expected, some reward system would be appropriate.

It is possible, however, to identify those programs in which a salary increase would be appropriate. One example would occur when a new process or equipment is introduced. Upon completion of that program, it is expected that performance will have changed and the organization will benefit from those changes. These benefits can be shared through salary increases in some equitable manner.

Authorize production differentials for trainees for short periods back on the job

This action addresses an interesting and often overlooked performance factor. When training is complete and a learner has achieved an acceptable level of performance, the general assumption is that this performance can immediately be transferred to the worksite. That may not be the case.

The protected environment of the training situation should have allowed the learner to explore new behaviors and to perform in ways different from those expected on the job. When the learner returns to the job, he or she tries to integrate the new learning into regular job performance. For a brief period of time during this integration process, performance may be lower than anticipated. This possibility should be recognized by upper management and the policy established to allow for that possible drop in performance. The specific limits and the application of that stated policy will be the concern of the supervisor.

The actions stated above are examples of ways in which upper management can demonstrate involvement in training. The specifics of each action will have to be explored in each situation by the HRD manager and the designer.

The next sections of this chapter deal with managers and supervisors (Figure 11-1).

MANAGERS AND SUPERVISORS INVOLVEMENT IN PRE-TRAINING

The actions by managers and supervisors should be directed to a specific training program. The HRD manager should encourage some of these actions, while the Designer should build others into the program.

These actions are not those of the Designer, but rather the actions of the supervisor. This means that the Designer must be able to work with the supervisor, provide some guidance, and recognize that the final decision on any action is the one the supervisor makes.

The term "supervisor" in this case is used to denote both the manager and the supervisor. The actions listed and discussed here are only some of those that supervisors should consider during the pre-training phase, that is, during the CEM before the Conduct Training event.

Participate actively in the design of the training program

This action has been emphasized repeatedly in the CEM and provision for this participation is built into E&FB in each event. Rather than repeat that material here, the Designer can return to the earlier pages of this book and identify some of the specific actions that supervisors can take.

The Designer can create a list of all those actions, recognizing that not every one is applicable for each supervisor or for each training program. Such a list can be helpful however in keeping the Designer aware of the need for identifying those specific participative actions.

Participate actively in the selection of internal instructors

This is being re-emphasized here because it is an area in which supervisors are very seldom asked to participate. Internal instructors are those employees of the organization who are not in the HRD unit, but who are used as instructors. Their basic jobs in the organization are *not* as instructors, so careful attention must be paid to this assignment.

Generally, the selection will occur in the Obtain Instructional Resources event, but indications of who can be an instructor may surface much earlier in the CEM. The Designer should develop the criteria for an instructor, and these criteria can begin to evolve very early in the CEM. For example, it may become apparent that a person used as a subject matter specialist in the Specify Job Performance event might serve as an instructor during the conduct of the program.

Care must be exercised that this instructional assignment is not viewed in any way as being a way to use a non-productive employee. Rather, assignment as an instructor should be seen as recognition and reward for high performers in the area related to the objectives of the training program. The announcement should be made in the most positive manner. It is preferable that a variety of qualified people seek such assignments. Being an instructor should not be considered as a way of getting out of work, but rather of working harder in an area where one can make an additional contribution to the organization and to one's career in the organization.

Selecting an instructor brings up the issue of training the instructor. As needed, supervisors should make adequate provision for the potential instructor's release from other duties for this training. The Designer should help the supervisor realize that such an assignment has benefits for the supervisor as well as for the assigned employee. The employee-instructor will return to the work unit with additional skills that can be helpful to the supervisor in carrying out other job training responsibilities and other instructional work at the job site.

Participate actively in selecting employees for training

As training is focused on problems and opportunities for employees in their present jobs, it is quite obvious that the supervisors must be involved in selecting those who will need the training. To reinforce this, the supervisor must take an active part in the selection process. For example, the supervisor should take the lead role in setting the criteria for selecting those to be trained.

In some situations, an Individual Development Plan (IDP) may be one of the criteria used by a supervisor to make that selection. The IDP, of course, will have been developed with the participation of the supervisor.

It is possible that the performance appraisal filled out by the supervisor indicates the need for training. It is not necessary for the supervisor to share all of the performance appraisal with the Designer. It would be extremely helpful, however, if the supervisor were to share that part that relates to the specific training program.

The Designer should urge the supervisor as part of selection to discuss the objectives of the program with the potential learner. As appropriate, the Designer might be part of that discussion. Of course, when a large number of employees are to be trained, the Designer will not have the time to sit in on all those discussions, but it would be helpful for the supervisor to invite the Designer to some of them.

In the selection process, the supervisor should use the program and learning objectives identified in the CEM. Those objectives should be shared with the learners being considered for selection.

Discuss training plans with union officials representing employees to be selected for training

This action, of course, would only apply if there was a union contract. Little reference has been made here to the role of unions. If the union is a significant factor in a particular organization, the Designer may have included union representation in some of the events. That is essentially a management decision.

At one time unions in the U.S. indicated only a slight interest in training and insisted that it not be used as a tactic for weakening the union or the contract. Generally, this attitude has changed because unions have recognized that training can improve job performance, which benefits both the union and management.

Designers are finding that it can be helpful to involve union leaders in training with management approval. The union leadership's lack of trust is partly due to history and partly due to an inadequate level of communication about training. Discussing a training program with union leadership provides an opportunity for a nonconfrontational meeting between management and the union leadership.

Notify employees of selection for training

The notification must be clear and specific and consistent with any notification from upper management. The supervisor however should provide more details to the employee.

The supervisor should provide notification, both oral and written, emphasizing the positive aspects of being selected for training—that training is being provided to solve a problem and improve performance. The communication must not contain any statement that suggests the training program is any kind of punishment. The manager and supervisor must communicate that this training is for the benefit of the individual, the work unit, and the organization. Obviously then, notification is much more than just sending out a notice.

The employee who was selected should have sufficient lead time to prepare both emotionally and physically. On the *emotional* side, concern should be shown if the employee has not been in a learning experience for a considerable length of time. The employee's self-image should also be considered. The employee might wonder "If I can be released from my job for training, might they discover they can do without me?" Another self-image factor may be that the employee wonders "Will my family and friends think I am being sent back to school?" The supervisor has to consider those factors and perhaps discuss them with the employees, so they will not start the training program with a negative attitude.

On the *physical* side, consideration must be given to the fact that the employee will be expected to be away from the plant or site. This applies to both upper management level personnel and lower levels of the organization. Arrangements have to be made for work coverage. When the training is on-site, those arrangements should assure that the learner is not disrupted during the training program. Some employees may have to make plans to cover their current work as well as the anticipated tasks that may arise while they are away from the job during training.

When training is not in the learner's home city, there are many considerations that should be covered by the notification. For some training programs, travel arrangements may be required, and for some employees, a travel advance may be necessary to avoid financial difficulty.

A supervisor may think that providing training shows concern for the employee, but the employee may not perceive it that way if notification does not cover some personal factors. The employee's family should be considered and the supervisor's should demonstrate concern through early discussions when notification is sent. For example, frequently two parents work, and there may be the need to make provision for children.

The learner should be allowed sufficient time for the emotional and physical preparation that is required. Some people may require more time than others, and the supervisor should explore this with potential trainees sufficiently in advance of the program, so that work and family needs related to the training program can be identified and dealt with.

Arrange for trainee to attend all sessions

When a training program has more than one session, and that is the general practice, supervisors should make all the necessary arrangements to permit uninterrupted attendance by the trainee.

Of primary importance, of course, is the need to make sure that the work of the trainee will be covered. It is important that the trainee not have to wonder about what work is accumulating on the desk or work site that will have to be dealt with on return. When that is a trainee's concern, it will detract from the training experience and cause the trainee to waste energy planning to "catch-up" rather than learn.

A policy should be established to provide for the training to be done on company time. That is the general rule among most U.S. companies, although there still are organizations that insist that the training be done on the trainee's time—"off the clock." This is highly controversial from many viewpoints. One is that such a practice diminishes the importance of the program. Another is a legal one, which cannot be addressed here, as to whether an employee has to be compensated for training required by the organization but offered outside of working hours.

When an employee is sent to an external program conducted away from the job site and offered by a different organization than the employer, the mutual expectations must be made clear. For example, an arrangement could be made for a tuition reimbursement program, where the employee attends a college or university and the employer pays. In such a situation, it is common for the employee not to expect any compensatory time. Of course, there is nothing to prevent the organization from providing time during work hours for such attendance. It is important that the organization have a clear policy on this so the supervisor can make arrangements accordingly.

When all the logistical elements are handled, no business reason should prevent a trainee from attending all sessions. Indeed, attendance at the training sessions should be considered the same as any other work assignment. Of course, an employee may miss work for health reasons and similarly may miss a training session.

An arrangement should be made so that whenever a trainee is absent from a session, no matter what the reason, the appropriate supervisor is immediately informed.

Assist in planning for evaluation

Planning for the evaluation should have taken place during the CEM. This action is included here to reinforce the fact that this planning should have taken place. It can also serve as a notice to supervisors that for evaluation to be effective and helpful, it must be a joint effort involving the supervisor and the HRD unit. Evaluation is included here because it is necessary for the supervisor to make pre-training performance data available if performance is to be evaluated at the end of the training program.

That data can take many forms depending upon the nature of the job, the objectives of the training program, practices in the organization, and the needs of the supervisors and the employees. In some situations the base line (pre-training) data may be gathered from co-workers or subordinates as well as from the potential learner.

MANAGERS AND SUPERVISORS INVOLVEMENT DURING TRAINING

The supervisor should not drop out of the picture once the training starts. Even during the training program, the learner is responsible to the supervisor as well as the instructor. That is the nature of the job assignment to a training program.

During the pre-training stage, supervisors will have made various provisions and arrangements that should be carried out during training. It is important that supervisors follow up to make sure that the arrangements are actually being implemented. The supervisor will also find it helpful to receive feedback from trainees and instructors regarding those arrangements in order to verify their effectiveness and make necessary changes in future pre-training activities.

Check up on work coverage arrangements

First and foremost, the supervisor must make sure that the trainee is actually released from regular duties. It is not uncommon, unfortunately, to find that the trainee is expected to report either by phone or by actual physical presence to the regular work situation some time during the training day. This is more commonly found among managerial and supervisory personnel than among employees who do not have those responsibilities. But even for other levels of employees, many instructors complain about trainees rushing for the phones during a break in order to call the office. This prevents the learners from using the break as a time to relax so they can return to the learning situation with renewed enthusiasm.

When the trainee leaves the job for an extended period of time, a replacement may be needed. Supervisors should not only provide for this, but should check to be sure that the replacement actually reports. The work unit will expect this to happen, but, if for any reason the replacement does not show up, chaos and recriminations may result. It is best for the supervisor to provide for a replacement as early as possible and to be sure that a possible absence of a replacement does not interfere with the trainee in the learning situation.

Some training programs use the spaced learning approach discussed in an earlier chapter. It is a situation where the trainee rotates between the learning situation and the job site. This can make for very good learning, but it also presents scheduling difficulties. When the Designer chooses to use spaced learning for a training program, the supervisor should have agreed previously to that instructional strategy. The supervisor should be made aware of the unusual demands that such an instructional strategy can make on work, scheduling, meetings, and other aspects of the work situation.

Avoid work-related interruptions of the trainees

It is too easy for a trainee to be interrupted during the training program, and thereby have added difficulty in reaching the training objectives. Interruptions may come from the supervisor who forgot that a particular employee was not available. The result is that the interrupted learner and the workforce feel that the supervisor does not really believe that training is really that important.

Emergencies can arise and there are times when interruption is unavoidable. The supervisor, at the outset, can establish the conditions under which an emergency interruption is permitted.

The supervisor should advise the trainee with that old adage, "don't call us, we will call you." This is not meant to block all communication with the job situation. Indeed, some training designs call for some communication back to the job site while the employee is in the training situation. There is a difference, however, between keeping the lines of communication open and interruptions.

Participate in one or more training sessions

To reinforce the value of training, supervisors should physically take part in the training on a planned basis. This should not be limited to only observing or making an unannounced visit. The supervisor's participation should be carefully planned and directly related to the training objectives and future performance.

Supervisors are excellent resource people, but they may need some assistance in actually making a presentation, particularly when the lesson plan calls for an interview, dialogue, panel, or similar instructional strategy. The session should be carefully chosen by the Designer and the supervisor, and the Designer should make sure that the supervisor has been provided with an adequate briefing and relevant preparation. This should be a positive experience for the supervisor, and can serve to reinforce the supervisor's involvement in training.

The supervisor can be more than just a resource person for a particular session. For example, the supervisor might meet with a trainee for lunch, when such a meeting would not interfere with the training program. Asking the supervisor to observe some training sessions could be helpful, but such observation visits must be carefully planned. It is disruptive for visitors to come and go during a training session, and without prior arrangement, the supervisor might observe a session that is of minor importance in the total program.

A Designer may also find that a supervisor who attends some training sessions also may be more helpful during future CEM design processes.

Award certificates on successful completion of the training

The completion of any training program should be signified by some kind of closing ceremony such as the award of some kind of certificate or letter to each trainee.

Supervisors, who generally have a higher level of educational achievement than their subordinates, may not realize the "psychological income" that some people get from those certificates. We have visited offices of supervisors (and even upper level management) who display training program certificates along with their university degrees on their office walls.

An all too common practice that should be avoided is to have the instructor hand out certificates at the final session of the program. Doing this can diminish the value of the certificate. The presentation should be made by some management level person in the organization, and preferably one in the direct management line of the trainees. (That, of course, would not include the HRD manager).

Whenever possible, the certificates should be distributed by a person who has obvious prestige in the eyes of the trainees. The actual distribution can be made at the last session of the program when all the trainees are present. One alternative is for the organization to host a lunch or dinner and to distribute certificates to the successful participants in a variety of training programs.

Another alternative is to award the certificates to the successful trainees at the work site. The supervisor should not just send the certificate through the mail or call the successful trainee into the office for a one-on-one distribution. When possible, all employees in the particular unit should be present during the award, although the disruption of usual work activities may be too costly.

The Designer may have to work with individual supervisors to identify the best award pattern for specific training programs and the individual work units.

MANAGERS AND SUPERVISORS INVOLVEMENT IN JOB LINKAGE

Linking training to the job is a crucial part of the support system, but it is an aspect that is all too frequently overlooked. If the new learned performance is to have an impact on the job, careful planning must link training to the job situation.

Returning to the job with new learning, has always been a difficult problem. One of the forces that contributed to the growth of the field of OD was the need to enable learners to bring new performance to the old job site. Too often the learner found that those who did not attend the training program tended to be unsympathetic or less than helpful when the learner tried to apply what had been learned in training.

Supervisors can take specific actions that will increase the possibility that the learning will be applied. This, however, must be planned for during the design process by both the Designer and the supervisor. The actions, however, must be taken by the supervisor. Some of these actions are described below.

Plan for evaluation when the trainee returns to the job

Evaluation should not come as a surprise to the learner. The Designer should have built several evaluation experiences into the training design.

The evaluation we are concerned with here is the supervisor's evaluation when the learner returns to the job. While in training, the learner should be told what to expect from this evaluation. The supervisor should work with the Designer to develop return evaluations. It is essential that the evaluation bear a direct relationship to the training program.

Because it is possible for training programs to change, even while they are being conducted, the supervisor should be in touch with the instructor and the Designer during the conduct of the program. That will enhance the possibility that the evaluation on the return to the job will be related to the training experience.

Help trainees set realistic goals

While in the training program, an employee can be swept up by the momentum of the challenge and opportunity presented by the learning experience. That is good, but it can prove counterproductive when the trainee returns to the work situation, unless the supervisor helps in setting realistic goals.

The work situation generally demands results. The training situation, however, should encourage and allow for trying out new behaviors rather than focusing on results. The supervisor must assist the trainee in bridging that gap.

As part of job linkage, supervisors should help trainees set realistic goals. This is best done while the trainee is still in the learning situation. Job linkage should not cause the trainee to lose interest in the challenges of the learning environment, but it should help him or her recognize that the challenges may be different on return to the job.

When a supervisor helps a trainee set realistic goals during the training program, some additional advantages may become apparent. A supervisor may see an employee in a new light, one not evident in the regular daily work on the job. The supervisor may also catch some of the enthusiasm that learners frequently experience when successfully acquiring new learning.

Prepare for the return of the trainee

Part of reentry is the kind of greeting or reception the trainee receives upon return to the job. A certain amount of teasing may occur, particularly if the training program was conducted at a pleasant site other employees perceive as a "country club." The greeting might be, "So you had a good time at the country club while the rest of us stayed here and worked like dogs." The intention may be light teasing, a kind of *rite of passage,* but if the supervisor does not present any alternatives the teasing can easily become bitter.

Supervisors should not try to stop the teasing—indeed, they probably cannot. The supervisor however should plan for alternatives so that teasing is not the only greeting the trainee receives upon return to the job.

While still in the program, the supervisor can discuss with the trainees some appropriate ways to facilitate returning to the job. Because the trainees may have been on the receiving end when others have returned from training, they may be aware of some alternatives that are not apparent to the supervisor. Also, because this discussion will take place while the trainee is still in the training program, it will communicate the supervisor's interest in making that transition as positive as possible.

The supervisor should also meet with the employees in the work group to get their ideas on the kind of greeting the trainee should receive. Doing this helps to bring everyone in the work unit into the support process.

Reinforce the use of new job performance by the trainee

If new learning is not used, it tends to fade and disappear. If nothing specific is done to link training with the job that is exactly what will happen.

There are times when the new learned performance cannot be used immediately. It may be necessary for the supervisor, working with the HRD unit, to devise some interim experiences to reinforce the learning until it is possible to use it on the job. After that, the new learning will be continually reinforced by direct use on the job.

It may seem that this action focuses on employees at the lower end of the organizational hierarchy, but that is not the case. For example, consider the manager who goes to a training course to improve skills in conducting staff meetings. Upon returning to the job, the manager may find that it is not possible to immediately use those skills at the next staff meeting. There could be many reasons for this, including changes in personnel, crisis, and other factors beyond the control of the manager.

That manager may tend to lose what had been learned in the training program and revert to previous performance patterns. By the time the crisis or need has been met, the manager is less likely to apply those new skills. The person above that manager should have built in ways to reinforce the new performance.

Provide for some work assignment related to the training

While the training program is still in progress, the supervisor should explore work assignments that will provide the returned trainee with appropriate opportunities for application. This may require temporarily assigning the returned trainee to a different unit or another part of the original work unit. Care must be taken so that the trainee is not permanently transferred, as that would thwart the purpose of the training program.

Output is measured in most production situations. Upon reentry, the trainee may produce at a lower level rather than a higher one. This condition is sometimes used as a criticism of training. Quite the contrary. The employee may need time to integrate new performance into existing situations. The trainee has an adjustment to make, and adjustments may also be required by those who did not attend the training but are influenced by the trainee's output. (See Figure 4-2 on input-output.)

If, when returning to the work site, the trainee is subjected to criticism for this temporary situation, the trainee can be expected to purposely forget what was learned and revert to earlier and less productive performance. During the period of integration, supervisors should provide for a possible dip in output, which will be more than compensated for later when integration is completed.

Provide for trainee to share the learning with others

As noted in the CEM, employees should be selected to attend a training program because there is a need. It is also possible, however, that there are other employees in the work unit who have a similar need, but for various reasons were not selected. The returned trainee is not expected to become a peer instructor but can still contribute to the general improvement of performance. When this is to happen, the supervisor and the employee should jointly prepare for this during the training program.

A common example might occur when an employee is sent to a conference or workshop outside of the organization and is expected to come back with new ideas and something of the "state of the art." The conference is a form of training program. Too often when the employee returns, very little is done to share what had been learned. The employee may be questioned, but too often those questions relate to the social aspects of the conference rather than the learning. The employee is not encouraged to share the learning with the others in the work unit, but rather is asked to tell grand stories about drinking and socializing. This makes the conference a fringe benefit rather than a training experience.

That can be changed. Working together, the supervisor and employee can arrange to share the learning with the others in the work unit or even with other parts of the organization. The focus should be on what was learned and how that learning can be applied in the work unit. The training may also make it possible to identify other needs that now exist.

The employee should anticipate having to share the learning on returning to the job from training. The supervisor should help the employee prepare for that and make arrangements so the sharing takes place. Sharing the learning can provide additional benefits to the employee because it can reinforce the learning. It can also provide indirect learning for those who did not attend the program.

Provide for meetings among trainee, instructor, HRD unit (Designer), and other supervisors

This action by the supervisor emphasizes that the employee, while in training, is still part of the work unit. It is too often the case that while in training the employee becomes a non-person to the supervisor. This is understandable because the employee is not on site and the supervisor has a lot to deal with in the on-site day-to-day operations. The more positive approach, which will support the training, is for the supervisor to retain some connection with the employee even during the training program.

The HRD unit could arrange for the meetings that should take place during the training program. As appropriate, such meetings can actually be built into the design by the Designer. At the very least, a meeting of the supervisor, employee, and selected others should be scheduled before the completion of the program. This may be a meeting with each trainee or a meeting with several of them.

The agenda for that meeting could include many different aspects such as employee reaction to the program, suggestions for improvement, plans to use the learning upon return to the job, and plans for the follow-up.

MANAGERS AND SUPERVISORS INVOLVEMENT IN FOLLOW-UP

This is the last part of the Support System model and should not be confused with evaluation. Follow-up is concerned with what happens after the learner has returned to the work situation. The actions described below should take place over a period of time, even several months after the return. Although the term *trainee* will be used, it is recognized that when follow-up takes place, the employee is no longer in training. The term is used here to differentiate the employee who has returned from training from the others who are on the job.

Initiate meetings with trainee after a period back on the job

Any efficient supervisor has frequent meetings with employees on a variety of topics, and some of those meetings should be a discussion of the training program. The meetings should have been planned for earlier under Job Linkage. In a reasonable period of time after return, the trainee should be asked to discuss aspects of the training program such as relevancy, effectiveness, and suggestions for improvement. The supervisor should be encouraged to share at least some of this information with the Designer.

The meetings can be valuable in helping the trainee understand something about the opportunities and problems the training program was designed to address. The opportunities may be obvious because the trainee may now be able to perform in ways that were unknown or unachievable before the training. Additional problems may occur if the trainee has new performance capabilities, but is not allowed to use them. If such problems are not explored and resolved, they can have a negative effect the next time the trainee goes for training and can also influence others who will be sent to training programs. The attitude that can be engendered by overlooking this aspect may be stated as, "Why bother to learn something new if they won't let me use it back on the job?"

Approve regular meetings of trainees

When several trainees have attended the same training program at different times, it can be helpful to arrange for them to meet periodically. This will not happen on the job unless the supervisor makes the appropriate arrangements.

The value of such meetings is that the trainees can reinforce each other and help to bring about the changes that were the program objectives of the training program.

A possible problem is that such trainees can become a subgroup or clique within a unit. There are ways to control this. For example, a time limit could be set that allows trainees to participate in such a meeting only up to a stated time (two months, for example) after their return.

Inform trainee of changes in job performance attributable to training

When a trainee returns and performance has improved, what feedback should the supervisor provide? Of course, the supervisor may take the improvement for granted because that was the purpose of the training program. Everyone expects performance to change and improve, but is that communicated directly to the trainee?

When the supervisor gives the trainee feedback on performance attributable to training, there will be several positive results. It will reinforce the new performance behavior. It can also reduce the possibility that training may be seen as punishment because the supervisor recognizes the learner's achievement. By providing the feedback, the supervisor will also communicate that training is not given as a fringe benefit, which is a perception held by some, but rather it is designed to help the trainee improve performance. The supervisor recognizes the improved performance that has resulted.

Provide continuing reinforcement

Although there is a good deal of research to show the benefits of reinforcing the learning received through training, reinforcement practices are not used as frequently as they should be. Reinforcement of learning is probably the single most important element of training. Reinforcement from the supervisor should be positive, even though there may be the need for criticism of the new performance. It is possible that supervisors need to be trained in techniques to provide feedback and criticism in a positive manner.

The supervisor can allow the trainee to directly participate in the reinforcement. When a supervisor asks a trainee how the new learning is being used on the job, that query serves as reinforcement. Of course, the supervisor must also take time to listen to the response.

During the CEM, the Designer can assist the supervisor in identifying some types of reinforcement that would be appropriate for the particular training program objectives.

Identify new learning needs

Learning should be a continuous process. One result of a good training experience is that the learner may discover that there is much to be learned about other areas.

Some adults hesitate to become involved in a learning activity because of past unfortunate experiences in learning. They may have failed, been cruelly criticized, or generally have had a negative experience. After a good training experience, it is not unusual to find that the trainee has increased confidence and becomes eager to become engaged in more learning.

As part of the follow-up, the supervisor should encourage the employee to identify other learning needs. It is important, however, that both the supervisor and the trainee have mutual understanding as to which of those needs relate to training for the present job and which might be more correctly considered as education for a future job.

CONCLUSION

If a support system for training does not exist in an organization, it is relatively easy to construct one. But it takes time and patience and involves more than just the Designer. The new system must be built into the organization slowly in many small increments.

With a good support system, the results of a training program can be greatly increased. The results would certainly be worth the effort. A good support system will complement the work done by a Designer (and the HRD unit) as well as the line people who use the Critical Events Model.

CHAPTER 12

Education

Up to this point, the focus of the CEM has been on training related to the *present* job of the learner. The focus of the next two chapters is on education, or those learning activities directed to preparing the learner for a different job. It will become obvious why a Designer should make that distinction when designing a program. It will also become obvious that the major difference between training and education is the learner. Therefore, let us look at the different types of learners who can be involved in education.

TYPES OF LEARNERS

There are essentially two types of learners: those currently employed by the organization and those newly hired. Those who are currently employed may need education for one of three reasons: promotion, lateral transfer, or downsizing. Of course, whether education is needed in an individual case can only be determined in the Identify the Needs of the Learner event. At this point, let us examine the three reasons that could create a need.

Current Employee

Promotion. Promoting the employee to a higher position in the organization is one of the most common reasons for education. Not every promotion may require education, but that can be determined by the application of the first events of the CEM.

For some promotions, such as to the first line of supervision, education virtually becomes a stated need (as discussed in Chapter 5). This kind of promotion can be one of the most traumatic changes in a person's work life (Gutteridge and Hutcheson, "Career Development" in [81]). Other promotions may not require as drastic a change, but may still require education.

Some organizations follow the practice of first promoting and then training. However, others have found it preferable to provide education first, for a number of reasons [77]. One of the most obvious is that education provides an opportunity for the employee who will be transferred to try out some of the new behaviors that will be required as a result of that promotion. It can also provide the organization with some assessment of the possibility of successful performance by that employee in the new position. As a result, the employee or the organization (a designated person or group) may decide unilaterally or mutually that the anticipated promotion is not beneficial.

Promotion and the use of the CEM can be linked with *career development.* An area of potential confusion exists between HRD (designing education programs) and career development (CD) [81]. Career development is important and usually has the goal of helping individuals move to other positions, usually within the same organization. This is evidenced when an organization encourages "internal mobility," in which people move around inside the organization as contrasted with "external mobility," in which the employees are brought into or leave the organization.

Career development for internal mobility can be planned without providing for any learning experiences, but generally that would be unwise. This frequently happens when an employee is promoted first and then trained. It is usually more effective to provide education to prepare the individual for the new position.

Lateral transfer. In this situation an employee is transferred to another and different job, but presumably at the same level in the organization. Lateral transfer assumes that no change in salary or status occurs, as would happen with a promotion.

There can be many reasons for a lateral transfer, and most of them can be positive. A lateral transfer may be an *organizational change* that can arise for several reasons. For example, an organization may choose to discontinue an operation or site. The employee might be transferred to a different operation or site, but at a position at the same level. If the new job is essentially the same, education may not be necessary. However, if the new position is not the same job, even though it is at the same level, education may be needed so the employee can function effectively on the new job. Providing education before the transfer will enable the employee to report to the new job and begin to function immediately.

Some of the same factors apply when the lateral transfer is to avoid *burnout.* This phenomenon was identified in the 1960s and has become even more of a factor in the intervening years. The term is used to identify an employee who has a good work record but seems to have slowed down. At first, the conjecture was that burnout was a factor of age because it seemed to occur in employees in their mid and late 40s. Research has shown that other factors were involved. For some people, the security of continuing to do the same thing on the job year after year was rewarding. For others, however, change was essential. They were good employees who did not want to continue to do the same job. They were not necessarily seeking a promotion but did want a different job within the same organization.

Education enabled those selected employees to learn about other lateral jobs and prepare for the transfer.

There are times when a lateral transfer is a form of *job rotation*. A common example occurs when a sales person is transferred to a manufacturing position or vice versa. Too often that transfer is made without education and it contributes to a negative experience. The employee being transferred or rotated knows little of what is expected on the new job, and the receiving supervisor must expend valuable resources on a comparatively nonproductive employee. That hardly contributes to making the rotation a positive experience for anyone.

Downsizing. There are different kinds of downsizing and it is done for many different reasons. No matter what the reason, the activity is virtually the same. An employee who is retained in the organization may be assigned to a lower level job than the one previously held. This generally means a loss in status, and very frequently, a loss in pay. Although there is nothing the Designer can do in those areas, it is possible through an effective education program to make that experience less negative for the employee and the organization.

The major reasons for shrinking the labor force of an organization are generally reorganization or the economy. With *reorganization,* the intent may be to retain the essential goals and activities of the organization, but to accomplish them using fewer people. Some of the employees may be "out placed," assisted in finding jobs in other organizations. Some employees may be retained to do different jobs from those they had been doing. If it is a lateral transfer, the discussion in the previous section will apply. An employee may also be assigned to a lower level job, which will be discussed below.

Reorganization and subsequent downsizing can also take place when the organization changes its products or services. Some production lines may be closed down or retail sites abandoned. If people working in those facilities are to be retained, they may need education to prepare them for their new jobs.

An organization may retain its essential goals and activities, but find that the impact of the *economy* forces it to cut costs. There are many ways to cut costs, and one is to reduce the workforce. Considering seniority and other factors, the executives may decide to cut from the lower levels and offer employees above those levels the opportunity to take lower level jobs. Once again, this may require education to make those employees effective in the lower level jobs.

Of course, it has been more common to cut at the middle levels because those people are paid more than lower levels. However, the various levels are relative in each organization, and no generalization can be made.

All of the above can result in what is essentially a *demotion* for an employee being retained, at a lower level of the organization. Demotion can also happen for other reasons such as poor performance. Whatever the reason, it can happen at any level of the organization. It is generally helpful if demotion is accompanied by some kind of job counseling provided by the organization. It is equally important to provide the education that will enable the employee to function effectively on the new job even though it is at a lower level.

New Employee

Education may be needed for a new employee at any level who has never worked for a particular organization before—or at least not recently. Time becomes a factor in this situation. Some organizations place a new employee on the new job immediately after hiring. In that situation, there may not be time for education, and training may have to be provided as soon as the new employee reports.

One problem with providing education for new employees is that of cost. Put another way, to whose budget will this design and education be charged? For some programs such as orientation (discussed below), it is customary to charge a general budget or to make provision for it in some human resource budget. When that is not the case, the Designer must determine where the budget will come from. That can affect the design process as well as the conduct of the education.

At the very least, there should be some kind of *orientation* program. This may take place after the employee is on the job. It can be considered training because the employee already has a job context and other employees will influence what is learned and how it is applied on the job.

Some organizations, however, put the new employee in a "hold" status and first provide orientation as education. The new employee does not have a job context and indeed does not need it for an effective orientation education program. The orientation may include factors that will determine the actual job placement that will take place at the end of the orientation-education program.

Other forms of education programs for new employees can also be offered. A common one that has been used in production situations is sometimes called *vestibule* education. The newly hired employee is put into a situation that is similar to the future job, but not actually that job. This enables the new employee to build up the necessary skills that are required prior to job placement.

If recruitment has been successful, the new employee will generally have at least the basic skills required for the new job. However, the new employee may have to learn to use those skills in ways that are consistent with the requirements of the specific job in this particular organization. Education before job placement can be effective in many ways, not the least of which is that it relieves the receiving supervisor of the task of providing training for the new employee.

THE SUPERVISOR

The supervisor is a crucial element in the design of learning programs. Because training is designed for the present job, the supervisor is clearly the person functioning in that capacity on the present job. With education, however, the identification of the supervisor is not always clear. If the Designer does not devote sufficient attention to this difference, the education program will invariably be less effective for the individual and less helpful to the organization.

In designing an education program for a current employee, two supervisors may be involved. The first is the supervisor the employee currently works for while he or she is in an education program. Because this supervisor will not be involved in the next job, consideration must be given to the unique role of this person. Although education will benefit the employee and the organization, it will not be of any direct benefit to the current supervisor. Therefore, it is important that appropriate actions be taken to assure that the current supervisor is not too hampered by the transition process.

For example, when the employee goes for education, the current supervisor loses the work input of that employee. If the education is for promotion, presumably the current supervisor had been involved in the selection process. Provision should be made for a replacement as soon as possible so as not to penalize that supervisor for helping an employee get promoted.

A similar situation may occur with a lateral transfer. The job will remain, but the employee who filled it will be involved in education, preparing for the next job.

With downsizing, the situation is much different because the job is expected to be vacated. The supervisor will be required to make an orderly dismantling of the existing unit.

A new employee, of course, has no current supervisor; therefore, there is no need to consider that situation.

The more complicated situation relates to the *receiving* supervisor—the one for whom the new employee will be working after reassignment. At times, it is possible to know exactly who that new supervisor will be, and that should be the general case for an education program. Whether the change is a promotion, lateral transfer, or downsizing, the job and the supervisor the employee will report to will be known.

Generally, a new employee will be told who the supervisor will be. There are some situations, however, when a new employee will be hired for a general classification of job, and the exact placement will not be determined until later. In that case, the receiving supervisor may not be as easily identified.

CONCLUSION

The design of education programs differs significantly from the design of training programs. Unfortunately, that distinction is not made often enough and "training" programs fail because they really are education programs.

CHAPTER 13

Using the CEM for Education

This chapter focuses on using the CEM for education. The same model is used as is shown in Figure 1-2. The events are the same, but some of the activities of the Designer are different. To see that, we need to start with another look at training and education, and the differences between them.

Training is learning related to the *current* job of the learner. Education is learning related to a *future* job of the learner.

When designing for an education program, the Designer must consider variables that relate to the job and the employee that do not exist when designing for training.

When designing for education, the Designer must first determine if the *job* already exists or if it is a new job. This should be fairly obvious, but the actions the Designer must take in respect to the job will vary significantly. What the Designer must consider and do will be discussed later.

The other variable is the *employee*. This can be the current employee who works for the organization but is being prepared to take a new job. The other type of employee is the new employee who has been recruited to work for the organization in either an existing job or a new one.

There are many reasons to provide education. A study we conducted highlights one of the benefits [73].

An organizational need came from an employment agency that made many people available for jobs. In some cases, these people were looking for a job, any job, but they did not remain on the job for a satisfactory period of time. (The reasons for it are discussed in the article.) Some of the organizations we studied had a real problem with turnover of new employees, and the organizations tried many approaches to deal with this. Several organizations decided to provide an education experience before the final selection of employees was made. Upon completion of the learning, the prospective employee and a selected member of the organization met to discuss the results of the education experience. The organization was represented by someone from the personnel office, a possible supervisor, and a staff member from the HRD unit. These meetings focused on the performance of the prospective employee during the education and the possible job placements. The group discussed additional learning needs that had been identified for specific learners as a result of the education experience.

Many benefits resulted. The major benefit was a significant reduction in turnover. One reason for this we were told was that education gave the newly hired employees an idea of what the job would be like. Some of the prospective employees decided they didn't want that kind of job.

Problems with Education

Education presents the possibility of some problems that do not arise when training is the focus of the CEM. The Designer must keep these in mind during the design process.

One of these problems is *time*—the interval between the end of the education program and the placement of the employee on that new job, which may be weeks or even months. Generally a gap in time will occur and the receiving supervisor is asked to invest time now for a possible return in the future (efficient new employee performance).

Another factor is inherent in the distinction between training and education. It is the possibility of a *lessened identification with the current work unit*. After training, the employee returns to the current job. At the end of education, the employee generally returns to the present job and awaits placement to the new job, which is the result of promotion, lateral transfer, or downsizing. In the interim, the employee can be expected to have lessened his or her identification with the present job. This is one reason so many supervisors are not enthusiastic about sending an employee for education.

It is also possible that the employee may successfully complete the education, but then decide to *leave the organization*. Particularly when education was for promotion, the employee may have acquired new skills and knowledge for which other organizations might offer an increased salary above what the employee can expect upon promotion. Education for promotion raises expectations, and these should be recognized as part of the support system.

The same problem can occur with an employee who has been educated for a lateral transfer. An employee who is to be moved to a different job as the result of downsizing can be expected to be less than enthusiastic. The Designer in that situation should explore what job counseling has taken place before the education program and determine whether such counseling should be built into the education program.

EVALUATION AND FEEDBACK

The major difference in E&FB between education and training is that in training it is fairly easy to identify the supervisor who should be involved. It is much different for education. The Designer must determine who is the right supervisor.

Obviously, the Designer can always identify the *current supervisor,* but because movement to another job is involved, it is not always possible to identify the *future supervisor.* When the Designer cannot make that determination, the design process must proceed without that supervisor being named.

With training, there was no question but that the learner would be returning to the same job at the end of the program. With education, that generally is the case, but not always, and not for long. Therefore, a current supervisor may not wish to invest the time taking part in an EF&B meeting when there may not be any benefit on the current job.

In addition to supervisors, the *decision makers* need to be involved. These could be individuals fairly high up in the organization who make changes and who therefore should be able to decide on how education would meet the needs that will arise.

IDENTIFY THE NEEDS OF THE ORGANIZATION

With training, every organization has needs. This chapter focuses on those needs that relate to education programs.

Looking at organizational needs for education is quite different than looking for training needs, although there may be some overlap and hence some confusion. Confusion can arise when a group gets together to explore organizational needs, but does not differentiate between those that exist currently and those that can be expected to be generated through future actions.

Anticipated and Unanticipated Change

Education focuses on changes, some anticipated, others not. Although these two factors are presented as alternatives, they really represent a continuum. In an organization, some changes are anticipated but do not ever occur, while others are anticipated, but no one knows when they might occur—in a week, a month, a year.

An *anticipated change* is one that is expected to occur or is planned to occur. It is common practice at management levels, for example, to have succession plans to anticipate changes in managerial postings. This is one of the most common anticipated changes, but there are many others related to people and performance.

The following is just a brief list.

- New product line. The decision is made to produce new products. This decision will require different jobs from those that now exist, current employees will have to be educated for those jobs, or new employees must be hired for those jobs that currently do not exist.
- New equipment. This involves more than just replacing old equipment. It could, for example, involve a management decision to use robots for some manufacturing functions. Education may have to be provided for those employees who will be replaced in order for them to get jobs in other parts of the organization. The introduction of robots will probably also require education for those employees who will repair these new pieces of equipment.
- New technology. The impact of new technology is no longer merely accepted after it happens. It can be anticipated. As a result, some existing jobs may be eliminated and new jobs developed for which current employees could be educated.
- Replacement of personnel. In the normal course of events, it can be expected that people will retire. Replacements should be educated much before that time so that they are ready to move immediately into the jobs vacated by retirees.
- New regulations. At times, it is possible for an organization to anticipate when the government will release new regulations that will have an impact on the organization.

An alert Designer will watch all elements of the organization to see what changes being planned can be anticipated.

There is also *unanticipated changes* or those changes that can be expected, although when they will occur is not known. If the organization uses a futurist or people in long range planning, the Designer should be in constant touch with them, even though it may not be clear exactly when the changes will take place. A brief list of unanticipated changes includes:

- Destruction of plant or equipment. This can occur as the result of a natural disaster (hurricane) or a local catastrophe (fire). The Designer should consider the kinds of education that would be helpful for these situations.
- New and previously unknown competitor. This has become a more frequent possibility with the burgeoning of technology. Some new competitors arise without having gone through the laborious and public process of obtaining investment capital.

By no means have all the changes, anticipated and unanticipated, been discussed. Books have been written on those changes. The intent in including this material here is to alert the Designer to the need to be involved in organizational planning for change.

Group and Individual Needs

Changes, whether anticipated or unanticipated, will create needs that the Designer must be sensitive to. Some of those needs will affect one individual (or a few individuals) while others will apply to groups of individuals.

Some of the needs of the organization can be viewed in terms of *individual needs*. It is not uncommon to find that after several years an employee wants to change jobs because, "They now expect me to do something I wasn't hired to do." One reaction to this is to offer a training program to such an employee, but what is the objective? The problem is not one of getting the employee to perform better on the present job. The employee is saying "I feel the need for a different job." One approach that management can take is to suggest that the employee go to another organization. Frequently, however, the employee has a good performance record, and many organizations provide for internal mobility or find another job for that employee within the organization and provide the education so the employee can be re-assigned. This is usually termed a *lateral transfer.*

The workforce is aging, and throughout the world retirement ages are going up. People change over the years, and the longer they remain in the workforce, the more changes will occur. Therefore, as changes occur, an employee may seek other challenges and opportunities within the organization. Education can be used effectively to prepare the individual to move to another job.

A new phenomena called "burnout" arose during the 1970s and is still with us, although it is perhaps not as significant today. A good employee reaches a point where continuing to do the same job is no longer challenging or interesting. If the economy is growing, the individual employee can meet this need by leaving the organization and going elsewhere. This however can be costly to the organization.

Burnout does not seem to be as important today because technology has caused many traditional jobs to disappear and new ones to emerge. Despite that fact, some individuals still prefer to do the more traditional jobs even though some of these jobs may not be as glamorous as those opened up by technological change.

In any case, line managers and the human resource units should be alert to burnout of individual employees. With appropriate job counseling, other jobs can be identified to which the individual can move, and education can help make that an effective change.

Most education is directed towards individual needs, but there are times when *group needs* exist. This may occur, for example, when there is a change in a government policy, such as opening promotional opportunities for designated minority groups. Just making jobs available can be meaningless, unless people in those groups are provided with education so they can move into those jobs.

A planned technological change may cause a job category to be reduced or eliminated, affecting a group of employees. If these employees are to be retained in the organization, education can be used to make the transition effective rather than disruptive to the group and the organization.

Timing

No matter what the source of the need, or whether it is for individuals or groups, the timing of education is important. The timing of training, as noted in Chapter 3, must be related to the nature of the problem and time by which it must be solved.

Frequently with education, some options exist particularly when anticipated change is planned. The Designer is faced with a delicate question. To educate too early may produce an educated employee with no place to go. This can result in the employee leaving and taking that new learning into another organization. Also, if too great a time lag occurs, the educated employee may lose the knowledge and skills that had been learned because of a lack of opportunity to use that new learning. On the other hand, if the education is delayed, the employee may have to move to the new position before the education has been completed.

Because timing is so crucial, the Designer must work closely with managers who make the decisions regarding the situation. Indeed, in E&FB the Designer must constantly check on the timing of the education as it relates to the time the employee is expected to use the new learning.

Alternatives to Education

There are alternatives to virtually any HRD program, including education. One of the most common is *recruitment,* recruiting, selecting, and hiring new employees from outside the organization. These employees may only need a good orientation program and some minimal training and could be placed on the job immediately.

When recruitment is used, the Designer should work with recruiters to identify the possible educational needs before recruitment starts. It is extremely important to do this when the HR people responsible for recruitment plan their activities. The nature and extent of the required education program can have a significant impact in many ways.

For example, it will undoubtedly help the recruitment people to determine what qualifications to look for and to take into account the cost in education to bring those new employees up to the performance level that will be required.

During this event, the Designer should raise the question of the budget for the design work and for conducting the education program.

SPECIFY JOB PERFORMANCE

With education, this event of the CEM is virtually the same as for training. One major difference will arise when the current or new employee is educated for a job that previously did not exist in the organization. Obviously, no performance can be observed nor is any data about the job available.

In such a case, the input-output discussed in Chapter 4 becomes even more necessary. The Designer may have to work with many people to reach an agreement on the input that is expected for the new job. Similarly, the probable output has to be planned and studied with those who expect to get the output of the new job. Then, it is possible for the Designer, working with those who designed the new job, to work towards completing this event of the CEM.

IDENTIFY THE NEEDS OF THE LEARNER

The greatest difference will be found when this event is used for education rather than training. Because neither current nor new employee has actually worked in that future job, no record of job performance related to that job exists. Of course, a work record for a current employee may have some relevance. Because the employee is transferring to a different job, some job performance behaviors may be applicable to the new job. To determine that, it may be necessary to put the current employee into a job simulation or similar experience to identify the specific needs. In other situations, some form of test might provide the same data. Indeed, it is possible to do this with new employees as well.

Consider what happens when an individual receives education to become a supervisor for the first time. The transition from being a subordinate to becoming a supervisor is the greatest change that most people make in their entire work career. A subordinate often perceives a supervisor as having a tremendous amount of power, many perks, and real control. When education is provided in presupervisory programs, the appearance of power and control are replaced with reality and fact. It is not unusual for an individual during or after a supervisor education program to decide to remain a subordinate. The common remark is "The pay isn't worth the hassle!"

Gathering data

Some of the same sources and methods to gather data about learner needs that were discussed in Chapter 5 can be applicable, but with an education program the task is more difficult. It is important for the Designer to first identify the population, those people who might be in the education program and their supervisors. If they are current employees, they may be fairly easy to access. When those to be educated are new employees, it may be difficult to identify them early enough before the start of the design process.

It is frequently not possible to have a *meeting* with the current employee because this would mean too much productive time spent away from the present job. In some cases however the sending supervisor might agree to it. A meeting might still be useful to compare the current employee's previous learning and experiences with the performance the employee thinks will be required on the new job. For the most part, this meeting will produce very subjective data and some of it will be unreliable. The employee, of course, is not hiding anything but is merely guessing about anticipated performance. A meeting can still be helpful, and even though the Designer should not expect too much specific data, it is worth the effort.

For new employees, a meeting might take place during the recruitment phase, but that is not too often feasible. When possible, the Designer might meet with the new employee as soon after selection as possible.

The *interview* is a valuable method, although *observation* of the present job generally is not too useful. Of course, some behavior on the present job may be transferable to the new job, and that should be explored.

The *questionnaire* is generally helpful. It allows the Designer to reach current employees who are not yet on the new job. For new employees, the questionnaire can highlight those learning needs that are essential before the individual is placed on the job and can determine which can be left for training after the new employee has been placed on the job.

DETERMINE OBJECTIVES

This event is used in a similar way for education and for training. The Designer must be very certain that the objectives relate to the new and different situation that the employee will be going to.

This is one event where including the possible new supervisor is very important. Without that supervisor, it is impossible for the Designer to know whether the program being designed will actually prepare the employee for the new position.

For example, a common problem arose recently in many countries and affected many organizations. It concerned education programs intended to include minorities in the workforce. The general program objective was to provide learning to enable those selected groups to move to higher level positions in organizations. This objective was not frequently stated in such specific terms, but rather it was implied when executives and managers made broad commitments in speeches and interviews. Designers, caught up in the idea, wrote program objectives focusing on minorities moving ahead in the workforce.

For some supervisors, however, such objectives came as a shock. Supervisors discovered when they reviewed the education objectives that they were supposed to provide for the promotion of their best minority employees. This meant the supervisor would lose a good employee and would have to deal with a replacement who would be an unknown. As in the past, program objectives very often have been overlooked or ignored. Supervisors did not tend to pay too much attention. Confrontation occurred when the minority employee completed the education program and sought the promotion. The supervisor, not having accepted the program objectives, looked upon the learning as a way to increase present performance. That problem could have been avoided if the supervisors had been involved in determining the program objectives.

BUILD CURRICULUM

This is another event in which the distinction between education and training is minimal, but one important difference relates to learning theory.

Most of what we learn is called *associative,* that is, new learning is associated to what was known or experienced previously. This concept is important in training, and even more so in education. It has two aspects.

With one aspect the Designer identifies previous experiences of the learner that can relate to the new position. For example, for a lateral transfers the Designer might be able to identify some limited performance from the current job that is appropriate to the new job. This performance could modify the curriculum for some employees. The Designer may also identify situations in the past in which the learner had some contact with the prospective unit. The contact certainly is not the same as actually working in that unit, but at least the learner has some idea of what is expected in that unit based on past experience. The Designer can design the curriculum in a way that associates the new learning with that past experience.

Another aspect of associative learning can be demonstrated with an example in which the Designer works on supervisory learning programs with a unit on dealing with grievances. For training, the learner can be asked to recall and associate previous situations in which the learner handled grievances as a supervisor.

However, when the learner has never been a supervisor and is being promoted to that position, he or she has no associative base for handling grievances except, perhaps, as an employee who has filed a grievance. The Designer then should build in simulations in which the learner can experience something of what can be expected upon promotion in dealing with grievances.

The *make-buy* decision may have more impact for education than for training. Consider the situation in which the organization purchases some new technology, which will mean new jobs. Current employees might be considered for later transfer into the new jobs and will need to know how to use the new technology. In that situation, the Designer should carefully explore whether the supplier of that technology is required to provide education (sometimes called training in the purchase contract). If that is the case, design work will not be needed because it is included in the buy decision on the new technology.

Not all new technology, and consequently new jobs, is accompanied by learning packages. However, learning programs may already exist for some of those jobs. Some programs may be purchased from suppliers of learning programs. Others may be available from professional colleagues who may have designed learning programs for that job in their organizations. In either case, the Designer may find it helpful to obtain these programs with or without having to actually pay for them.

When the program is purchased from a supplier, the Designer must recognize that it has been designed for general consumption, that is, a large market. A good deal of customizing may be necessary to make it applicable to the particular situation in the organization. The previous experience of the learner may be quite different from the experience that was anticipated when the program was designed for a broad market.

If the Designer is able to obtain a program from a professional colleague, some customizing will probably be necessary. In addition to different learners, the Designer may have to consider the differences among organizations that should be built into the curriculum.

SELECT INSTRUCTIONAL STRATEGIES

This is another event in which little difference exists between designing programs for education or for training.

For a *current employee,* the Designer will know which instructional strategies have been experienced as well as the general climate of learning in the organization. Both of these factors will influence the selection of instructional strategies.

When the learner is a *new employee,* the situation can be much different. It is unlikely that the Designer will know the previous learning experiences of that employee. Confusion could arise in the following situation. Let us assume that within this organization there is a great deal of self-directed learning, small group work in learning situations, and provision for influence by the learner. The new employee, however, may have come from an organization where the emphasis was on the didactic, the lecture, and where the learner was expected to be passive. Therefore, the Designer has to select strategies carefully. That does not mean that the Designer should not select interactive learning strategies, but it means that provision must also be made to enable the learner to shift into this different learning mode.

OBTAIN INSTRUCTIONAL RESOURCES

This event can be significantly different when used for education and confusion may result unless the Designer has prepared carefully for the needed resources.

Consideration must be given to the *financial* resources that will be required. A budget for the design work becomes extremely important here and must be explored, for without a budget there cannot be a program. With training, supervisors generally have either a provision in their own unit's budget for training or can readily or readily approve a budget allocation for training.

The situation with education is much more complicated. It is possible for each supervisor to have the budget to educate employees for promotion particularly if the organization recognizes that as a supervisory responsibility. Unfortunately, that is not the general practice.

Supervisory budgets rarely make provision for education for lateral transfers or for downsizing. Therefore, the Designer must determine where the budget will come from to conduct the education program. If possible, that determination should take place during the first event, Identify the Needs of the Organization.

The *physical* and the *human* resources required for education are much the same as those for training. One difference concerns the scheduling of the learners. If the learners are current employees, the factors discussed earlier related to loss of work must be carefully considered. If new employees, it may be necessary to coordinate the scheduling with the human resource unit, principally recruiting.

CONDUCT EDUCATION

This event will be similar for education and training programs except for factors such as released time for education and accountability.

The evaluation "back on the job" cannot take place, of course, until the learner has transferred to that new job.

SUPPORT SYSTEMS FOR EDUCATION

Less has been done to explore the use of the Support System Model (SSM) for education than for training. Nevertheless, Designers should explore ways in which to use the SSM as support for education.

Upper management involvement

This part of the model is crucial in education. A good deal of education provided for current employees comes about as a result of upper management decisions.

Managers and Supervisors Involvement in Pre-education

An important action of the Designer is to identify the managers and supervisors to whom the learner will be reporting after education and placement.

A major task of the Designer is to find ways to involve the receiving supervisor prior to the conduct of education. Of course, involvement in the CEM is one apparent way that this can be done.

Managers and Supervisors Involvement During Education

The problem again arises of involving the receiving supervisor who at the time of the education program may have little interest in the employee. When the assignment to the new position is firm, the receiving supervisor probably will be interested in becoming involved with the employee during education. When the assignment is not firm, the response of the receiving supervisor will vary depending on many factors such as the degree of involvement of upper management in education.

Managers and Supervisors Involvement in Job Linkage

This part of the SSM can only work where the future work unit of the employee has been specified and the receiving supervisor is known. Actually, job linkage activities can be extremely helpful to the receiving supervisor as a way of getting to know the new employee outside of the work unit. The receiving supervisor can build progressive activities while the employee is still in education to help integrate that employee into the work unit.

Unless the work assignment and supervisor are known, it is not possible to do much about job linkage because the future job is too indefinite.

Managers and Supervisors Involvement in Follow-up

The follow-up steps for education are much the same as for training. It probably will not be necessary, however, for the employee to share the education with those already working in the unit because they probably will not have any need for it. The receiving supervisor could couple the follow-up activity with the usual feedback an employee should be given during the early days of working in a new situation.

An effective support system for education reinforces the work of the Designer and has value for the organization and for all the individuals involved.

Appendix

INSTRUCTIONAL STRATEGIES

Volumes have been written about the range of instructional strategies, but few books have ever achieved any significant general acceptance. Obviously, some core instructional strategies never seem to change (for example, lecture) and others shift under the impact of constantly emerging technology (for example, computer conferencing).

In the listing that follows, we endeavored to include those instructional strategies of which Designers should be aware. We do not claim that the list contains every single strategy in existence, but neither does it contain just a few of the more commonly used strategies.

We made no attempt to classify these strategies because up to now no classification has evolved that has proven generally useful. Also, some semantic problems become apparent concerning labels, perceptions of some strategies, and so on. These semantic discrepancies are dealt with in the "related" item under each strategy. Because of space limitation, the brief description under each strategy probably will not provide all the information a particular Designer may want. The listings, however, provide the Designer with a place to begin searching for other sources, data banks, and publications.

Action maze: A highly structured written variation of the case study in which the problem unfolds, one incident at a time, as a consequence of a series of decisions made (or action taken) by the learner.
Related: case study, simulation, game.

Alter ego: Used to facilitate communications whereby one person observes the learner in a situation and provides immediate or delayed feedback to the learner on observed communication and behavioral components.
Related: coaching, counseling.

Annotated reading list: A list of readings on a particular subject, characterized by a short description, explanation, or evaluation of the entry.
Related: handout, bibliography.

254   *Designing Training Programs*

Apprenticeship: A means of learning a craft or skill by which the learner (apprentice) works with an experienced worker on the job. This is generally supplemented with some formal instruction.
Related: OJT, vestibule learning, coaching, JIT.

Audience reaction: Used with a guest speaker in order to provide for interaction with the learners. A small group of learners is selected, usually not more than five, who ask questions or make comments on the speaker's presentation.
Related: listening team, interview.

Audio tape: Sound is recorded on specially prepared tape by a recorder. The most common recorder today is the cassette, which comes in various sizes depending upon the playback machine. Recordings are easy to make, and professional recordings are available with tapes by leading professionals or thinkers. Audio tape can also be used as a job aid to provide simple routine instructions.
Related: video tape, recordings, job aid.

Audio visual: Refers to the entire range of instructional materials that uses sight and/or sound to aid or reinforce learning.
Related: video, films, filmstrips, overhead projectors, opaque projector.

Bibliography: A list of books that relates to the topic of the learning experience. Can also be extended to lists of other nonprinted resources. A bibliography should indicate sufficient information so the learner can obtain a desired resource.
Related: annotated reading list, handout.

Brainstorming: A technique to encourage the generation of ideas without any evaluation. Can also be used in conjunction with problem solving and various forms of creativity. Emphasis is on ideas, not on solutions, produced in a free-wheeling and non-judgmental atmosphere.
Related: creative thinking, think tank, synectics.

Buzz group: A large group divided into small units, usually of no more than six learners, that meet simultaneously to react to a topic or to a charge given to them. Emphasis is on ideas because time is usually limited to 10 minutes or less. Provision must be made for feedback.
Related: group discussion, workshop, work group.

Cable television: Franchised transmission of multiple channels over coaxial cable to individual homes or institutions for a fixed monthly fee or subscription for a particular transmission. Requires special equipment for reception.

Related: closed-circuit TV, video-tape.

Case study: An oral or written account of an event, incident, or situation used to develop critical thinking skills and to gain new perceptions of concepts and issues.

Related: action maze, in-basket, incident process, role play.

Chalkboard: Vertical upright surface that can be written on with chalk (and easily erased or modified) to be viewed by groups.

Related: magnetic board, flannel board, white board.

Clinic: A session or part of a session in which the learners react to some common experience they have shared previously. Can also be used when part of the group has an experience they would like the others to react to. The instructor serves as a resource person and observes carefully to avoid losing the objective of the session.

Related: workshop, work group, laboratory, group discussion.

Closed circuit TV (CCTV): Cable TV within one or more buildings owned by the institution. Used to broadcast prepared tapes or live presentations.

Related: video tape, cable television.

Coaching: One-on-one, intensive learning through demonstration and practice characterized by immediate feedback and correction.

Related: counseling, alter ego, interactive modeling.

Colloquy: A modification of the panel that uses six to eight persons. Half the panel represents the audience, the other half serves as resource persons or experts.

Related: panel, audience reaction team, listening team.

Computer-assisted instruction (CAI): Highly structured and self-paced, a series of learning segments is presented by a computer and the learner is asked to make a response. The computer electronically processes the response and provides immediate feedback to the learner. Also called computer-assisted learning (CAL).

Related: programmed instruction.

Conference: A group of people discussing a common problem or need. Not all conferences focus on learning objectives. Generally uses a variety of strategies during the course of the activity.

  Related: forum, symposium, workshop.

Confrontation, search, and coping (CSC): A three-part experience in which the learner is faced with a problem or a need (confrontation) and is responsible for searching for a solution (search) and applying the solution to the problem (cope).

  Related: DPT, laboratory learning.

Contract: A written document developed by the learner and reviewed by the instructor. Contains the objectives, methods of reaching them, and evaluation. Although time-consuming, a learning contract can result in improved learning for each learner who develops one. Contracts can be renegotiated during the course of the learning.

  Related: peer-mediated learning, home study, confrontation/search/coping, correspondence.

Correspondence: Self-directed learning characterized by written interaction between the learner and the facilitator and implemented through the mail.

  Related: home study, contract.

Creative thinking: A way of thinking that uses several ways to generate fresh patterns, new relationships, and unconventional kinds of thinking.

  Related: think tank, brainstorming, problem solving.

Critique: Participants analyze the strengths and weaknesses of a learning experience and make suggestions for improvements as well as assessing their own learning.

  Related: coaching, laboratory.

Debate: Two individuals or teams take opposing sides of a clearly specified issue. They can compete based on a grading system or present the opposing views for an audience or other participants. Requires a high level of verbal ability and stage presence.

  Related: panel, colloquy.

Delphi technique: A method of organizing larger groups of materials or people into smaller groups by a system of narrowing choices.

  Related: small groups.

Demonstration: A presentation that shows ways to perform an act or procedure. Can be done by direct presentation or through a prepared video cassette. Should be brief, allow for interaction with the learner, and then proceed to the next point.
   Related: observation, behavior modeling, mock up.

Diagnosis, prescription, treatment (DPT): The learner's needs and weaknesses are uncovered by some instrument or procedure (diagnosis), a course of action or a plan of study is developed to meet the need (prescription), and the learner follows the prescribed treatment in order to correct the diagnosed weakness (treatment).
   Related: confrontation/search/cope, peer-mediated learning, coaching.

Dialogue: A conversation between two individuals in front of a larger group. The individuals could be invited resource people or class members discussing an assigned topic. They need not present opposing views but should explore the topic in some depth from their prior learning and experience.
   Related: discussion, interviewing, dyad, debate.

Discussion: A relatively unstructured exchange of ideas among members of a group on a topic of mutual interest.
   Related: dyad, dialogue, colloquy.

Drill: Repetitive, structured practice that can be written, oral, or motor to reinforce previous learning.
   Related: exercise.

Dyad: Another name for a pair of individuals or a situation in which two participants work together or talk together. The dyad can remain in the room or move to another convenient place. Usually some form of feedback is required when using a dyad.
   Related: peer-mediated instruction, discussion, dialogue, buzz groups.

Exercise: A structured learning experience usually using some instrumentation or guide sheets. May be used to introduce a new topic for skill practice, review, or evaluation.
   Related: games, drill, learner-response system, workbook.

Feedback mechanisms: A response system (mechanical or nonmechanical) that provides feedback on learning to both facilitator and learner.
   Related: audience reaction team, CAI, learner-response system, programmed instruction, teaching machine.

Field trip: A carefully arranged group visit to an object or place for on-site observation and learning. It should not be used for recreation. Field trips require careful planning, coordination, and an analysis of the learning upon return.
Related: demonstration, guided tour.

Film: Visual and audio presentation characterized by motion. Can be purchased or produced in-house. Generally, film has been replaced by video, but some films are still available.
Related: video, audio/visual.

Fishbowl: A discussion group that is divided in two (not necessarily in half). The inner circle discusses while the outer group listens and observes. Member of outer group may "tap in" or exchange places with a member of the inner group.
Related: discussion, laboratory.

Flannel board: A flannel-covered board used for presentations to groups in which materials are prepared to stick to the boards.
Related: chalkboard, newsprint, magnetic board, flipchart, white board.

Flipcharts: Previously prepared material, usually permanent, that can be mounted on an easel. The pages are flipped over to disclose the material.
Related: newsprint, easel, flannel board.

Forum: A type of question-and-answer period. Can be used after a formal presentation when the entire group is encouraged to ask questions of the presenter(s). Encourages interaction between the participants and the presenter(s).
Related: discussion, panel, symposium.

Games: An activity characterized by structured competition to provide the opportunity to try out previous learning. Generally scored so that a winner is identified.
Related: simulation, exercise.

Handout: Printed materials distributed as part of a learning experience made available at the appropriate time before, during, or after the session. Ample copies must be provided so that each participant has an individual copy.
Related: annotated reading list, bibliography.

Home study: A learning activity that is largely self-directed. Facilitator-learner interaction is accomplished by mail.
Related: correspondence course, contract learning.

In-basket: A simulated, reinforcing exercise in which the learner responds to a collection of memos, directives, and problems that force the learner to prioritize, make decisions, and handle the difficulties that might be faced on the job.
Related: case study, action maze.

Incident process: A variation of the case study in which the learner is given only some basic data and then must question the instructor further to obtain the additional data required to complete the assignment. The instructor must have carefully prepared data sheets available that can be given to the learner when the appropriate question is asked.
Related: case study, simulation, game, exercise, action maze.

Interactive modeling: A means for learning new behaviors by observing model or ideal behavior, trying new behavior, and receiving feedback. The cycle is repeated until the new behavior is learned. Sometimes called behavior modeling.
Related: role play, demonstration.

Internship: Supervised practical experience used for advanced learners who are entering new roles (internship: white collar; apprenticeship: blue collar).
Related: apprenticeship, OJT, practicum, JIT, vestibule learning.

Interview: A strategy for using a resource person without a speech. The resource person is asked questions while the learners listen. The questions can be spontaneous or given to the interviewee earlier to allow for preparation.
Related: audience reaction team, colloquy, dialogue, panel.

Job aid: Material specifically related to a job or a part of a job that enables the person to learn a particular task without formal instruction. Essentially used by individuals.
Related: apprenticeship, internship, JIT

Job instruction training: A form of on-the-job training characterized by supervisory responsibility for training of employees.
Related: coaching, apprenticeship, OJT.

Job rotation: A change of jobs for a specified period of time with learning as the objective.
Related: OJT, coaching.

Laboratory: An environment conducive to experimentation and testing by the learner. Can be used for a variety of objectives including cognitive, affective, and psychomotor.
Related: T-groups, sensitivity (one kind of laboratory).

Learner response systems: Devices, usually mechanical, used by learners to provide immediate and individual feedback to instructors on their learning.
Related: feedback mechanisms, programmed instruction, teaching machine.

Lecture: A one-way presentation in which a speaker addresses participants. It can and usually should be supplemented with other strategies. Must be limited in time and content.
Related: forum, audience reaction team, interview.

Listening groups: Participants are divided into several groups, each of which is assigned the task of listening to and observing an assigned part of a speech, demonstration, panel, or similar strategy.
Related: audience reaction team.

Magnetic board: A device used to display prepared materials that are magnetized. Allows for showing movement, relationships, and so on.
Related: chalkboard, flannel board, newsprint, white board.

Mock up: A full-sized replica built accurately to scale, but not the real object.
Related: model, simulation.

Model: Usually used to present a physical item in a different form than usual (smaller but to scale) in order to facilitate learning. Can also be used to present ideas and show the flow of a series of actions. Is not the real thing, but represents the real thing or idea.
Related: mock-up, diagram, flowchart.

Newsprint: Large sheets of paper usually provided in pads written on with felt tip markers or crayons (may be called flipchart pads). The pads may be mounted on easels with provision for removing the individual sheets to be posted and/or saved.
Related: chalkboard, flannel board, magnetic board, white board.

Nonverbal learning: A learning experience that does not use any spoken communication. However, the instructor may use speech to give instructions

and must use speech to enable learners to process the learning after completion of the nonverbal experience.
Related: exercise, laboratory.

Observation: The learner observes and reports on an action or incident. This may be highly structured with checklists or may consist only of general instructions.
Related: demonstration, field trip.

Opaque projector: A device capable of reproducing an image of greater size than the original from a nontransparent master such as a book.
Related: overhead projector, slide projector.

Overhead projector: A device capable of reproducing an image of greater size than the original, from a transparent master. Masters (called slides or transparencies) can be commercially produced or made by the instructor or the learners. Special marking pens allow for flexibility, and if nonpermanent, can be easily erased.
Related: opaque projectors, slides.

Panel: A group of several persons having a purposeful conversation on an assigned topic in the presence of participants.
Related: forum, discussion, debate, colloquy, dialogue, symposium.

Peer-mediated learning (PML): Learners are grouped with their peers and facilitate each others' learning under the guidance of a peer group leader who provides them with specially prepared materials.
Related: internship, observation.

Practicum: A study program that allows the learner to pursue a special project under the guidance of a learning facilitator.
Related: tutorial, internship, apprenticeship.

Programmed instruction: Subject matter presented in a series of small carefully graduated, sequential steps that allow the student to achieve mastery of the material presented. It is self-paced and usually used by individuals rather than groups.
Related: teaching machine, CAI, feedback mechanism, computer-assisted instruction.

Project: A specially assigned task in which the participants work independently or in a small group on a specific assignment.
Related: field trip.

Puppets: Less than life-size figures through which the learners can express ideas and thoughts that might not be possible in direct conversation.

Related: skit, role play.

Question: An inquiry designed to test, stimulate thought, or clarify. In some situations, the instructor should prepare carefully thought out questions prior to the learning experience. In other situations, questions may arise spontaneously. Learners should be encouraged to ask questions of the instructor and each other.

Related: discussion, audience reaction group, small groups.

Reading assignment: Assigned readings in textbooks, manuals, periodicals, and other printed media followed by a specific and positive activity such as a written report or class presentation.

Related: textbook, bibliography, annotated reading list, project.

Role play: Interaction among two or more individuals on a given topic or situation. Often used to allow learners to practice using previously presented material. Consists of many variations including multiple role play and role reversal. Can be scripted or spontaneous.

Related: interactive modeling, simulation, case study, laboratory.

Seminar: A form of learning in which each learner in the group is expected to be at a sufficient level to actively participate. The instructor serves as a resource person, with the seminar members responsible for the interaction during the seminar.

Related: workshop, clinic, discussion.

Sensitivity training: Not only training but also education. It involves a group that is purposely deprived of a leader, an agenda, and norms. As the group struggles to fill those gaps, members exhibit behaviors that are then used as the basis for learning.

Related: laboratory, T-groups.

Simulation: A situation that is designed to enable learners to try out new behaviors with no risk of punishment. It differs from a game in that there is no winner and no loser. Everyone wins by being able to experience a new situation.

Related: game, role play.

Slides: A transparency capable of being enlarged and projected onto a screen. Can be synchronized with an audio tape or used as support for a speaker. Requires a projector.
Related: filmstrip, audio visual.

Skit: A short, rehearsed dramatic presentation involving two or more persons acting from a prepared script and dramatizing an incident that illustrates a problem or situation.
Related: role play.

Still pictures: Photographs usually offered in a sequence to illustrate a point or to show the learner a view that would not ordinarily be seen. Can be used on a computer when appropriate equipment is available.
Related: diagrams, field trip, observation, flipchart, computer assisted learning.

Study guide: Provides an organized progressive learning experience in written form that leads towards predetermined objectives. Useful for individual learning, although it can be used with groups.
Related: workbook, handouts.

Symposium: A series of related speeches by several people who are qualified to speak with authority on different phases of the same topic or closely related topics.
Related: colloquy, debate, dialogue, interview, panel.

Teaching machine: A mechanical device (simple or complex) that carries a programmed learning activity that provides immediate feedback to individual learner responses.
Related: CAI, PI.

Team building: A concept that uses various instructional strategies to promote effective group interaction.
Related: exercises, role play, laboratory, games, simulation.

Telecon: Prearranged conference by telephone and/or close circuit TV.
Related: CCTV.

Test: Any means that measures skill, knowledge, intelligence, or aptitudes against some standard. General categories are pencil and paper and performance.
Related: question, exercise, feedback.

Textbook: A manual of instruction or a book containing a presentation of the principles of a subject used as a basis for instruction.

Related: workbook.

Think tank: A group of people assigned the task of generating fresh ideas using a combination of strategies. Generally, they meet several times and use different kinds of techniques related to creative thinking.

Related: brainstorming, creative thinking.

Tutorial: One-on-one experiences (facilitator and learner) designed to help the learner engage in self-directed learning with periodic consultation on the individual's progress and problems.

Related: directed study, DPT, contract, correspondence, coaching.

Video cassette: A specially treated ribbon (tape) capable of retaining pictures and sound that have been recorded on its surface. Can be in color or black and white. Cassettes can be produced in-house or purchased commercially.

Related: film, audio-visual.

VCR (video cassette recorder): An electromechanical device capable of recording and/or playing back a video tape.

Related: film, projector.

Vestibule learning: Off-line, instructor-led training designed to bring the learner up to production standards before assuming on-line responsibilities.

Related: OJT, JIT, apprenticeship, simulation.

White board: Similar to a chalkboard but is white rather than some darker color. Comes in a variety of sizes and can be mounted or portable. Uses a washable nonpermanent marker that is easily removed with an eraser or damp cloth. Colored markers are available.

Related: chalkboard, flannel board, newsprint.

Workbook: A book of questions or written exercises that provides space for the learner to write answers.

Related: drill, exercise.

Work group: Learners working together toward stated objectives to produce a tangible product.

Related: discussion, laboratory, performance team.

Work study: An activity in which learners work on a job related to their studies part of the time and study part of the time. Designed to reinforce learning as soon as possible in a work situation.

    Related: cooperative education, internship, apprenticeship.

Workshop: A group learning experience with the purpose of producing a product by having the participants highly involved.

    Related: seminar, conference.

Bibliography

We provide two bibliographies here. The first is a list of *models* to provide the reader with resources to other models or alternative ways of designing training and education programs. Often an author does not differentiate between training and education and the reader therefore should be cautious when selecting a particular resource. The second bibliography is on *instruction strategies.*

For both bibliographies, we generally only listed publications since 1980. Some good material has been published prior to that date, but sometimes it is less accessible.

MODELS

1. Abella, Kay Tyler. *Building Successful Training Programs: A Step-by-Step Guide.* Reading: Addison-Wesley, 1986.
2. Birnbrauer, Herman. *The Design, Development and Installation of Technical Training Programs.* Philadelphia, PA: Institute for Business and Industry, 1983.
3. Birnbrauer, Herman (editor). *The ASTD Handbook for Technical and Skills Training,* Vol. 2. Alexandria: American Society for Training and Development, 1986.
4. Blank, William E. *Handbook for Developing Competency-Based Training Programs.* Englewood, NJ: Prentice-Hall, 1982.
5. Briggs, Leslie, Kent Gustafson, Murry Tillman (editors). *Instructional Design: Principles and Applications,* Second Edition. Englewood Cliffs, NJ: Educational Technology Publications, 1991.
6. Broad, Mary. *Identification of Management Actions to Support Utilization of Training on the Job.* Unpublished Ed.D. dissertation. School of Education and Human Development, The George Washington University, 1980.
7. Broad, Mary L. and John W. Newstrom. *Transfer of Training.* Reading, MA: Addison-Wesley, 1992.
8. Broadwell, Martin M. *The Supervisor as an Instructor: A Guide to Classroom Training.* Reading, MA: Addison-Wesley, Fourth Edition, 1984.
9. Broadwell, Martin. *The Supervisor and On-The-Job Training,* Third Edition. Reading, MA: Addison-Wesley, 1986.

10. Caffarella, Rosemary S. *Program Development and Evaluation Resource Book for Trainers.* New York, NY: John Wiley, 1988.
11. Carnevale, Anthony P., Leila J. Gainer, and Ann S. Meltzer. *Workplace Basics Training Manual.* San Francisco, CA: Jossey-Bass Publishers, 1990.
12. Clark, C. C. *Developing Technical Training: A Structured Approach for the Development of Classroom and Computer Based Instructional Materials.* Reading, MA: Addison-Wesley, 1989.
13. Cole, Henry P. and others. *Measuring Learning in Continuing Education for Engineers and Scientists.* Phoenix, AR: Oryx Press, 1984.
14. Commons, Michael J., Francis A. Richards and Cheryl Armon. *Beyond Formal Operations: Late Adolescent and Adult Cognitive Development.* New York, NY: Praeger, 1984.
15. Conroy, Barbara. *Learning Packages to Go: A Directed and Guide to Staff Development and Training Packages.* Phoenix, AZ: Oryx Press, 1984.
16. Craig, Robert L. (editor). *Training and Development Handbook: A Guide to Human Resource Development,* Third Edition. New York, N.Y.: McGraw Hill, 1987.
17. Craig, Robert L. and Leslie Kelly (editors). *Sales Training Handbook: A Guide to Developing Sales Performance.* New York, NY: Prentice-Hall, 1989.
18. Cross, Patricia K. *Adults as Learners: Increasing Participation and Facilitating Learning.* San Francisco, CA: Jossey-Bass, 1981.
19. *Customer Service Training Guide.* Tucker, GA: Selin Corporation, 1985.
20. Decker, Philip J. and Barry R. Nathan. *Behavior Modeling Training: Principles and Applications.* New York: Praeger, 1985.
21. Deming, Basil S. *Evaluating Training Programs: A Guide for Training the Trainer.* ASTD, 1982.
22. *Designing and Managing Instructional Programs.* Alexandria: GP Courseware, 1983.
23. Donaldson, Les and Edward E. Scannell. *Human Resource Development: The New Trainer's Guide,* Second Edition. Reading, MA: Addison-Wesley, 1985.
24. Foshay, Wellesley, Kenneth Silber, and Odin Westgaard. *Instructional Design Competencies: The Standards.* Batavia, NY: International Board of Standards for Training, 1986.
25. Francis, David and Don Young. *Improving Work Groups: A Practical Manual for Team Building.* San Diego, CA: University Associates, 1983.
26. Frantzreb, Richard B. (editor). *Training and Development Handbook.* Englewood Cliffs, NJ: Prentice-Hall, 1990.
27. Friedman, Paul G. and Elaine A. Yarbrough. *Training Strategies from Start to Finish.* Englewood Cliffs, NJ: Prentice-Hall, 1985.
28. *Fundamentals of Classroom Instruction.* Alexandria, VA: GP Courseware, 1983.
29. Gael, Sidney. *Job Analysis: A Guide to Assessing Work Activities.* San Francisco, CA: Jossey-Bass, Inc., 1983.

30. Goad, Tom W. *Delivering Effective Training.* San Diego, CA: University Associates, 1982.

31. Goldstein, Irwin L. *Training in Organizations: Needs Assessment, Development, and Evaluation,* Second Edition. Monterey, CA: Brooks/Cole, 1986.

32. Greer, Michael. *ID Project Management: Tools and Techniques for Instructional Designers and Developers.* Englewood Cliffs, NJ.: Educational Technology Publications, 1992.

33. Hackman, J. Richard and Greg R. Oldham. *Work Redesign.* Reading, MA: Addison-Wesley, 1980.

34. *Handbook of Training Techniques.* Madison, CT: Business and Legal Reports, 1989.

35. Hannum, Wallace and Carol Hansen. *Instructional Systems Development in Large Organizations.* Englewood Cliffs, N.J.: Educational Technology Publications, 1989.

36. Head, Glenn E. *Training Cost Analysis: A Practical Guide.* Washington, DC: Marlin Press, 1984.

37. *The Instructor's Survival Kit: A Handbook for Teachers of Adults.* Blaine, WA: Training Associates, Ltd., 1987.

38. Juch, Bert. *Personal Development: Theory and Practice in Management Training.* New York: John Wiley, 1983.

39. Kaufman, Roger. *Planning Educational Systems: A Results-Based Approach.* Lancaster, PA: Technomic Publishing Co., 1988.

40. Kearns, David T. and David A. Nadler. *Prophets in the Dark: How Xerox Reinvented Itself and Beat Back the Japanese.* New York, NY: Harper, 1992.

41. Kearsley, Greg. *Cost, Benefits, Productivity in Training Systems.* Reading, MA: Addison-Wesley, 1982.

42. Kearsley, Greg. *Training and Technology: A Handbook for HRD Professionals.* Reading, MA: Addison-Wesley, 1984.

43. Kearsley, Greg. *Training for Tomorrow.* Reading, MA: Addison-Wesley, 1985.

44. Klevins, Chester (editor). *Materials and Methods in Adult and Continuing Education.* Canoga Park, CA: Klevins Publications, 1987.

45. Knox, Alan B. *Helping Adults Learn: A Guide to Planning, Implementing, and Conducting Programs.* San Francisco: Jossey-Bass Inc., 1986.

46. Knowles, Malcolm. *The Adult Learner: A Neglected Species,* Third Edition. Gulf Publishing, 1984.

47. Knowles, Malcolm S. and Associates. *Andragogy in Action: Applying Modern Principles of Adult Learning.* San Francisco: Jossey-Bass, Inc., 1984.

48. Knowles, M. S. *Using Learning Contracts.* San Francisco, CA: Jossey-Bass, 1986.

49. Kolb, David. *Experiential Learning: Experience as the Source of Learning and Development.* Englewood Cliffs, NJ: Prentice Hall, 1984.

50. Kubr, Milan and Joseph Prokopenko. *Diagnosing Management Training and Development Needs.* Albany, NY: ILO Publications Center, 1989.

51. Laird, Dugan and Ruth House. *Training Today's Employees.* Glenview, IL: Scott, Foresman and Co., 1984.

52. Langenbach, Michael. *Curriculum Models in Adult Education.* Malabar, FL: Krieger Publishing, 1988.
53. Leatherman, Dick. *The Training Trilogy.* Amherst, MA: Human Resource Development Press, 1990.
54. Leshin, Cynthia B., Joclyn Pollock, and Charles M. Relgeluth. *Instructional Design Strategies and Tactics.* Englewood Cliffs, NJ.: Educational Technology Publications, 1992.
55. London, Manuel. *Managing the Training Enterprise.* San Francisco, CA: Jossey-Bass, Inc., 1989.
56. Long, Huey B. *Adult Learning: Research and Practice.* Follett, 1982.
57. Lutterodt, Sarah A., and Deborah Grafinger. *How to Write Learning Objectives.* Columbia, MD: GP Courseware, 1985.
58. Mager, Robert F. *The New Mager Library.* Belmont, CA: David S. Lake Publishers, 1984.
59. Mager, Robert F. *Preparing Instructional Objectives,* Second Edition. Belmont, CA: Lake Publishing, 1992.
60. Mager, Robert F. *Making Instruction Work.* Belmont, CA: Lake Books, 1989.
61. Mager, Robert and Peter Pipe. *Analyzing Performance Problems: Or You Really Oughta Wanna,* Second Edition. Belmont, CA: Lake Publishing, 1992.
62. Margolis, Frederic H. and Chip R. Bell. *Managing the Learning Process.* Minneapolis: Training Books, 1984.
63. Margolis, Frederic H. and Chip R. Bell. *Understanding Training: Perspectives and Practices.* Minneapolis, MN: Lakewood Publications, 1989.
64. Marsick, Victoria J. (editor). *Enhancing Self Development in Diverse Settings.* San Francisco, CA: Jossey-Bass, Inc., 1987.
65. Mayo, G. Douglas and Philip H. DuBois. *The Complete Book of Training: Theory, Principles, and Techniques.* San Diego, CA: University Associates, 1987.
66. McInerney, Diane. (editor). *The Best of Technical and Skills Training.* Alexandria, VA: American Society for Training and Development, 1989.
67. Merwin, Sandra. *Effective Evaluation Strategies and Techniques: A Key to Successful Training.* San Diego, CA: University Associates, 1986.
68. Miller, K. *Retraining the American Workforce.* Reading, MA: Addison-Wesley, 1989.
69. Mills, G., R. W. Payce, and B. D. Peterson. *Analysis in Human Resource Training and Organization Development.* Reading, MA: Addison-Wesley, 1989.
70. Marquardt, Michael J. and Dean W. Engel. *Global Human Resource Development.* Englewood Cliffs, NJ: Prentice Hall, 1993.
71. Munson, Lawrence. *How to Conduct Training Seminars.* New York: McGraw Hill, 1983.
72. Nadler, David and Associates. *Organizational Architecture: Designs for Changing Organizations.* San Francisco, CA: Jossey-Bass, Publishers, 1992.

73. Nadler, Leonard, "Training People Before Hiring Them—It Sounds Funny But It Saves Money." *Training: The Magazine of Human Resource Development.* January, 1975, pp. 28–29, 32.
74. Nadler, Leonard, "Research: An HRD Activity Area," *Training and Development Journal.* May, 1979, pp. 60–66.
75. Nadler, Leonard, "The Organization as a Micro-Culture," in Bell, Chip and Leonard Nadler. *Clients and Consultants: Meeting and Exceeding Expectations,* Second Edition, Houston, TX: Gulf Publishing, 1985.
76. Nadler, Leonard, "Helping the Hard Core Adjust to the World of Work," *Harvard Business Review.* March–April 1970, pp. 117–126.
77. Nadler, Leonard and Zeace Nadler. *The Conference Book.* Houston, TX: Gulf Publishing Co., 1977.
78. Nadler, Leonard and Zeace Nadler, "Methods and Techniques: A Selected Sample of Application for Cross-Cultural Consulting," in Gordon L. Lippitt and David S. Hoopes (editors) *Helping Across Cultures.* International Consultants Foundation, 1978, pp. 31–51.
79. Nadler, Leonard and Zeace Nadler. *The Comprehensive Guide to Successful Conferences and Meetings: Detailed Instructions and Step-by-Step Checklists.* San Francisco, CA: Jossey-Bass Publishers, 1987.
80. Nadler, Leonard and Zeace Nadler. *Developing Human Resources,* Third Edition. San Francisco, CA: Jossey-Bass Inc., 1989.
81. Nadler, Leonard and Zeace Nadler (editors). *The Handbook of Human Resource Development,* Second Edition. New York: John Wiley & Sons, 1990.
82. *Needs Assessment Instruments.* Alexandria, VA: American Society for Training and Development, 1990.
83. Nilson, Carolyn. *Training Program Workbook and Kit.* Englewood Cliffs, N.J.: Prentice Hall, 1990.
84. Odiorne, George S. and Geary A. Rummler. *Training and Development: A Guide for Professionals.* Chicago, IL: Commerce Clearing House, 1988.
85. Peterson, David A. *Facilitating Education for Older Workers.* San Francisco, CA: Jossey-Bass Inc., 1983.
86. Phillips, Jack J. *Handbook of Training Evaluation and Measurement Methods,* Second Edition. Houston, TX: Gulf Publishing, 1991.
87. Priestley, Michael. *Performance Assessment in Education and Training: Alternative Techniques.* Englewood Cliffs, NJ: Educational Technology Publications, 1982.
88. Powers, Bob. *Instructor Excellence: Mastering the Delivery of Training.* San Francisco, CA: Jossey-Bass, 1992.
89. *Principles of Instructional Design.* Alexandria, VA: GP Courseware, 1983.
90. Rae, Leslie. *How to Measure Training Effectiveness.* E. Brunswick, NJ: Nichols Publishing, 1986.
91. Richey, Rita. *Theoretical and Conceptual Bases of Instructional Design.* E. Brunswick, NJ: Nichols Publishing Co., 1986.
92. Robinson, Kenneth R. A *Handbook of Training Management,* Second Edition. Columbia, MD: Boswell Publishing, 1988.

92A. Roethlisberger, F. J. and William J. Dickson. *Management and the Worker,* Cambridge, MA: Harvard University Press, 1939.
92B. Rokeach, Milton, *The Nature of Human Values,* Free Press, 1973.
93. Romiszowski, A. J. *Designing Instructional Systems: Volume I, Theory and Design.* E. Brunswick, NJ: Nichols, 1981.
94. Romiszowski, A. J. *The Selection and Use of Instructional Media,* Second Edition, E. Brunswick, NJ: Nichols Publishing, 1988.
95. Rossett, Allison. *Training Needs Assessment.* Englewood Cliffs, NJ: Educational Technology Publications, 1987.
96. Rothwell, William J. and H. C. Kazanas. *Mastering the Instructional Design Process: A Systematic Approach.* San Francisco, CA: Jossey-Bass, 1992.
97. Schein, Edgar H. *Organizational Culture and Leadership,* Second Edition. San Francisco, CA: Jossey-Bass Publishers, 1992.
98. Schmidt, Renata V., Sarah A. Lutterodt and Deborah Grafinger. *Classifying Learning Objectives.* Columbia, MD: GP Courseware, 1985.
99. Shea, Gordon F. *The New Employee.* Reading, MA: Addison-Wesley, 1981.
100. Sheal, Peter R. *How to Develop and Present Staff Training Courses.* E. Brunswick, NJ: Nichols Publishing, 1989.
101. Smith, B. J. and Delahaye, B. L. *How to Be an Effective Trainer,* Second Edition, New York, NY: John Wiley, 1987.
102. Smith, Judson and Janice Orr. *Designing and Developing Business Communications Programs That Work.* Glenwood, IL: Scott, Foresman, 1985.
103. Smith, Robert M. *Learning How to Learn: Applied Theory for Adults.* New York, NY: Follett, 1982.
104. Spaid, O. A. *The Consummate Trainer: A Practitioner's Perspective.* Englewood, NJ: Prentice-Hall, 1986.
105. Sredl, Henry J. and William J. Rothwell. *The ASTD Guide to Professional Training Roles and Competencies,* Second Edition. Amherst, MA: Human Resource Development Press, 1993.
106. Steele, Fritz and Stephen Jenks. *The Feel of the Workplace.* Reading, MA: Addison-Wesley, 1977.
107. Sudman, Seymour and Norman M. Bradburn. *Asking Questions: A Practical Guide to Questionnaire Design.* Jossey-Bass Inc., 1982.
108. Sullivan, Richard L., Jerry L. Wicenski, Susan S. Arnold, and Michelle Sarkes. *The Trainer's Guide: A Practical Manual for the Design, Delivery, and Evaluation of Training.* Rockville, MD: Aspen Publishers, 1989.
109. Tracey, William R. *Human Resource Development Standards.* AMACOM, 1981.
110. *The Trainer's Library: Techniques of Instructional Development.* Reading, MA: Addison-Wesley, 1988.
111. *The Trainer's Library: Developing Instructor and Student Guides.* Reading, MA: Addison-Wesley, 1988.
112. *Train the Trainer.* Amherst, MA: HRD Press, 1989.
113. *The Training and Development Strategic Plan Workbook.* Englewood Cliffs, NJ: Prentice-Hall, 1992.

113A. *TQC and Quality Circles.* The Cambridge Corporation, Tokyo, Japan, 1981.

114. Ulschak, Francis L. (editor). *Human Resource Development: The Theory and Practice of Needs Assessment.* Reston, VA: Reston Publishing, 1983.

115. von Bertalanffy, Ludwig. *General System Theory: Foundation, Development, Applications.* New York: George Braziller, 1968.

116. Waldron, Mark W. and George A. B. Moore. *Helping Adults Learn: Course Planning for Adult Learners.* Toronto, Canada: Thompson Education Publishing, 1991.

117. Ward, Gary. *High Risk Training: Managing Training Programs for High Risk Occupations.* E. Brunswick, NJ: Nichols Publishing, 1988.

118. Wolfe, Patty *et al., Job Task Analysis: Guide to Good Practice.* Englewood Cliffs, NJ.: Educational Technology Publications, 1992.

119. Winfield, Ian. *Learning to Teach Practical Skills,* Second Edition. E. Brunswick, NJ: Nichols Publishing, 1988.

120. Zemke, Ron and Thomas Kramlinger. *Figuring Things Out: A Trainer's Guide to Needs and Task Analysis.* Reading, MA: Addison-Wesley, 1982.

121. Zemke, Ron. *Computer Literacy Needs Assessment.* Reading, MA: Addison-Wesley, 1984.

122. Zemke, Ron and Linda Standke (editors). *Designing and Delivering Cost-Effective Training and Measuring the Results.* Minneapolis, MN: Training Books, 1981.

INSTRUCTIONAL STRATEGIES

Barker, John, Richard Tucker, and Paul Bacisch (editors). *The Interactive Learning Revolution: Multimedia in Education and Training.* East Brunswick, NJ: Nichols Publishing, 1990.

Barker, P. *Multimedia Computer-Assisted Learning.* New York, NY: Nichols Publishing, 1989.

Bianchi, Susan and Jan Butler. *Warmups for Meeting Leaders.* San Diego, CA: University Associates, 1989.

Bouton, Clark and Russell Y. Garth (editors). *Learning in Groups.* (New Directions for Teaching and Learning #14). Jossey-Bass Publishers, 1983.

Brandt, Richard C. *Flip Charts: How to Draw Them and How to Use Them.* San Diego, CA: University Associates, 1989.

Burke, Robert L. *CAI Sourcebook.* Edgewood, NJ: Prentice-Hall, 1982.

Casner-Lotto, Jill *et al., Successful Training Strategies.* San Francisco, CA: Jossey-Bass, 1988.

Christopher, Elizabeth and Larry E. Smith. *Leadership Training Through Gaming.* Minneapolis, MN: Lakewood Publications, 1990.

Christopher, Elizabeth M. and Larry E. Smith. *Negotiation Training Through Gaming: Strategies, Tactics and Maneuvers.* New York, NY: Nichols, 1991.

Collins, Michael. *Competency in Adult Education: A Relevant Perspective and New Direction.* Lanham, MD: University Press of America, 1987.

Conroy, Barbara. *Learning Packages to Go: A Directed and Guide to Staff Development and Training Packages.* Phoenix, AZ: Oryx Press, 1984.

Davis, Gary (editor). *Training Creative Thinking.* New York: Holt, Rinehart & Winston, 1971.

Davis, Michael, Gary M. Gray, and Harry Hallez. *Manuals That Work: A Guide for Writers* (Revised). E. Brunswick, NJ: Nichols Publishing, 1990.

de Bono, Edward. *Serious Creativity: A Systematic Approach to Take You Beyond the Power of Lateral Thinking.* New York, NY: Harper Business, 1992.

Dean, Christopher and Quentin Whitlock. *A Handbook of Computer Based Training,* Second Edition. E. Brunswick, NJ: Nichols Publishing, 1989.

Decker, Phillip J. and Barry R. Nathan. *Behavior Modeling Training: Principles and Applications.* New York: Praeger, 1985.

Draves, William A. *How to Teach Adults.* Manhattan, KS: Learning Resources Network, 1984.

Drumm, David E. *The Computer in Training and Development.* Amherst, MA: HRD Press, 1985.

Duffy, Thomas M. and Robert Waller (editors). *Designing Usable Texts.* Orlando, FL: John Wiley, 1985.

Duning, Becky S., Marvin J. Van Kekerix, and Leon M. Zaborowski. *Reaching Learners Through Telecommunications.* San Francisco, CA: Jossey-Bass, 1993.

Eitington, Julius. *The Winning Trainer,* Second Edition. Houston, TX: Gulf Publishing, 1989.

Ellington, Henry, Eric Addinall, and Fred Percival. *Case Studies in Game Design.* Chicago, IL: Nichols, 1984.

Forbess-Greene, Sue. *The Encyclopedia of Icebreakers: Structured Activities That Warm-Up, Motivate, Challenge, Acquaint, and Energize.* San Diego, CA: University Associates, 1989.

Francis, D. *50 Activities for Unblocking Organizational Communication.* Brookfield, VT: Gower Publishing Co., 1987.

Futrell, M. and P. Geisert. *The Well-Trained Computer.* Englewood Cliffs, NJ: Educational Technology Publications, 1984.

Gailbraith, Michael W. (editor). *Adult Learning Methods: A Guide for Effective Instruction.* Melbourne, FL: Krieger Publishing, 1990.

Gayeski, Diane M. *Corporate and Instructional Video: Design and Production.* New York, NY: Prentice-Hall, 1982.

Gayeski, Diane M. (editor). *Multimedia for Learning.* Englewood Cliffs, NJ: Educational Technology Publications, 1992.

Gentry, Jim (editor). *Guide to Business Gaming and Experiential Learning.* East Brunswick, NJ: Nichols Publishing, 1990.

Goodlad, Sinclair and Beverly Hirst. *Peer Tutoring: A Guide to Learning by Teaching.* New Jersey: Nichols Publishing, 1989.

Hannum, Wallace. *The Application of Emerging Training Technology.* Alexandria, VA: ASTD, 1990.

Hartley, James. *Designing Instructional Text,* Second Edition, New York: Nichols Publishing, 1985.

Heerman, Barry (editor). *Personal Computers and the Adult Learner.* San Francisco: Jossey-Bass, 1986.

Heinich, Robert, Michael Molenda and James D. Russell. *Instructional Media and the New Technologies of Instruction.* New York: John Wiley & Sons, 1982.

Heron, John. *The Facilitators' Handbook.* E. Brunswick, NJ: Nichols Publishing, 1989.

The Instructor's Survival Kit: A Handbook for Teachers of Adults. Blaine, WA: Training Associates, Ltd., 1987.

Jones, Ken. *A Source Book of Management Simulations.* E. Brunswick, NJ: Nichols Publishing, 1989.

Jones, Ken. *Interactive Learning Events: A Guide for Facilitators.* New York, NY: Nichols Publishing, 1988.

Kemp, Jerold E., and Don C. Smellie. *Planning, Producing, and Using Instructional Media.* New York, NY: Harper & Row, 1989.

Lambert, Michael P. and Sally R. Welch (editors). *Home Study Course Development Handbook.* Washington, DC: National Home Study Council, 1988.

Lewis, Linda H. (editor). *Experiential and Simulation Techniques for Teaching Adults.* San Francisco: Jossey-Bass, 1986.

Lowman, Joseph. *Mastering the Techniques of Teaching.* San Francisco: Jossey-Bass, Inc., 1984.

Margolis, Frederic H. and Chip R. Bell. *Instructing for Results.* San Diego, CA: University Associates, 1986.

Margolis, Frederic H. and Chip R. Bell. *Managing the Learning Process.* Minneapolis: Training Books, 1984.

Mill, Cyris R. *Activities for Trainers; 50 Useful Designs.* San Diego, CA: University Associates, 1983.

Misanchuk, Earl R. *Preparing Instructional Text: Document Design Using Desktop Publishing.* Englewood Cliffs, NJ.: Educational Technology Publications, 1992.

O'Shea, Tim and John Self. *Learning and Teaching with Computers: Artificial Intelligence in Education.* New York: Prentice-Hall, 1983.

Parker, L.A. (editor). *Teleconferencing Resource Book.* New York: Elsevier Science Publishing Co., 1984.

Pfeiffer, J. William. (editor). *The 1990 Annual: Developing Human Resources.* San Diego, CA: University Associates, 1990 and other years.

Pfeiffer, J. William (editor). *The Encyclopedia of Group Activities.* San Diego, CA: University Associates, 1989.

Picciotto, Ian Robertson, and Ray Colley. *Interactivity: Designing and Using Interactive Video.* Columbia, MD: Boswell Publishing, 1989.

Pike, Robert. *Creative Training Techniques Handbook: Tips, Tactics, and How-To's for Delivering Effective Training.* Minneapolis, Minn.: Lakewood Books, 1989.

Piskurich, George M. (editor) *The ASTD Handbook of Instructional Technology.* New York, NY: McGraw Hill, 1992.

Platt, S., R. Piepe and J. Smyth. *Teams: A Game to Develop Group Skills.* Brookfield, VT: Gower Publishing Co., 1988.

Podracky, John. *Creating Slide Presentations: A Basic Guide.* New York, NY: Prentice-Hall, 1982.

Race, P. *The Open Learning Handbook.* New York, NY: Nichols Publishing, 1989.

Rae, Leslie. *How to Measure Training Effectiveness.* Chicago: Nichols Publishing, 1986.

Reddy, Brendan W. and Clenard Henderson (editors). *Training Theory and Practice.* San Diego, CA: University Associates, 1987.

Reiser, Robert and Robert M. Gagne. *Selecting Media for Instruction.* Englewood Cliffs, NJ: Educational Technology, 1983.

Reynolds, Angus and Ronald H. Anderson. *Selecting and Developing Media for Instruction,* 3rd Edition. New York, NY: Van Nostrand Reinhold, 1992.

Romiszowski, A. J. *Developing Auto-Instructional Materials.* New York: Nichols Publishing, 1985.

Ross, Paul. *Open Learning and Open Management: Leadership and Integrity in Distance Management.* E. Brunswick, NJ: Nichols, 1990.

Rossett, Allison and Jeanetter Gautier-Downes. *A Handbook of Job Aids.* San Diego, CA: Pfeiffer & Co., 1991.

Roundtree, Derek. *Teaching Through Self-Instruction: A Practical Handbook for Course Developers.* New York: Nichols Publishing, 1986 and 1989.

Scannell, Edward and John Newstrom. *Still More Games Trainers Play.* New York, NY: McGraw-Hill, 1991.

Schindler-Raiman, Eva and Ronald Lippitt. *Taking Your Meetings Out of the Doldrums,* Revised Edition. San Diego: University Associates, 1988.

Silberman, Mel. *Active Training.* Lexington, MA: Lexington Books, 1990.

Smith, Terry C. *Making Successful Presentations: A Self-Teaching Guide.* New York: John Wiley & Sons, 1984.

Sork, Thomas J. (editor). *Designing and Implementing Effective Workshops.* San Francisco, CA: Jossey-Bass In., 1984.

Taylor, M. H. *Planning for Video: A Guide to Making Effective Training Videos.* New York, NY: Nichols Publishing, 1989.

The Trainer's Library: Developing Training Media. Reading, MA: Addison-Wesley, 1988.

Van Ments, Morry. *The Effective Use of Role Play: Handbook for Teachers and Trainers,* Second Edition. New York, NY: Nichols Publishing, 1989.

Varney, Glenn H. *Building Productive Teams: An Action Guide and Resource Book.* San Francisco, CA: Jossey-Bass Inc., 1989.

Wilson, John P. (editor). *Materials for Teaching Adults: Selection, Development, and Use.* San Francisco: Jossey-Bass, Inc. 1983.

Woodcock, M. *50 Activities for Teambuilding.* Brookfield, VT: Gower Publishing Co., 1989.

Index

National Training Laboratories (NTL), 159
Needs, 90–91
 felt, 91, 98
 group, 244–245
 implied, 91, 98
 individual, 244–245
 learning, 88, 96, 169
 listing and organization, 100
 organizational, 242
 stated, 91
Newsprint, 261
Nonprofit organizations, 43
Nonverbal learning, 261
Notification of participants, 195–196

Objectives, 22, 105–123, 144, 146,
 149–150, 159, 187, 200, 247–248
 program, 108, 122
Observable, 150
Observation, 82, 98–99, 247, 261
Opaque projector, 261
Open model, 7–9
Organismic, 126–127
Organization architecture, 51
Organization climate, 67–68
Organization development, 34, 51,
 212, 227
Organizational change, 38, 51, 235
Organizational culture. *See* Culture,
 organizational.
Orientation, 3–4, 237
Osborne, Alex, 159
Output, 60–63
Overhead projector, 261

Packaged programs, 131, 139–140,
 179–180, 249
 cost, 141
Panel, 261
Part-time assignment, 130
Participative behavior, 23–25
Participative management, 98
Pavlov, I.P., 127
Peer-mediated learning (PML), 12,
 115, 261
Peers, 58, 69
Performance, 5, 17, 54–55, 64, 90,
 91, 99, 103, 111, 116–118, 121,

123, 149–150, 170, 194, 214,
 229, 232, 246
 analysis, 45
 appraisal, 17, 70, 94, 117
 learning and, 5
Platform positions, 48
Posttests, 204
Practicum, 261
Pretests, 204
Preview of training programs, 215
Priorities, 108
Privacy, 103
Process of Training, 14
Production or service, 36
Production/output records, 93
Professional societies, 38, 132
Program director, 202–203, 207
Programmed instruction, 159, 262
Project, 262
Promotion, 234
Psychomotor, 111
Puppets, 262
Purchasing a program, 131

Quality, 39, 62–63, 93, 118
 and quantity, 63, 118
Quality circles, 43, 98
Quantified, 62–63, 65, 93
Question, 262
Questionnaire, 73, 75, 99, 247

Reading assignment, 262
Reading file, 71
Recognition
 for instructors, 206–207
 for participants, 205–206
Records and reports, 70
Recruitment, 245
Redesign of jobs, 49–50
Reentry, 138, 229
Regulations, 37–38, 50
Reinforcement, 232
Research, 19
Rogers, Carl, 113, 127, 136
Role play, 152, 166, 262

Sampling technique, 92
Scheduling, 181–182, 250

Here is perhaps the single most important tool available to HRD professionals for creating cost-effective, productivity-oriented training programs. The first edition of this popular book was used extensively by business organizations and as a text in many universities. Now this revised second edition updates the unique training model called the Critical Events Model, which HRD professionals can readily adapt to their particular training situations. The model is presented in a series of steps called "events" that provide the designer with a straightforward, easy-to-follow system for designing training programs to improve performance and efficiency in the workplace.

The authors cover all aspects of training, including ways to identify company and individual needs that necessitate training, involve supervisors and managers in the training, obtain resources for training, and use specific instructional strategies. An evaluation and feedback session at the conclusion of each event allows the trainer to constantly evaluate the program.